MURDERS IN THE UNITED STATES

Crimes, Killers, and Victims of the Twentieth Century

R. BARRI FLOWERS
H. LORAINE FLOWERS

MURDERS IN THE UNITED STATES
Crimes, Killers, and Victims of the Twentieth Century

ISBN: 1724622331
ISBN-13: 978-1724622334

OTHER TRUE CRIME TITLES
BY R. BARRI FLOWERS

MYSTERY & THRILLER FICTION TITLES
BY R. BARRI FLOWERS

Before He Kills Again: A Veronica Vasquez Thriller
Dark Streets of Whitechapel: A Jack the Ripper Mystery
Dead in Pukalani: An Eddie Naku Maui Mystery
(Book 1)
Dead in Kihei: An Eddie Naku Maui Mystery (Book 2)
Deadly Defense: A Grace Gaynor Christian Mystery
Justice Served: A Barkley & Parker Mystery
Killer in The Woods
Murder in Maui: A Leila Kahana Mystery (Book 1)
Murder on Kaanapali Beach: A Leila Kahana Mystery
(Book 2)
Murder of the Hula Dancers: A Leila Kahana Mystery
(Book 3)
Persuasive Evidence: A Jordan La Fontaine Legal
Thriller
State's Evidence: A Beverly Mendoza Legal Thriller

PRAISE FOR TRUE CRIME BOOKS
BY R. BARRI FLOWERS

"Will appeal to public library true-crime buffs...and is suitable for academic study in disciplines such as criminal justice and criminology." — Booklist on Murders in the United States

"Selected as one of Suspense Magazine's Best books." — John Raab, CEO/Publisher on The Sex Slave Murders

"A gripping account of the murders committed by husband-and-wife serial killers Gerald and Charlene Gallego." — Gary C. King, true crime author on The Sex Slave Murders

"R. Barri Flowers always relates an engrossing story." — Robert Scott, true crime author on The Sex Slave Murders

"A model of exposition not to be missed by anyone interested in the annals of American criminal behavior." — Jim Ingraham, Ph.D., professor emeritus of American Studies at Bryant University on The Pickaxe Killers

"Striking, well-written tales sparkle in this ocean of murder." — Diane Fanning, true crime author on Masters of True Crime

"This book should be a mandatory purchase and read for any true-crime buff." — Steven A. Egger, Ph.D., associate professor on Masters of True Crime

"Incredible cases, psychopathic killers, unwitting victims, along with the very best writers, make for an exciting, no-holds-barred, soon-to-be true-crime classic." — Dan Zupansky, host of True Murder on Masters of True Crime

"Vivid case studies of murder to complement this well researched criminology text." — Scott Bonn, Ph.D., criminology professor on The Dynamics of Murder

"An indispensable sourcebook for anyone interested in American homicide, from law-enforcement professionals to armchair criminologists." — Harold Schechter, true crime historian on The Dynamics of Murder

* * *

CONTENTS

PREFACE

According to recent FBI figures, the number of murders being committed in the United States is on the decline. This is good news in the early part of the 21st century. Indeed, with recent crime legislation, stiffer penalties for offenders, and more law enforcement personnel on the streets, most forms of violence appear to be lessening in their incidence and impact on society. However, there are still tens of thousands of people murdered each year in this country, with such horrific examples as the September 11, 2011, terrorist attack and recent cases of mass murder at an elementary school in Newtown, Connecticut; a nightclub in Orlando, Florida; and a country music festival in Las Vegas, Nevada. Killers and homicide victims range from spouses or lovers, to children and young adults, to serial killers and mass murderers or organized crime killers, to hate crime killers and sex-related or politically motivated murderers, to gangland killers, to insane and random murderers. What this tells us is that society is heterogeneous when it comes to murder and those involved. It also tells us that history is our best teacher in recording and understanding the when's, why's, motives, methods, and madness in this decisive type of violence and how we might reduce it further, if not prevent it altogether for future generations.

Murders in the United States: Crimes, Killers, and Victims of the Twentieth Century takes a unique look at the crime of murder from 1900 to 1999 in America, providing a summary of events, killers, and victims. It will include homicides that were headliners, heinous, shocking, familial, serial, sexual, singular, mass, unbelievable, or otherwise unforgettable or of historical significance or interest as part of our country's shameful past century. Among the murders profiled are those driven by greed, jealousy, sex, love triangles, hatred, politics, profit, racism, vendettas, perversions, insanity, and other causes or motivations.

The book is divided into four parts. Part I recounts many of the more unforgettable and significant murder cases of the 20th century. Part II focuses on murderers in the 1900s, subdivided into men, women, and juvenile killers; pair and group killers; hate crime killers; and school killings.

Part III looks at notable victims of murder in 20th century America. Part IV contains noteworthy murderers and murders in other countries in the last century. A glossary is provided for understanding terms. Finally, a comprehensive reference section can be found at the end of the book for more detailed study of specific murder crimes, killers, and victims in the 1900s.

The book is an excellent reference tool for historians, true crime buffs, researchers, writers, scholars, students, criminal justice professionals, laypersons, and others with an interest in the crime of murder and its varied participants in the 20th century.

INTRODUCTION

The specter of murder at the dawn of the 1900s may be most memorable for some shocking murders and murderers near the turn of the century. These would, in many respects, set the tone for homicides that would occur throughout the 20th century. Perhaps the most unsettling crime of murder in the late 19th century occurred in Massachusetts on August 4, 1892, when banker Andrew Borden, sixty-nine, and his second wife, Abby, sixty-four, were bludgeoned to death with an axe in their home. Suspected of the brutal slayings was Andrew's youngest daughter, thirty-two-year-old Lizzie Borden. She was put on trial and acquitted of the heinous crime of parricide, but suspicions of guilt and insanity dogged Borden until her death in 1927.

Another vicious axe and gun crime of murder occurred on May 26, 1896, in the Santa Clara Valley of California, when James C. Durham went berserk and killed four members of his family and two employees. The mass murderer used an axe, a .45-caliber pistol, and a .38-caliber revolver to kill his twenty-five-year-old wife, Hattie, her mother and stepfather, brother, and the two hired helpers for the family. The only one spared was Durham's infant son. Speculation was that the murders were caused by parental interference in their lives and the resultant family friction. Durham escaped on his brother-in-law's horse. In spite of being hunted by a posse and reportedly spotted in various places over the years, he was never apprehended.

Other turn of the century murders in America that gained attention for their brutality, familial, or intimate nature included one in Chicago in 1897 when Adolph Luetgert murdered his wife. The sausage maker dissolved her body with potash found at his factory. Teeth and bone fragments of the victim were discovered some weeks later. Luetgert was convicted of killing his wife and sentenced to life imprisonment.

One year later in 1898, San Franciscan Cordelia Botkin—who had been having an affair with a married man, John Dunning—became jealous. She poisoned to death his wife and his sister-in-law by lacing chocolate bonbons with the poison, which the victims ate. Botkin was convicted of first-degree murder and given a life sentence in prison. Though insisting on her innocence, she spent the rest of her life behind bars.

In spite of the heinous nature of these killings, the latter part of the 19th century also produced one of America's worst mass and serial murderers. Herman Webster Mudgett, also known as Harry Howard Holmes, was born in 1860 in New Hampshire. By the early 1890s, Mudgett had honed his skills as a swindler, cheating husband, and sexual murderer, and moved to Chicago where he managed a boarding house referred to as "Holmes Castle," "Murder Castle," and

"Nightmare House." The names were apt in describing a death house where it is believed that Mudgett drugged, tortured, and murdered at least twenty-seven guests, including an untold number who disappeared during the World's Fair in Chicago in 1893. He was finally apprehended after a vengeful-minded insurance accomplice reported a murder plot. He was sentenced to death in November 1895 and executed on May 27, 1896.

It is worth noting that murder was also making news and terrorizing citizens on the other side of the Atlantic in the 19th century. For example, in 1811, John Williams, a sailor, was convicted of the Ratcliffe Highway murders in which two families in London, England's East End were stabbed and bludgeoned to death. Robbery was thought to be the motive. The violent nature of the murders was a prelude of murders to come.

Perhaps the most infamous murderer of all time was Jack the Ripper. The mutilating sexual serial killer hunted down prostitutes in London in the fall of 1888, stabbing and disemboweling five streetwalkers, before vanishing without a trace. A bit earlier, in 1867, Frederick Baker, a Hampshire clerk, kidnapped and murdered seven-year-old Fanny Adams and then dismembered her body. He was convicted and executed that year. In Paris, France, in 1880, twenty-year-old Louis Menesclou abducted, strangled, and dismembered a four-year-old girl. The literature is replete with other examples of various types of homicides in other countries near the turn of the century.

Murder in the 20th century proved to be equally horrific—both in America and abroad—producing sexual killers, serial killers, mass murderers, black widows, intimate killers, juvenile killers, and other combinations of murderers and victims.

PART I

A CENTURY OF
UNFORGETTABLE MURDERS

THE 1900s: THE FIRST DECADE

The first decade of the 20th century was marked, most notably, by the assassination of President William McKinley, the shocking kidnap and murder of seven-year-old Walter Lamana, the murder of famed architect Stanford White, and the murder-for-profit killings of serial murderers Johann Hoch and Belle Gunness.

The Assassination of President William McKinley

On the afternoon of September 6, 1901, President William McKinley was assassinated in Buffalo, New York, in what many called the "Queen City's Darkest Moment in History." McKinley, the 25th President of the United States, was attending a reception just after four p.m. in the Temple of Music at the Pan-American Exposition. While extending his hand to shake that of his would-be assassin, he was shot twice. The first bullet struck the President's breast, the second entered his abdomen, tearing into his stomach. He died eight days later.

The shooter was quickly apprehended by secret service agents and taken into custody. The killer was identified as Leon Czolgosz, a twenty-eight-year-old blacksmith from Cleveland, Ohio. Czolgosz described himself as a disciple of anarchist Emma Goldberg, whose doctrines rejected this type of government. He had come to Buffalo three days earlier for the express purpose of killing the President. He succeeded in his objective when he pulled the gun from under a handkerchief and fatally wounded McKinley as he greeted him.

Czolgosz was beaten severely by an angry mob en route to Buffalo Police Headquarters but survived to stand trial on September 23, 1901, for the assassination of President William McKinley. A jury found him guilty of first-degree murder and sentenced him to death. On October 29, 1901, Leon Czolgosz was strapped into the electric chair at Auburn Prison where his sentence was carried out. *See also* Adult Victims, McKinley, William; Politically Motivated Killers – Men, Czolgosz, Leon.

The Death of Marie Walcker

On January 12, 1905, Marie Walcker, a Chicago sweet shop owner, became one of six wives who would be poisoned by serial murderer Johann Hoch in the late 1800s and early 1900s. Hoch was born as Johann Schmidt in Germany in 1860. He abandoned his wife and children and made his way by boat to the United States in 1887. By 1905, Hoch had married at least a dozen women—murdering half of them, usually for their money or other assets. Shortly after the mysterious death of Marie Walcker, Hoch married her sister, Julia. She too might have become another victim or an abandoned and swindled wife had her suspicions about Johann Hoch not frightened him off while she alerted authorities.

Marie Walcker's body was exhumed—her cause of death had been misdiagnosed as due to nephritis—and a post-mortem detected an unusual amount of arsenic in her stomach and liver. The case drew national attention. Hoch, who had fled to New York under another assumed name, was identified by his photograph, arrested, and returned to Chicago to stand trial for the murder of Marie Walcker. He was convicted and sentenced to death. After an appeal was rejected, Johann Hoch was put to death by hanging on February 23, 1906.

Some speculate that murder-for-profit killer Hoch may have murdered more wives than believed during his time in America, as his first known victim came after he had already been in the country for nearly a decade.

The Murder Case of Harry Thaw

On June 25, 1906, celebrated architect Stanford White was watching a rooftop musical performance at the first Madison Square Garden in New York City when millionaire Harry K. Thaw shot him to death. The thirty-five-year-old Thaw had stormed over to the table and accused White of ruining his wife, ex-showgirl Evelyn Nesbit, before shooting the fifty-two-year-old twice in the head, killing him instantly. Thaw was quickly apprehended and charged with murder.

During two highly publicized trials, it was revealed that both men had an unnatural sexual attraction to young females. Evelyn Nesbit was sixteen when she became White's mistress in the early 1900s, seen as a step toward achieving stardom in the theater. Thaw, who inherited his wealth, was taken with the seventeen-year-old Nesbit in 1901, pressuring her to dump White in favor of him. She succumbed to his advances and married Thaw in 1905. Only then did she learn how insecure, jealous, and violent he was, frequently being battered by her husband at his irrational whim.

Thaw's first trial ended in a hung jury, and he was acquitted by reason of temporary insanity in the second trial. He was committed to the New York Asylum for the Criminally Insane. After fleeing to Canada in 1913, Thaw divorced Nesbit and was eventually re-institutionalized for other violent behavior and released once more in 1922. Harry Thaw continued his life as a playboy and litigant in lawsuits involving other showgirls and actresses until his death in 1947.

The Kidnapping and Murder of Walter Lamana

In June 1907, seven-year-old Walter Lamana became a murder victim of the Mafia or "Black Hand," when he was kidnapped in New Orleans' Italian district. Shortly thereafter, a ransom demand of $6,000 was made to his father. The abduction was apparently meant to further secure the Mafia's grip on power in that section of New Orleans, where many Italians had been forced for years to pay "protection money" to the Black Hand.

An investigation led to the capture of Black Hand members Frank Gendusa and Ignazio Campisciano, the latter by a posse. Campisciano led authorities to a swamp where the corpse of Walter Lamana was discovered in a blanket. He had been bludgeoned to death with a hatchet.

Four of Lamana's kidnappers were tried, including the man who had abducted the boy, Tony Costa. All were found guilty but avoided the death penalty. Two other participants in the crime—siblings Leonardo Gebbia and Nicolina Gebbia—went to trial several months later because of public outrage. Both were convicted. Leonardo was hanged and Nicolina received a sentence of life in prison. The actual killer of Walter Lamana was never brought to justice. However, the Black Hand's grip on power in New Orleans was destroyed.

The Gunness Farmhouse Fire

On April 27, 1908, a roaring fire destroyed a farmhouse in a rural area in Indiana near the town of La Porte. The farm belonged to Belle Gunness, one of America's most infamous female serial murderers and Black Widows. Nicknamed Lady Bluebeard due to her penchant for murdering for profit, Gunness was born in 1859 as Brynhild Paulsdatter Størseth. She is estimated to have taken as many as forty-nine lives between 1896 and 1908. Victims died most often by poisoning and included two husbands and a number of her children.

Belle Gunness herself may have become a victim of murder on that night in April. The charred bodies of three young children and a headless woman were uncovered beneath the rubble. Though the head was never found, it was assumed that the woman was Gunness when her dental bridge was uncovered amongst the debris. Arrested and charged with multiple murders and arson was Ray Lamphere, ex-handyman and lover of Gunness. That very day, Belle Gunness had reportedly accused a vengeful Lamphere of intending to burn her farmhouse down.

However, suspicions abound about Gunness when authorities discovered that her property was littered with the skeletal remains of various suitors and hired hands. Many had been dismembered or found in the hog pen. It turned out that Belle Gunness had been the beneficiary of life insurance or otherwise robbed many of the victims of their assets.

In spite of these revelations, Ray Lamphere went to trial for four murders and arson. A doctor testified that poison was found in the bodies of all four victims, suggesting murder and possibly suicide before the fire. On November 26, 1908, Lamphere was found guilty of arson and not guilty on four counts of murder. He was sentenced to twenty years in prison, where he died shortly thereafter of consumption.

Many believe that Belle Gunness actually faked her own death and lived to a ripe old age, continuing as Lady Bluebeard well after the farmhouse fire. *See also* Black Widow Killers – Women, Gunness, Belle.

THE 1910s

The 1910s were characterized by the murder of thirteen-year-old Mary Phagan and the subsequent hanging of her alleged killer, Leo Frank; a serial killer in New Orleans dubbed the "Mad Axeman"; and a poisonous black widow killer named Lydia Trueblood.

The Murder of Mary Phagan

On the Saturday morning of April 26, 1913, thirteen-year-old Mary Phagan went to pick up her paycheck at the National Pencil Factory in Atlanta, Georgia, where she worked putting erasers into the metal casing atop pencils. It was the last time she was seen alive. The following morning, a night watchman found her body in the basement of the pencil factory, beaten and strangled to death. There were indications that she may also have been sexually assaulted.

A number of suspects surfaced. Given the racial climate of the day—fresh off the Jim Crow era of discrimination and segregation in the South—not too surprisingly the perpetrator was suspected of being black. This belief was, no doubt, aided by the discovery of two scrambled notes near Phagan's body that suggested her killer was a black man. Among the chief suspects were the night watchman who discovered the body, Newt Lee, and James Conley, a factory sweeper and career criminal. Under interrogation, Conley confessed to writing the two notes but claimed someone else had ordered him to.

Leo Frank, the plant superintendent and part owner, emerged as a suspect. The twenty-nine-year-old Frank was born in Brooklyn, New York, and Jewish. He had seen Mary Phagan the day the murder occurred to give her her paycheck. Some other female employees had told police of Frank's offensive attempts at romancing them. The frail, thin Frank was arrested and charged with Phagan's murder.

With Conley as the prosecution's chief witness, Leo Frank was found guilty of murder on August 25, 1913, and sentenced to death by hanging. However, Frank's supporters believed he had been unjustly convicted and questioned the verdict enough to cause the governor to commute his sentence to life imprisonment on June 21, 1915.

There was equally strong support for Frank's guilt and death sentence, with anti-Semitism running high in the South. On August 17, 1915, a lynch mob of some twenty-five men calling themselves the Knights of Mary Phagan overpowered guards at the Milledgeville state prison where Frank was being held. They abducted Frank and drove him to Mary Phagan's hometown of Marietta, Georgia, where he was blindfolded and hung from an oak tree. Leo Frank's killers were never apprehended, but his death ignited further violence by such hate groups as the Ku Klux Klan. *See also* Child Killers – Men, Frank, Leo; Child Victims, Phagan, Mary.

The Mad Axeman of New Orleans

On May 23, 1918, Italian grocer Jake Maggio of New Orleans awoke to gurgling sounds coming from the next room where his brother Joe and his wife were sleeping. Maggio was horrified to find that the two had been viciously attacked with an axe that was found near the bodies, and their throats cut with a razor. Mrs. Maggio's head had nearly been severed from the horrific attack. Both Maggios died.

Seven years earlier, three similar axe killings of Italian grocers and their spouses occurred, including the Rosettis, the Curtises, and the Schiambras. At the time, these were believed to be the work of the Black Hand organized crime syndicate in New Orleans. Now it appeared as though an independent serial murderer was on the loose, targeting Italians. The killer became known as the "Mad Axeman."

As the attacks continued, hysteria hit New Orleans. Finger-pointing led to various people being arrested for the attacks that were said to have been committed by a large, menacing white man brandishing an axe. Included among the suspects were Italian grocer Frank Jordano and his father Iorlando. In March 1919, the two were accused of killing the baby of and attempting to kill grocer Charles Cortimiglia and his wife, Rosie, who made the accusation. The Jordanos were tried in May 1919 and convicted. Frank was given a death sentence and Iorlando life behind bars.

Only the attacks continued after their imprisonment. On December 7, 1920, Rosie Cortimiglia admitted to authorities that she lied about the Jorandos attacking them as part of a vendetta, and they were released.

As for the real Mad Axeman of New Orleans, one possibility is career criminal and New Orleans resident Joseph Mumfire. He was shot and killed in Los Angeles on December 2, 1920. His killer was identified as Mrs. Mike Pepitone, whose husband was the Mad Axeman's last known victim on October 27, 1919. Pepitone claimed she had seen Mumfire running from the scene of the crime. She went to trial in April 1921 and pleaded guilty. Mrs. Pepitone received a sentence of ten years. Whether or not Joseph Mumfire was the Mad Axeman will never be known for sure.

Black Widow Murderess Lydia Trueblood

On September 7, 1919, Edward Meyer of Idaho died of mysterious circumstances while hospitalized. The woman he had recently married, Lydia Trueblood, came under suspicion after a postmortem of Meyer indicated that he had died of arsenic poisoning. She had attempted to take out an insurance policy on her new husband, but the insurance company had rejected it.

It turned out that Lydia Trueblood was on her fourth husband—all who had died, along with a brother-in-law and one of her children, for insurance policy payoffs. Trueblood was a classic example of a Black Widow, marrying and murdering for money. Similar to another American Black Widow, Amy Archer-Gilligan—who murdered five husbands between 1901 and 1914 to profit from their life insurance—Missouri born Lydia Trueblood was cold, calculating, and vicious. From 1915 to 1919, she set up her victims and then murdered them by poisonous means.

Yet Trueblood managed to evade the law until the murder of her unsuspecting husband, Edward Meyer. Before the police could close in on her, she fled Idaho for California. In 1920, feeling safe from prosecution, Trueblood wed her fifth husband, a seaman. However, before she could take out an insurance policy on his life, the authorities managed to track her down. She was arrested and returned to Idaho to face charges in the murder of Meyer.

In 1921, Lydia Trueblood went to trial and was convicted of Edward Meyer's death. She was sentenced to life in prison where she eventually died of natural causes. *See also* Black Widow Killers – Women, Trueblood, Lydia.

THE 1920s

The roaring 1920s saw a number of notable murder crimes over the decade, including the murder of well-known director William Desmond Taylor, the killings of Reverend Edward Hall and choir singer Eleanor Mills, the Southern Pacific train robbery-murder, the deaths of fourteen-year-old Bobby Franks and twelve-year-old Marion Parker, and the St. Valentine's Day Massacre.

The Murder of William Desmond Taylor

On the evening of February 1, 1922, silent film director William Desmond Taylor was shot and killed in his apartment in Los Angeles, California. The forty-five-year-old Taylor, who was considered a ladies' man, was the victim of two .38-caliber bullets in his chest. His servant, Henry Peavey, discovered his body. Before the authorities arrived, various associates of the dead director came to the apartment upon hearing of his death, compromising evidence of the crime. Visitors included a couple of young actresses, Mabel Normand and Edna Purviance, along with executives from Paramount Studio—all seeking to remove incriminating materials from the premises, such as love letters or bootleg whiskey.

The police investigation and allegations gained national press coverage in the tabloids. Taylor was discovered to have changed his name from William Deane Tanner and had abandoned a wife and daughter years earlier. The director of such films as "The Top of New York" and "Diamond From the Sky" became the president of the Screen Directors Guild and was rumored to have had numerous relationships with female stars.

Among the suspects in Taylor's death was his secretary, Edward Sands, who had vanished in 1921 after stealing from Taylor and forging checks in his name. Another suspect was Charlotte Shelby, whose seventeen-year-old daughter, actress Mary Miles Minter, was having an affair with Taylor. Shelby, who had a .38 revolver and was jealous of her daughter, was rumored to have been involved with the director herself. Authorities also considered that Taylor might have been the victim of a hired killer due to his lifestyle. William Desmond Taylor's killer was never caught.

The Murders of Reverend Edward Wheeler Hall and Choir Singer Eleanor Mills

On September 16, 1922, a shocking discovery on a New Brunswick, New Jersey, "lover's lane" led to the bodies of Reverend Edward Wheeler Hall and choir singer Eleanor Mills. The forty-one-year-old married pastor and the thirty-four-year-old attractive singer, who was married to the sexton of the church, were brutally murdered. Hall was shot once in the head and Mills was shot three times in the forehead and her throat was slashed and tongue severed. Steamy love letters were scattered about the bodies.

There were no arrests made in the double murder and the case seemed to be going nowhere for four years until the New York *Daily Mirror* began publishing stories about the Hall-Mills homicides. The newspaper suggested that Frances Hall, the Reverend's wife, and her brothers and cousin were behind the horrific murders of Hall and Mills. A secret witness to that effect led to the indictment of Mrs. Hall, her brothers Henry and Willie Stevens, and her cousin Henry Carpender. Carpender would face a separate trial.

The trial of Frances Hall and her brothers in 1926 drew international coverage. Eleanor Mills' daughter, Charlotte, testified that the love letters belonged to her mother. The prosecution was able to establish that the pastor and singer were engaged in a passionate affair. The prosecutor's star witness was a woman named Jane Gibson, dubbed the "Pig Woman," because of her pig farm near the death scene. She identified the defendants as being there and that she had heard arguing and shots fired.

The defense countered by attacking Gibson's credibility and memory. The jury took only a few hours to find the defendants not guilty. The case against the cousin, Henry Carpender, was dismissed. Frances Hall and her brothers sued the *Daily Mirror* for libel and the case was settled out of court. In spite of the continuing suspicions of guilt against the accused, the murders of Hall and Mills were never solved.

The Train Robbery-Murder on the Southern Pacific

On October 12, 1923, an Old West type train robbery turned into cold-blooded murder and a sensation of the day. Along the border of California and Oregon, the Southern Pacific train "Gold Special" was en route to San Francisco when three robbers equipped with a shotgun, Colt .45, and box of dynamite approached it. When Edwin Daugherty, the mail clerk, refused to open the bolted car door, one of the robbers tossed the dynamite on the sill and the mail car almost immediately became a blazing inferno. Along with killing Daugherty by the blast, the robbers used their guns to eliminate other witnesses including the engineer, Sidney Bates, the brakeman, and fire fighter before fleeing into the hills.

The railroad authorities employed the services of American criminologist Edward Oscar Heinrich to help solve the case. Heinrich, who lived in Berkeley, California, had often been compared to the fictional British detective Sherlock Holmes, much to his chagrin. Though some of his methods and conclusions were questionable, Heinrich found a registered mail receipt in a pair of overalls left behind by the bandits. It was traced to an Oregon logger by the name of Roy D'Autremont. He and his brothers, Ray and Hugh D'Autremont, became the chief suspects in the botched robbery-murder.

It took four years—along with reward money paid in gold and "Wanted" posters placed in train stations nationwide—before the elusive trio was captured. The D'Autremont brothers were tried and convicted for their murderous crimes in Medford, Oregon, in 1927.

Roy D'Autremont was found to be insane after spending twenty years in prison. Hugh D'Autremont, stricken with stomach cancer, was paroled in 1958. Ray D'Autremont was paroled in 1961.

The Kidnap and Murder of Bobby Franks

On May 21, 1924, fourteen-year-old Bobby Franks was kidnapped and brutally murdered in Chicago, Illinois, in one of the most shocking crimes of the 1920s and, indeed, the 20th century. Franks, son of multimillionaire Jacob Franks, was on his way home from school when his killers lured him to a car. They abducted him and bludgeoned him to death.

The murderers, Richard A. Loeb and Nathan F. Leopold Jr., were surprisingly also from two of Chicago's wealthiest families. Eighteen-year-old Loeb and nineteen-year-old Leopold were both attending graduate school at the University of Chicago. Spoiled by wealth, intelligence, jealousy, and perhaps boredom, they concocted a plan to commit the perfect crime of murder. The two rented a car that fateful afternoon in search of prey. Franks was the random victim of time and opportunity. After crushing his skull with a chisel, the teenage killers drove Franks to marshland on the outskirts of the city. They poured hydrochloric acid over his nude body to make it difficult to identify him. He was then stuffed in a drainage culvert made of concrete.

The killers then tried to collect ransom from the Franks family, demanding $10,000 in unmarked bills. However, before the money could be paid, Bobby Franks' remains were discovered. It was not long before Leopold and Loeb were arrested and their perfect crime unraveled by mistakes and overconfidence. Loeb was the first to confess to the murder and Leopold followed his lead, though both sought to blame the other for the crime.

An outraged and unforgiving public expected nothing less than both killers to be executed for the murder of Bobby Franks. Famed defense attorney Clarence Darrow was hired by Leopold and Loeb's families to prevent them from being hanged. Darrow succeeded. The chief justice hearing the case, Judge John R. Caverly, sentenced Leopold and Loeb to life in prison for the murder of Bobby Franks and ninety-nine years for his kidnapping.

On September 11, 1924, the two murderers entered the Illinois State Prison at Stateville before they were eventually transferred to a Joliet, Illinois, penitentiary. In 1936, Richard Loeb was stabbed to death by an inmate. Nathan Leopold was paroled in 1958 and died from heart problems on August 30, 1971. *See also* Child Victims, Franks, Bobby; PAIR AND GROUP KILLERS, Leopold, Nathan.

The Kidnap and Murder of Marion Parker

In December 1928, twelve-year-old Marion Parker was kidnapped from her school in Los Angeles, California. The kidnapper signed his name as "The Fox" on the ransom note sent to Marion's father, banker Perry Parker. Wanting only to get his daughter back alive, Parker tried to cooperate with the kidnapper, who sent more notes demanding $1,500 and clearly seemed to take sadistic pleasure in maintaining his advantage in the kidnapping plot.

When Perry Parker was finally able to arrange an exchange of money for his daughter, it turned out to be too late. While "The Fox" took the money, he left Marion Parker dead and mutilated. Her legs had been severed and left in a park not far from her body.

Police investigating the horrific murder of young Marion Parker were able to trace a shirt her legs were wrapped in to a twenty-year-old named Edward Hickman. The suspect confessed quickly enough, claiming to have needed the money to pay for college. He also admitted to holding a grudge against Perry Parker, whom he blamed for time served in prison for forgery.

The publicity of the murder case and trial was a prelude of another kidnapping-murder that was to capture the attention of the American public four years later—the Lindbergh baby abduction and murder. Edward Hickman was found guilty of the kidnapping-murder of Marion Parker and sentenced to death. In 1928, he was hung at San Quentin.

The St. Valentine's Day Massacre

On February 14, 1929, an organized crime mass murder gained national attention for Al Capone. A group of hit men seeking to murder the competition—gangster George "Bugs" Moran—executed seven bootleggers in a garage in Chicago, Illinois, in what became known as the St. Valentine's Day massacre. Except Moran—who battled Capone for years for control of the Chicago underworld—was not at the garage, having shown up late for the set-up to assassinate him and his entire gang.

Under Capone's orders, Jack "Machine Gun" McGurn assembled an assassination squad that included Fred "Killer" Burke, James Ray, John Scalise, Albert Anselmi, Joseph Lolordo, and Harry and Phil Keywell. Wearing stolen police uniforms and trench coats, the assassins entered the garage that was Moran's headquarters and pretended that they were raiding the place. They ordered the seven bootleggers to line up against the wall and then opened fire, using two machine guns, a .45-caliber gun, and a sawed-off shotgun. All seven men died and the killers escaped in a stolen police car.

The massacre and publicity surrounding it catapulted Al Capone and his crime syndicate to national status of infamy and glamorization. Though Capone and McGurn were believed to have orchestrated the mass murder, proving it was a different story. Capone had been enjoying the good life in Florida at the time and McGurn had a solid alibi in his girlfriend, Louise Rolfe, whom he later married so she couldn't testify against him. No one was ever convicted for the St. Valentine's Day massacre. *See also* Bandits, Outlaws, and Organized Crime Killers - Men, Capone, Alphonse.

THE 1930s

The 1930s were identified by the kidnapping and murder of baby Charles Augustus Lindbergh, the Kansas City Massacre, and the outlaw and gangster killings and deaths of Charles "Pretty Boy" Floyd, Bonnie and Clyde, and John Dillinger.

The Lindbergh Baby Kidnapping and Murder

On the night of March 1, 1932, twenty-month-old Charles Augustus Lindbergh Jr., son of the famed aviator Charles Lindbergh, was abducted from the family home near Hopewell, New Jersey. A ransom note demanding $50,000 was found on the windowsill in the nursery where the child had been sleeping. A few days later, the ransom went up to $70,000. A series of ransom related notes would follow.

On April 2, 1932, retired school principal Dr. John F. Condon, acting as a go-between, delivered $50,000 to the alleged kidnapper who was using the name "John," and received instructions as to where the Lindbergh baby could be found. The search proved unsuccessful with no sign of the missing baby.

On May 12, 1932, the badly decomposed corpse of an infant was discovered partially buried a few miles from the Lindbergh home in Mercer County. It was positively identified as the kidnapped Lindbergh baby. His head had been crushed and some body parts were missing.

The New Jersey State Police was in charge of the investigation into the kidnapping-murder, led by Superintendent Colonel H. Norman Schwarzkopf. However within weeks, the FBI began to play a major role in the investigation. On October 19, 1933, an official announcement was made giving the FBI exclusive federal jurisdiction of the case, which had included work done by the IRS Intelligence Unit.

Leads about the kidnapper came in from across the United States and various suspects were investigated. Two men—Gaston B. Means, a con artist, and Norman T. Whitaker, a disbarred lawyer—were arrested and convicted of conspiracy to defraud charges in relation to the kidnapping, though they were unconnected with it per se.

Bruno Richard Hauptmann, a German carpenter who had lived in the United States for more than a decade, became the chief suspect in the Lindbergh kidnap-murder when gold ransom certificates were traced to him. He was further identified by Condon as "John" and through handwriting analysis of the ransom notes. The thirty-five-year-old Hauptmann was indicted for murder on October 8, 1934.

His trial began on January 3, 1935, and lasted five weeks. A jury found Hauptmann guilty of first-degree murder and sentenced him to death. After various federal appeals, Bruno Richard Hauptmann was electrocuted on April 3, 1936. *See also* Child Killers – Men, Hauptmann, Bruno; Child Victims, Lindbergh, Charles Augustus Jr.

The Deadly Saga of Bonnie and Clyde

On October 11, 1932, Howard Hall was murdered during the holdup of a grocery store in Sherman, Texas. His killers were Clyde Barrow and Bonnie Parker. Few outlaws, past or present, have gained the notoriety and fascination of the public as the girl-boy bandits known as Bonnie and Clyde. The two are believed to have killed thirteen people in a bloody career of bank, grocery store, and gas station robberies during the early 1930s. Other well-known criminals of the day, such as John Dillinger, viewed Bonnie and Clyde as strictly amateurs in their small-time killings and robberies across the Midwest.

Barrow, born in 1909, and Parker, born in 1910, met in January 1930 in Texas. At the time, the nineteen-year-old Bonnie was married to a convicted killer in prison. She and the twenty-one-year-old Clyde Barrow hit it off immediately and began a life of crime together—often as part of a Barrow gang that included Clyde's older brother, Marvin Ivan "Buck" Barrow and his wife, Blanche, along with Raymond Hamilton. Bonnie and Clyde became famous for their daring robberies, breaking into prison, shootouts with police, and their ability to evade capture. They were usually heavily armed with Barrow typically relying on a Browning automatic rifle in their robberies or to outgun pursuers. The couple often escaped the law in their trademark V-8 Ford automobiles.

The spectacular end for Bonnie and Clyde came on May 23, 1934, when they were ambushed on a highway between Gibsland and Sailes, Louisiana. A posse, led by Texas Ranger Frank Hamer, opened fire on the notorious pair's automobile with high-powered rifles, riddling the car and its occupants with 167 bullets. Bonnie Parker and Clyde Barrow were killed, though their legend lives on. *See also* PAIR AND GROUP KILLERS, Barrow, Clyde.

The Kansas City Massacre

On June 17, 1933, a mass killing occurred at the Union Railway Station in Kansas City, Missouri, taking the lives of four law officers and their prisoner in what later became known as the Kansas City Massacre. The deadly ambush was designed to assist federal prisoner, Frank Nash. The career criminal and prison escapee had been recaptured on June 16, 1933, in Hot Springs, Arkansas, and was being transported by authorities aboard a Missouri Pacific train to Kansas City. A plot to free Nash was orchestrated by a group of outlaw associates including Richard Tallman Galatas, "Doc" Louis Stacci, Herbert Farmer, and Frank B. Mulloy. The actual task of helping Nash escape was to be carried out by Charles "Pretty Boy" Floyd, Vernon Miller, and Adam Richetti.

After arriving at Union Station, as Frank Nash entered a car surrounded by FBI agents and other law enforcement personnel, the three gunmen appeared with machine guns and opened fire. When the carnage was over, Frank Nash had been killed by his would-be captors. Also murdered was FBI agent R. J. Caffrey; McAlester, Oklahoma Police Chief Otto Reed; and two police officers from the Kansas City Police Department, W. J. Grooms and Frank Hermanson.

The killers got away and the search was on to find them. Vernon Miller, thirty-seven, who led the mass murder, was found dead near Detroit, Michigan, on November 29, 1933—the apparent victim of an underworld killing. It would be nearly a year before the other killers were cornered.

On October 20, 1934, Adam Richetti survived a shootout in Wellesville, Ohio, to be captured. Two days later, a wounded Charles Floyd gave up on a farm near Clarkson, Ohio, before dying from his injuries. On March 1, 1935, Richetti was indicted in Kansas City on four counts of first-degree murder. On June 17, 1935, two years after the massacre, a jury found the twenty-five-year-old guilty in the murder of police officer Frank Hermanson and gave him the death penalty. After his appeal failed, Adam Richetti was put to death in the Missouri State Penitentiary gas chamber on October 7, 1938.

The four men that conceived the plan to free Frank Nash—Galatas, Stacci, Farmer, and Mulloy—were indicted by a federal grand jury on conspiracy charges. Each was found guilty on January 4, 1935, and given prison sentences.

The Life and Death of Public Enemy Number One, John Dillinger

On January 15, 1934, Patrolman William O'Malley was killed during a robbery of the First National Bank in East Chicago, Indiana. The murderer was believed to be John Herbert Dillinger, who committed the robbery along with two other men. This was to be the only homicide blamed directly on Dillinger, who captured the imagination of the public and the ire of the FBI and other law enforcement officials during a colorful career as a bank robber during the 1930s.

Born in Indiana in June 1903, Dillinger's exploits as a cunning and elusive criminal—who associated with other Depression Era outlaws such as George "Baby Face" Nelson and Charles "Pretty Boy" Floyd— embarrassed authorities for his ability to evade capture and escape from custody. On March 3, 1934, Dillinger gained infamy and glamorization historically when he used a wooden gun to break out of the Lake County jail at Crown Point, Indiana, where escape was said to be all but impossible. He had been captured by authorities in Tucson, Arizona, on January 25, 1934, in connection with the murder of patrolman O'Malley and the bank robbery.

As part of his attempt to elude the law, Dillinger had plastic surgery done on his face and fingerprints in May 1934. So determined was the FBI to recapture him that John Dillinger became the country's first Public Enemy Number One on June 22, 1934. In a set-up orchestrated by ex-madam, Anna Sage, Dillinger was shot and killed on July 22, 1934, by federal agents and police as he left the Biograph Theater in Chicago with Sage and his girlfriend, Polly Hamilton. *See also* Bandits, Outlaws, and Organized Crime Killers – Men, Dillinger, John Herbert.

THE 1940s

The decade of the 1940s was marked notably by the William Heirens triple murder case, the sensationalized murder of "The Black Dahlia" Elizabeth Short, the Lonely Hearts Killer tandem of Raymond Fernandez and Martha Beck, and the mass murder spree of Howard Unruh.

The William Heirens Triple Murder Case

On June 3, 1945, Josephine Alice Ross, a widow, was stabbed to death in her Chicago apartment. Her face and neck had multiple lacerations, as did other parts of her nude body. The murderer used adhesive tape to cover some of the stab wounds on the victim. Several other women were attacked by an unknown assailant in the coming months, before Frances Brown, a secretary, was found viciously stabbed to death in her studio apartment on December 10, 1945, in a manner similar to Josephine Ross. The killer left a message on the wall in the living room using the victim's red lipstick that read: "For heaven's sake catch me before I kill more. I cannot control myself." On January 7, 1946, six-year-old Suzanne Degnan was abducted from her bed, murdered, and dismembered.

In June 1946, police arrested William George Heirens, a seventeen-year-old student at the University of Chicago, after he was caught burglarizing an apartment. Heirens, a habitual burglar, confessed to the murders of Ross, Brown, and Degnan under police interrogation. He claimed that it was his alter ego "George Murman" who had committed the crimes.

With his sanity questionable, prosecutors allowed William Heirens to plead guilty to murder and did not seek the death penalty. He was given three consecutive life sentences behind bars. Heirens eventually recanted his murder confession, claiming it was forced out of him. After spending more than sixty-five years in prison, William Heirens died in March 2012 at the age of eighty-three. He was found dead in his cell at Dixon Correctional Center in Dixon, Illinois.

The Case of the Black Dahlia

On the dreary morning of January 15, 1947, housewife Betty Bersinger and her three-year-old daughter were walking to a shoe repair shop in the Leimert Park area of Los Angeles, California, when they came upon the grisly remains of a young woman in a vacant lot near Norton and 39th Street. The chalky white nude victim's body had been cut in two, separated at the waist. Her arms were lifted over her shoulders and legs spread-eagle. The dead woman's face had been horribly disfigured with multiple lacerations and there were rope marks on her neck, wrists and ankles.

The gruesome scene quickly attracted reporters, photographers, curiosity seekers, and the police in this shocking homicide case. In using the *Los Angeles Examiner's* new Soundphoto service, the victim's fingerprints were identified by the FBI as belonging to Elizabeth Short, a twenty-two-year-old aspiring actress. During World War II, Short had worked as a clerk at the Camp Cooke Army Base near Santa Barbara, California, which had required her prints to be taken.

The name "Black Dahlia" was given to Short in Hollywood because of her penchant for wearing all black clothing, her long jet-black hair, pale white skin, and her bright red lipstick and matching nail polish. Born in Massachusetts in 1924, Short left home at sixteen and eventually made her way to California hoping to make it in Hollywood. Elizabeth Short quickly gained a reputation as one who loved the Los Angeles night scene, often innocently flirting with the men she met. However, suggestions that Short was promiscuous appear unlikely after the pathologist who performed the autopsy on her reported that she had an abnormally developed vaginal canal. As such, she was physically incapable of having a normal sex life.

The horrible nature of Short's death captured the imagination of the public and immortalized the Black Dahlia for her almost ghostly beauty, sexuality, and ultimate victimization. The homicide investigation of what was considered to be a sexual crime, though there was no proof that Short had been raped, produced no solid evidence against anyone. Thus, the case was never officially solved.

The only somewhat credible suspect was a man named Arnold Smith, who claimed in the 1980s that an associate named Al Morrison killed Elizabeth Short before leaving her mutilated body in the lot. Police investigators suspected that Smith and Morrison might have been the same person. Before authorities could interview Smith, he died in a fire apparently caused by a cigarette he was smoking while intoxicated. The death of the Black Dahlia remains a mystery. *See also* Adult Victims, Short, Elizabeth.

The Lonely Hearts Murders

In December of 1948, sixty-six-year-old Janet Fay was bludgeoned with a hammer and strangled to death in Long Island, New York. This was after she had been bilked of her savings in hopes of marriage. Her unlikely killers were Raymond Fernandez and Martha Beck. Between 1947 and 1949, the serial team murderers are believed to have killed as many as twenty women. Dubbed by the press as the "Lonely Hearts Killers," Fernandez and Beck lured their victims to their deaths through advertising and notices in lonely hearts clubs sections of newspapers and other publications. The motivation was to seduce and con them into parting with their assets.

Raymond Fernandez, born in Hawaii in 1914, had been well into the confidence scheme of taking advantage of lonely women as a gigolo and con artist. In Pensacola, Florida, in 1947, he placed advertisements in lonely hearts clubs personals, seeking new women to victimize. Martha Beck responded. Six years his junior, the lonely nurse weighed almost 300 pounds and was only too happy that the smooth talking, handsome

Fernandez seemed to show an interest in her. In fact, what Fernandez saw was the perfect accomplice in his fraudulent schemes.

The mismatched couple formed a deadly duo of swindlers and killers, with Beck often posing as Fernandez's sister in the scams. Victims were disposed of in various ways including poisoning, bludgeoning, strangulation, drowning, and shooting to death.

The Lonely Hearts Killers' last victims were twenty-eight-year-old Delphine Dowling and her two-year-old daughter, Rainelle. Dowling had invited the pair to move into her Michigan home, which proved to be a lethal mistake. Fernandez and Beck robbed her of everything they could take, before shooting Dowling to death and drowning her young daughter. Suspicious neighbors reported them missing and police soon discovered their remains buried under the basement floor.

Fernandez and Beck were arrested for the homicides and confessed to killing Fay and the Dowlings but denied other murders attributed to them. The killer couple was extradited to New York, where they had the death penalty. They went to trial in July 1949 on multiple murder charges. On August 22, 1949, Raymond Fernandez and Martha Beck received the death penalty. After all appeals were exhausted, the two lovers were executed together on January 2, 1951, in Sing Sing prison's electric chair. *See also* PAIR AND GROUP KILLERS, Fernandez, Raymond Martinez.

The Mass Killing by Howard Unruh

On the morning of September 5, 1949, World War II veteran, Howard Unruh, went berserk in his hometown of Camden, New Jersey, and committed mass murder. Apparently set off by a prankster who had removed a gate from his garden fence, the twenty-nine-year-old Unruh, described as withdrawn and a "mama's boy," left his house with a German Luger pistol and began firing randomly at everyone he came upon. Within minutes, he had killed thirteen people, including a young child, a shoemaker, a barber, and three members of a single family.

The murder spree shocked the town of Camden and distinguished Unruh as the country's first mass murderer. After barricading himself in his bedroom following the killings, the police finally convinced Unruh to surrender. He was found to be insane and never went to trial for his deadly crimes. Instead, he was committed to the Trenton State Psychiatric Hospital. In 1980, a judge dismissed the thirteen murder indictments against Unruh, but he remained institutionalized.

In 1996, a psychiatrist described Howard Unruh as schizophrenic, but a "problem free" patient. However, in every commitment hearing, it was ruled that Howard Unruh was insane and remained a danger to himself and the community.

After sixty years of confinement, Unruh died in October 2009 at the age of eighty-eight in a nursing home in Trenton, New Jersey. *See also* Mass Murderers – Men, Unruh, Howard.

THE 1950s

The 1950s saw an increase in sex-motivated and serial murders compared to earlier decades. However, the decade was perhaps most memorable for a mass murder in the sky, the shocking murder of Marilyn Sheppard and the Clutter family, and the abduction and murder of an infant boy named Peter Weinberger.

The Murder of Marilyn Sheppard

On the morning of July 4, 1954, Marilyn Reese Sheppard was beaten to death while in bed in her lakefront suburban home in Cleveland, Ohio. The Independence Day brutal murder of the thirty-one-year-old housewife and mother—who was four months pregnant—drew national headlines and has had a rippling effect that has lasted nearly five decades.

Charged with the murder was Marilyn Sheppard's husband, Dr. Samuel H. Sheppard. The thirty-year-old neurosurgeon claimed that a "bushy-haired intruder"

40

had broken into the house, killed his wife, and knocked him unconscious twice during struggles. Authorities believed otherwise and Sheppard was indicted for murder on August 17, 1954.

The sensational murder trial began on October 28, 1954, and drew massive media coverage. On December 21, 1954, a jury found Sheppard guilty of second-degree murder. He was sentenced to life in prison. The Sheppard family's troubles continued. Two weeks later his despondent mother, Ethel Niles Sheppard, committed suicide. Shortly after that, his father, Dr. Richard A. Sheppard, died of stomach cancer.

The U.S. Supreme Court overturned Sam Sheppard's conviction in June 1966. After a second trial, he was found not guilty of Marilyn Sheppard's death on November 16, 1966. In spite of this vindication, the severely depressed Sheppard was a broken man and died of liver disease on April 6, 1970, at the age of forty-six.

Suspected of being the real killer is convicted murderer, Richard Eberling. The interior decorator was once a window washer at the home of the Sheppards. In July 1989, he was found guilty of aggravated homicide in the murder of Ethel May Durkin. Eberling, who died in prison in 1998, denied involvement in Marilyn Sheppard's murder.

Samuel Reese Sheppard, who was seven years old and sleeping in the next room when his mother was murdered, has tried valiantly in recent years to completely clear his father's name in his mother's death. In April 2000, a Cleveland civil jury ruled against Sheppard in a wrongful imprisonment lawsuit that could have resulted in a declaration of innocence for the late Dr. Samuel Sheppard.

The enduring national interest in the unsolved murder mystery was the inspiration for two television series and a motion picture all titled "The Fugitive." *See also* Adult Victims, Sheppard, Marilyn.

The Deadly Explosion Aboard Flight 629

On November 1, 1955, at 6:52 p.m., an explosion occurred on United Airlines Flight 629, while in flight, killing all forty-four people aboard. The DC-6B had taken off from Stapleton Airport in Denver, Colorado, eleven minutes earlier en route to Seattle, Washington. Killed instantly were thirty-nine passengers and five crew members in what turned out to be one of the nation's worst mass murders.

The Federal Bureau of Investigation led the grim task of identifying the victims, while the Civil Aeronautics Board was spearheading the investigation of the tragedy. On November 7, 1955, the Civil Aeronautics Board made an official statement that Flight 629 appeared to have been sabotaged. The FBI began a criminal investigation into the deaths of the forty-four passengers aboard the ill-fated airliner.

Amongst the personal effects recovered from the debris were a number of items that belonged to passenger Daisie E. King. These included newspaper clippings and a receipt for a safety deposit box. Investigators soon learned that Mrs. King's son, Jack Gilbert Graham, had been charged with forgery by the Denver County District Attorney and put on their "most wanted" list in 1951. Background investigations further revealed that there were three life insurance policies on Daisie King. Jack Graham was the beneficiary of the largest policy, which was in the amount of $37,000.

Graham, born in 1932, was married with two young children. A small time con, he hated his mother and wanted her dead so he could collect the insurance money. He was arrested and charged in the mass killing. On May 5, 1956, a jury found him guilty of murder in the first degree and recommended that he be put to death. The judge concurred, sentencing Graham to die in the gas chamber. On January 11, 1957, Jack Graham was executed in the Colorado State Penitentiary. *See also* Mass Murderers – Men, Graham Jack Gilbert.

The Kidnapping and Murder of Peter Weinberger

On July 4, 1956, one-month-old Peter Weinberger was abducted from his family's suburban home in Long Island, New York. It was reminiscent of two earlier child kidnappings—Marion Parker in the 1920s and Charles Lindbergh Jr. in the 1930s. However, the family was not well to do, bringing the threat of such a crime much closer to the average household.

On this particular Independence Day, Peter had just been taken to the patio and put in his carriage by his mother, Betty Weinberger. Minutes later he was abducted. The kidnapper left a ransom note requesting $2,000 and promising the baby's safe return when the money was paid.

The story made the front page of the *New York Daily News* in spite of attempts by the parents to prevent it. The FBI entered the case after a mandatory seven-day waiting period. They examined nearly two million handwriting samples from federal and state probation records, the New York State Motor Vehicle Bureau, and other sources in an attempt to match the ransom note.

On August 22, 1956, a tentative match was made through the probation file on Angelo LaMarca, a taxi dispatcher, who had been arrested at his home in Plainview, New York. LaMarca, who had financial difficulties, initially denied his involvement in the Weinberger abduction, but confessed after being shown the handwriting analysis. He claimed he had abandoned the infant in a heavy brush area off the highway after being scared off by the publicity over his ransom demands.

Searching the area, the FBI discovered Peter Weinberger's decomposed remains. Since he had not crossed state lines, LaMarca could not be charged under the federal kidnapping statute. He was bound over to Nassau County authorities to face state charges.

On December 14, 1956, after being tried and convicted of the kidnapping and murder of Peter Weinberger, Angelo LaMarca was sentenced to death. His appeals went all the way to the Supreme Court before he was executed in the electric chair at Sing Sing prison on August 7, 1958.

As a result of the Weinberger case, a new law was enacted lowering the mandatory waiting period for FBI involvement from seven days to twenty-four hours. *See also* Child Killers – Men, LaMarca, Angelo; Child Victims, Weinberger, Peter.

The Model and Lonely Hearts Murders

On August 1, 1957, Judy Van Horn Dull was lured from her Hollywood, California, apartment by a man claiming to be a photographer. The attractive nineteen-year-old model mistakenly trusted the bespectacled, mild mannered man who called himself Johnny Glynn. Nearly five months after vanishing, a ranch worker found Judy Dull's skeletal remains in the desert on December 29, 1957.

A similar disappearance occurred on March 8, 1958, when twenty-four-year-old Shirley Ann Loy Bridgeford went out on a blind date and never returned. The lonely divorcee had joined a Lonely Hearts Club in Los Angeles and had been set up with a man named George Williams. Based on his description, authorities quickly came to believe that Johnny Glynn and George Williams were one and the same and that a serial killer was on the loose in Hollywood.

He struck again on July 23, 1958, when Ruth Rita Mercado was abducted from her Los Angeles apartment. The twenty-four-year-old stripper and nude model had vanished without a trace.

The police finally got the break they were looking for on October 27, 1958, when a California Highway Patrolman spotted what appeared to be a couple struggling on a road some thirty-five miles southeast of Los Angeles. The woman was pointing a gun at the man, insisting he was trying to rape and kill her. The patrolman raised his gun and held both at bay while radioing for backup.

The woman was identified as Loraine Vigil, a secretary and aspiring model. The man was identified as Harvey Murray Glatman, a thirty-year-old TV repairman. Authorities learned that Glatman had a record and had been previously incarcerated. Under interrogation, he confessed to raping and murdering Dull, Bridgeford, and Mercado after tricking them by posing as a photographer or while on a blind date. The police found photographs of the victims and other mementoes the sex killer had taken from them.

In November 1958, Harvey Glatman pled guilty in a San Diego courtroom to the homicides of Shirley Bridgeford and Ruth Mercado. Glatman openly stated his wish to be put to death rather than spend the rest of his life in prison. A judge granted him his wish and the sexual serial killer was executed in San Quentin's gas chamber on September 18, 1959. *See also* Serial Killers – Men, Glatman, Harvey.

The Clutter Family Massacre

In the early morning on November 14, 1959, the town of Holcomb in Kansas was the scene of a massacre when four members of the Clutter family were brutally slain in their home. Their killers were Richard Eugene Hickock and Perry Edward Smith, ex-convicts who were looking to rob the Clutters. Truman Capote dramatized the violent mass murder and subsequent conviction and execution of the murderers in his best-selling true crime novel, *In Cold Blood*.

The victims of the shocking small town crime were wealthy farmer Herbert Clutter, his wife Bonnie, the two youngest of their four children, Nancy, sixteen, and Kenyon, fifteen. Each was shot in the head at close range. Herbert Clutter was also stabbed and his throat was slashed. The Clutter family was amongst the more prosperous in Finney County. Forty-eight-year-old Herbert Clutter was a college graduate who raised cattle and produced grain. He had served as an advisor on the Farm Credit Board during President Dwight Eisenhower's administration and founded the Kansas Wheat Growers Association.

Recently released from prison, thirty-one-year-old Perry Smith and twenty-eight-year-old Richard Hickock chose the Clutters to rob because they mistakenly believed them to keep large sums of money in a safe in the house. This was not the case. By the time they had slaughtered the family, Smith and Hickock fled with less than $50 in cash, along with a transistor radio and pair of binoculars.

The two killers were captured in early January 1960 in Las Vegas, Nevada. Eventually, they confessed to the multiple murders and went to trial on March 22, 1960. Smith and Hickock were convicted on all counts on March 29, 1960, and sentenced to death. On April 14, 1965, Richard Hickock and Perry Smith, who had actually been the shooter in all the deaths of the Clutter family, were sent to the gallows at the Kansas State Penitentiary. *See also* Adult Victims, Clutter, Herbert; PAIR AND GROUP KILLERS, Smith, Perry Edward.

THE 1960s

The murderous decade of the 1960s was marked by racial unrest, racism, campus violence, and political killings. This included the murders of civil rights workers in Mississippi, mass murder at the University of Texas, the Charles Manson led Tate-Folger-LaBianca murders, and the assassinations of John F. Kennedy, Malcolm X, Martin Luther King, and Robert Kennedy.

The Assassination of President John F. Kennedy

On November 22, 1963, President John Fitzgerald Kennedy was shot to death as he rode in an automobile procession through Dealey Plaza in Dallas, Texas. The shots heard around the world gripped the nation in tragedy and disbelief. The assassin's bullets were believed to have come from an upper floor window in the Texas School Book Depository. Arrested for the murder later that afternoon was former Marine and depository employee, Lee Harvey Oswald. Two days later, he was shot and killed by local nightclub owner, Jack Ruby.

Born in Brookline, Massachusetts, in 1917, John Kennedy was a Harvard graduate, served in the Navy during World War II, and won the Pulitzer Prize in 1957 for his book, *Profiles in Courage*. Following stints in both houses of Congress, in 1960 Kennedy became the thirty-fifth President of the United States and the first Roman Catholic to be elected to office, defeating Vice President Richard Nixon. At the time of his death, Kennedy was only forty-six-years-old and the fourth president to be assassinated.

His alleged assassin, Lee Harvey Oswald, was born in New Orleans in 1939. After growing up in Fort Worth, Texas, Oswald joined the Marines in 1956, before moving to the Soviet Union in 1959 as a Marxist, intending to renounce his U.S. citizenship. He returned to America in 1962 with a Russian wife and daughter. He eventually settled in Dallas, where he took a job at the depository in October 1963.

Following the assassination of the President, Oswald fled the depository, later shooting to death a policeman who was pursuing him, before being arrested in the Texas Theater and charged with the two murders. With Oswald insisting that he was merely a patsy, the world was denied ever seeing him go to trial. Just two days after Kennedy's assassination, on November 24, 1963, while in the basement of the Dallas city jail, Lee Harvey Oswald was shot to death while millions watched on national television. His killer, Jack Ruby, was the proprietor of a Dallas nightclub called The Carousel Club. Ruby claimed that in silencing Oswald forever, he was simply doing his patriotic duty out of grief and anger. Jack Ruby died on January 3, 1967 from a blood clot in his lungs, while awaiting a second trial after a previous conviction for Oswald's murder was reversed on appeal.

In 1964, the Warren Commission concluded that Lee Harvey Oswald acted alone in assassinating President Kennedy and rejected the notion of a conspiracy. However, in 1979, a U.S. House of Representatives committee concluded that a conspiracy was "likely." Today many continue to support conspiracy theories in the murder of Kennedy. With Oswald long dead, the world will probably never know for certain. *See also* Adult Victims, Kennedy, John Fitzgerald; Politically Motivated Killers – Men, Oswald, Lee Harvey; Ruby, Jack.

The Mississippi Freedom Summer Murders of 1964

On the night of June 21, 1964, three civil rights workers—James Chaney, Andrew Goodman, and Michael Schwerner—were severely beaten and shot to death by members of the Ku Klux Klan in Neshoba County, Mississippi. Chaney, a Mississippian from Meridian, and New Yorkers, Goodman and Schwerner, were volunteers in assisting African American voters to register in the Deep South during the Freedom Summer of 1964. That day, they visited the burned out ruins of the Mount Zion African Methodist Episcopal Church where the three were helping to register voters.

They were later arrested by police on a trumped up charge of speeding. After being released that night, the civil rights workers were forced from the blue station wagon they were in on an isolated, dark road. They were then murdered and buried. Their burned out vehicle was found near a swamp two days later.

Six weeks passed before FBI investigators discovered, with the help of a paid informant, the remains of Chaney, Goodman, and Schwerner in an earthen dam near Philadelphia, Mississippi, on August 4, 1964. Within four months, the sheriff of Neshoba County, Lawrence Rainey, and his chief deputy, Cecil Price, were under arrest for conspiracy in connection to the crime. Sixteen members of the Ku Klux Klan were indicted for federal civil rights violations in the deaths of the three civil rights workers. Seven of the Klansmen, including Price and Imperial Wizard Sam Bowers, were convicted and received prison sentences of three to ten years. None of the convicted men spent more than six years behind bars.

Sheriff Rainey was never convicted of a crime in connection with the case. No state murder charges were ever brought against any of the men who had deprived Goodman, Chaney, and Schwerner of their civil rights by murdering them.

However, Klan leader Sam Bowers was convicted in August 1998 in the murder of another civil rights black activist, Vernon Dahmer, whose house was firebombed on January 10, 1966. Bowers was given a life sentence in prison. He died in prison in November 2006 at the age of eighty-two.

In January 2005, Edgar Ray Killen, believed to be the mastermind behind the attacks, was indicted by a Neshoba County grand jury on three counts of murder. On June 21, 2005, the eighty-year-old Killen was convicted of manslaughter in the deaths of the civil rights workers and received three consecutive terms of twenty years behind bars. In 2007, the verdict was upheld by the Mississippi Supreme Court. He died on January 11, 2018, at the Mississippi State Penitentiary.

The racially motivated murder of James Chaney, Michael Schwerner, and Andrew Goodman shocked the nation and helped galvanize the civil rights movement of the 1960s. The murder case inspired the motion picture "Mississippi Burning" and a number of books. *See also* Adult Victims – Dahmer, Vernon; HATE CRIME KILLERS, Bowers, Samuel H.

The Assassination of Malcolm X

On February 21, 1965, Malcolm X, a former minister of the Nation of Islam, was shot to death while giving a speech in the Audubon Ballroom in Harlem, New York. Arrested and charged with the murder of the thirty-nine-year-old—who had changed his name to El-Hajj Malik El-Shabazz—were three men associated with the Nation of Islam, Talmadge Hayer, Norman Butler, and Thomas Johnson.

Born in 1925 in Omaha, Nebraska, as Malcolm Little, Malcolm had been a hustler, pimp, and drug dealer before being convicted of robbery in 1946 and sent to prison. It was there that he became a follower of Elijah Muhammad, the leader of the Black Muslim movement. He became a minister upon his release from prison in 1952 and replaced is surname with the letter X.

His combative style and outspokenness helped expand the movement's reach across the country and made Malcolm X one of its most powerful figures, causing resentment among some other Black Muslim leaders. In March 1964, after becoming critical of Elijah Muhammad, Malcolm X left the Nation of Islam and established the Muslim Mosque, Inc. In June 1964, he formed the Organization of Afro-American Unity and traveled through Africa and Europe espousing his views.

On February 14, 1965, the home Malcolm X shared with his wife and six children in Queens, New York, was firebombed. A week later, he was assassinated. Hayer, Butler, and Johnson were convicted of first-degree murder in his death in March 1966. Butler, who changed his name to Muhammad Abdul Aziz, was paroled in 1985 and appointed in 1998 by current Nation of Islam leader Louis Farrakhan to head a Harlem mosque. Johnson, who became Khalil Islam, was paroled in 1987, and Hayer, who changed his name to Mujahid Halim, was released in 2010.

In June 1997, Malcolm X's widow, Betty Shabazz, died at age sixty-one, after she was critically burned in an apartment fire set by her grandson. *See also* Adult Victims – X, Malcolm; PAIR AND GROUP KILLERS, Hayer, Talmadge.

Massacre at the University of Texas

On August 1, 1966, just after eleven in the morning, the University of Texas was stunned by a mass murder that was a prelude of other school violence to come in later decades. Charles Joseph Whitman—heavily armed with a shotgun, three rifles, and three handguns—perched himself on the observation deck of the university's watchtower building, thirty stories high. He took aim at students and anyone else in sight some 370 feet below and began firing. Before it was over, fifteen people on the campus were dead, including the shooter, with thirty others wounded.

The twenty-five-year-old Whitman was a former Marine and sharpshooter who had been court-martialed on an illegal weapon's charge and sentenced to thirty days of hard labor, before being given an honorable discharge. The previous evening, he had written a suicide note complaining of severe headaches and homicidal tendencies. Afterward, he went to his mother's apartment and stabbed and shot her to death. A few hours later, he stabbed his sleeping wife to death, before preparing for his deadly day on campus.

By the time more than one hundred police arrived, there was utter chaos on the ground beneath the tower as Whitman fired away indiscriminately and people ran, ducked, rolled, and prayed for their lives. Whitman fully intended to take as many as he could before his own life ended. That happened at about one-thirty in the afternoon when police broke through a barricade he had constructed on the observation deck and shot Charles Whitman to death.

An autopsy performed on the mass murderer revealed that he had a brain tumor. However, it was concluded that his homicidal rampage could not be directly attributed to the small tumor in his head. *See also* SCHOOL KILLINGS, Whitman, Charles.

The Assassination of Dr. Martin Luther King Jr.

On the morning of April 4, 1968, thirty-nine-year-old black civil rights leader Dr. Martin Luther King Jr. was mortally wounded from an assassin's bullet while he stood on the balcony of the Lorraine Hotel in Memphis, Tennessee. His killer was identified as James Earl Ray, whose 30.06 Remington Gamemaster hunting rifle and a pair of binoculars were found outside a boarding house near the hotel. The escaped prisoner and murder suspect fled the scene afterward as news spread of the shooting.

Born in Atlanta, Georgia, in 1929, King was a Baptist minister and campaigner for civil rights who advocated nonviolence. In 1957, he founded the Southern Christian Leadership Conference. In 1964, he was awarded the Nobel Peace Prize. In honor of King's prominence as a civil rights worker and black leader, his birthday is observed every third Monday of January as a national holiday.

On June 8, 1968, King's killer was apprehended by law enforcement authorities in England. James Earl Ray was extradited to America to stand trial for murder. Ray pleaded guilty on March 10, 1969, and was sentenced to ninety-nine years in prison for the death of Martin Luther King Jr.

Three days after his trial, Ray filed a motion to withdraw his guilty plea. He insisted he was completely innocent and requested a trial to prove it. Ray contended that he was a fall guy in a conspiracy to kill King and that a mystery man named "Raoul" had manipulated him into being there, leaving his rifle near the scene of the crime, and fleeing.

Ray maintained this position for more than three decades, fueling fire into conspiracy theories in King's assassination. The civil rights leader's style and approach to racial equality angered black militants and made him the target of extensive investigations by the federal government, particularly the FBI. Some believe such a conspiracy could have involved the FBI, CIA, or organized crime.

In 1978, the House Select Committee on Assassinations concluded that Martin Luther King's death was likely the result of a conspiracy and that

James Earl Ray was his killer. Following the release of the committee's final report in 1978, the records, transcripts, and documents were ordered sealed for fifty years.

After a long battle with liver disease, James Earl Ray died on April 23, 1998, at age seventy, maintaining his innocence to the very end. Among his supporters are Dr. Martin Luther King's family members who believe that justice has not been served in getting to the bottom of King's assassination with Ray's death. *See also* Adult Victims, King, Martin Luther Jr.; HATE CRIME KILLERS, Ray, James Earl.

The Assassination of Robert F. Kennedy

On June 5, 1968, Senator Robert Francis Kennedy was shot to death at the Ambassador Hotel in Los Angeles only minutes after a victory speech upon winning the presidential primary in California. Born in 1925 in Brookline, Massachusetts, Kennedy was the brother of the late President John F. Kennedy. He had served as U.S. Attorney General under him before being elected to the Senate in 1964.

Robert Kennedy was killed by Sirhan Bashara Sirhan, a twenty-five-year-old Palestinian. Born in Jerusalem, Sirhan was thought to be an anti-Israeli. Though he never clearly explained the motivation behind the deadly shooting, it was believed to be a form of protest against Israeli control over the Palestinians and perhaps due to a particular resentment of Kennedy for the sale of fifty American fighter jets to Israel.

Sirhan used a .22-caliber pistol to assassinate Kennedy while the senator was leaving through the hotel kitchen to avoid the huge crowd outside. The assassin was immediately wrestled to the ground with the murder weapon still in his hand. Robert Kennedy died the following day from a head wound at the age of forty-two.

Sirhan was arraigned in Los Angeles on August 2, 1968, and pleaded not guilty. His trial began on January 7, 1969. The defendant claimed he did not remember anything about the moments leading up to and after the shooting. The fifteen-week trial ended on April 14, 1969. After three days of deliberation, a jury found Sirhan Sirhan guilty of murder in the first degree and five counts of assault with a deadly weapon in the assassination of Robert Kennedy. On May 21, 1969, the convicted killer was sentenced to die in the gas chamber. His sentence was commuted to life in prison in 1972 when California abolished the death penalty.

While some believe there was an assassination conspiracy and more than one shooter, Sirhan Sirhan remains incarcerated at Richard J. Donovan Correctional Facility in San Diego County, as Kennedy's sole assassin. He has been denied parole numerous times. *See also* Adult Victims, Kennedy, Robert Francis; Politically Motivated Killers – Men, Sirhan, Bashara Sirhan.

The Tate-Folger-LaBianca Cult Murders

Shortly after midnight on August 9, 1969, intruders entered the grounds of an estate in Beverly Hills, California, belonging to actress Sharon Tate and her husband, movie director Roman Polanski. In a shockingly brutal crime, five people were slaughtered that night—including Tate who was eight months pregnant; coffee heiress Abigail Folger; her writer-producer boyfriend, Wojciech Frykowski; hair stylist Jay Sebring; and Steven Parent. The victims were viciously stabbed multiple times, bludgeoned, and/or shot.

Two days later, on August 11, 1969, intruders broke into the nearby home of businessman Leno LaBianca and his wife, Rosemary. The LaBiancas were also murdered by being stabbed multiple times—Rosemary LaBianca had forty-one stab wounds. In both crimes, the killers used the victims' blood to write the word "pig" and other phrases on the walls and doors.

The horrific murders within forty-eight hours of one another were committed by followers of cult leader Charles Manson, as the start of "helter skelter," a twisted belief by cult members of a race war in which the Manson Family would be left in a controlling position. Manson, a career criminal and ex-con who used sex, drugs, and violence to control his Family, ordered the mass slayings. The murders were carried out by Charles Watson, Patricia Krenwinkel, Leslie Van Houten, Susan Atkins, Linda Kasabian, and Mary Brunner. Manson himself, however, was present at the LaBianca's house—tying up the victims before leaving it up to his Family to finish the job of murder.

Authorities caught on to the cult's role in the senseless murders when Family member Susan Atkins talked about it to a cellmate while in jail on prostitution charges. On December 1, 1969, Charles Manson and his followers were arrested on charges of murder. Following a sensational trial, Manson, Atkins, Krenwinkel, and Van Houten were found guilty on April 19, 1971, and sentenced to death for what became known as the Tate-LaBianca murders. Charles Watson was convicted in a separate trial in 1971 on seven counts of homicide and conspiracy and given the death penalty. Kasabian and Brunner turned state's evidence and were not charged in the killings. (Brunner was later convicted of murder in another case).

When the U.S. Supreme Court abolished the death penalty in 1972, the sentences of the Manson Family members were commuted to life in prison.

Susan Atkins died on September 24, 2009, while battling brain cancer, and Charles Manson died of natural causes on November 19, 2017.

The other participants remain behind bars and their applications for parole have been repeatedly denied. *See also* Adult Victims, Tate, Sharon; PAIR AND GROUP KILLERS, Manson, Charles.

THE 1970s

The decade of the 1970s had a plethora of sexual serial murders such as the sex slave murders committed by Gerald and Charlene Gallego, and the sexual assault homicides by Ted Bundy. However, it was also marked by a number of high-profile intimate and family murders including the MacDonald family killings, the murder of Olympic skier Vladimir Sabich, the murder of Mormon multimillionaire Franklin J. Bradshaw, and a love triangle homicide perpetrated by famed horse trainer Howard Jacobson.

The Fort Bragg Murder Case

On the early morning of February 17, 1970, Colette MacDonald and her two young daughters—five-year-old Kimberley and two-year-old Kristen—were the victims of a vicious murder in their residence at Fort Bragg, North Carolina. The victims were the family of Green Beret surgeon Dr. Jeffrey R. MacDonald. It was

MacDonald who phoned military police to report the massacre. His twenty-six-year-old pregnant wife had been stabbed some sixteen times in the face and chest with a knife, and twenty-one times with an ice pick. She was also beaten across the head with a club. The two daughters were also victims of multiple stab wounds and bludgeoning. The word "pig" was written in blood in the couple's bedroom on their headboard.

According to MacDonald, who suffered only minor injuries, the attackers were a bat wielding black man in Army clothing, and two white men and a white woman dressed as hippies. The woman reportedly chanted "acid is groovy" and "kill the pigs." The inconsistencies in MacDonald's story, along with fiber evidence and his comparatively limited injuries, gave the Army's Criminal Investigation Division cause to believe he had murdered his own family. Following a six-week pre court-martial hearing, the charges against MacDonald were found to be untrue and dismissed. He was given an honorable discharge from the Army and moved to California, where he resumed his medical practice.

However, when one of his previous supporters, Freddy Kassab—the stepfather of MacDonald's wife— became convinced of his guilt, his efforts almost single-handedly resulted in the former Green Beret doctor being indicted by a federal grand jury in 1975. In August 1979, Jeffrey MacDonald was convicted of the murders of Colette, Kimberley, and Kristen MacDonald and sentenced to three consecutive life terms in prison.

Since then, numerous appeals have been filed by MacDonald's defense team asserting a travesty of justice in the government's case against him. MacDonald's supporters have remained loyal and have perhaps even grown over the years. However, the convicted triple murderer remains behind bars today. His story has been the basis of a number of books and a television miniseries. *See also* Familial Killers – Men, MacDonald, Jeffrey.

The Murder of Martha Moxley

On October 30, 1975, Martha Moxley was beaten to death with a 6-iron golf club in the exclusive Belle Haven area of Greenwich, Connecticut. The body of the fifteen-year-old victim of the bludgeoning and stabbing was discovered the next day under a pine tree located on the Moxley family's three-acre estate. Authorities discovered the golf club murder weapon belonged to the Skakel family, whose residence was across the street from the Moxley's.

The night of her death, Martha Moxley attended a pre-Halloween party at the Skakel house, along with other neighborhood youth. She was said to have left the Skakel residence between nine-thirty and eleven p.m. headed for home some 150 yards away. Her killer prevented her from succeeding, attacking Moxley in the family's driveway. Though the victim's jeans and underwear were pulled down, there was no indication that she had been sexually assaulted.

The case became a media event because two of the murder suspects were related to the Kennedys. Thomas Skakel, seventeen, and his brother Michael Skakel, fifteen—who were hosting the party Martha attended that night—were the nephews of Ethel Skakel Kennedy and the late Senator Robert Kennedy. Thomas was rumored to have been the last person to see Moxley alive, while Michael reportedly had a romantic crush on the girl.

It would take a quarter of a century before authorities could make a case against Skakel in the Martha Moxley homicide. On January 19, 2000, following a grand jury investigation that found there was sufficient evidence to make an arrest, Michael Skakel was taken into custody after surrendering to Greenwich police. The thirty-nine-year-old murder suspect was charged as a juvenile because he was fifteen at the time of the crime.

On August 17, 2000, a juvenile court judge ruled that there was sufficient evidence for Skakel to stand trial for the nearly twenty-five-year-old murder. In January 2001, Skakel's case was transferred to adult court.

On June 7, 2002, Michael Skakel was found guilty of the murder of Martha Moxley and sentenced to twenty years to life behind bars. On May 4, 2018, the conviction was vacated by the Connecticut Supreme Court. *See also* Child Victims, Moxley, Martha.

The Murder of Champion Skier Vladimir Sabich

On March 21, 1976, champion skier Vladimir "Spider" Sabich was shot to death in his home in Aspen, Colorado. Implicated in the thirty-one-year-old Sabich's death was his thirty-four-year-old lover, Claudine Longet. Sabich and the former actress and showgirl Longet were living together with her three children from a previous marriage to singer Andy Williams when the killing occurred.

Sabich was well liked in the Rocky Mountain resort town where he had taken up residence while capitalizing on Olympic success through product endorsements. He and Longet had been together for two years, but the relationship showed signs of souring with reported nasty public confrontations between the two. Sabich died of a bullet wound to his abdomen. According to Longet, it was an accidental shooting from his .22-caliber gun that he was reportedly showing her how to operate.

Authorities were suspect of Longet's account and on April 8, 1976, she was charged with reckless manslaughter. In June 1976 at a preliminary hearing, she pled not guilty. In spite of the Colorado Supreme Court ruling key evidence against Longet to be inadmissible—including blood and urine tests and contents of her diary—on January 14, 1977, Longet was convicted of criminally negligent homicide. The misdemeanor charge carried a maximum sentence of two years in prison and a $5,000 fine.

On January 31, 1977, Claudine Longet was given a sentence of thirty days in jail, put on two years' probation, and fined $250 for killing her lover, Vladimir Sabich. *See also* Adult Victims, Sabich, Vladimir "Spider"; Celebrity Killers – Women, Longet, Claudine.

The Murder of Multimillionaire Mormon Franklin J. Bradshaw

On July 23, 1978, multimillionaire businessman Franklin J. Bradshaw was shot to death with a .357 magnum at point-blank range in his warehouse in Salt Lake City, Utah, in what turned out to be a murder in the family motivated by greed and domination. The seventy-six-year-old Bradshaw was a Mormon who made his fortune as owner of an auto parts store chain and from federal and state gas and oil leases. He was married to Berenice Bradshaw and they had four children, including Frances, whom her mother had a soft spot for.

Frances Schreuder emerged as the principal figure in her father's death. Living in an apartment on the Upper East Side of Manhattan, the socialite had three children from two marriages, both of which ended in divorce. She was described as manipulative and dominating over her children, abusive, and greedy in her quest to climb the social ladder at all costs. During the summer of 1977, Schreuder allegedly sent her boys—Larry and Marc—to kill her father by poisoning him. While the murder plot did not succeed, Bradshaw's grandsons managed to steal over $200,000 from him in checks, stock certificates, and merchandise, giving a portion of it to their mother.

It was in October 1980 that the true depths of Frances Schreuder's greed and desperation came to light. When the murder weapon used against Franklin Bradshaw was turned over to authorities by Frances's sister, Marilyn, it was traced to Marc Schreuder, who was seventeen at the time of the killing. He was arrested in 1981 for first-degree murder. In 1982, he was convicted of second-degree murder and sentenced to five to ten years in prison.

Frances Schreuder, who was believed to have ordered the murder of her father to keep from being disinherited, was also charged with first-degree murder but fought extradition to Salt Lake City from New York. However, she lost the battle and was brought to Salt Lake City to stand trial for the murder of Franklin Bradshaw. Her convicted son, Marc, testified that he had shot his grandfather to death on her directive. In 1983, forty-five-year-old Frances Schreuder was found guilty of first-degree murder and sentenced to life in prison. After serving time at Utah State Prison, Marc Schreuder was paroled in 1995 and Frances was paroled in 1996. She died on March 30, 2004. *See also* Adult Victims, Bradshaw, Franklin J.; Familial Killers – Women, Schreuder, Frances.

The Murder of Restaurateur Jack Tupper

In August 1978, Jack Tupper, a divorced owner of a restaurant, was brutally beaten, stabbed, and shot to death in an apartment on the Upper East Side of Manhattan, New York. Arrested and charged with the murder was famed horse trainer and real estate investor Howard "Buddy" Jacobson. The forty-nine-year-old Jacobson—considered one of the top horse trainers in the United States, and owner of a modeling agency—killed Tupper out of jealousy over his relationship with fashion model Melanie Cain. The twenty-three-year-old Cain had ended a long relationship with Jacobson and had taken up with Tupper, moving in with him in the same apartment building Jacobson lived in.

Howard Jacobson had a reputation as a womanizer in spite of his attraction to and obsession with Cain, whom he met and began an affair with in 1973. The two formed the modeling agency My Fair Lady after Jacobson wooed Cain from the Ford Agency. Cain soon discovered that her lover was seducing other young models and she tried to break off the relationship with the man who was more than twice her age.

It was shortly after Melanie Cain told Jacobson that she was in love with Jack Tupper in 1978 that he was killed. Jacobson sought to dispose of the victim's remains by burning the corpse. At his highly publicized trial, the horse trainer pleaded not guilty to murder.

In 1979, Howard Jacobson was convicted of second-degree murder, based largely on Cain's testimony and circumstantial evidence. On May 31, 1980, Jacobson escaped from jail where he was awaiting sentencing by switching clothes with another man who owed him a favor. The escaped convict fled to California with his new girlfriend, a twenty-two-year-old model named Audrey Barrett.

Forty days later, Jacobson was apprehended in Manhattan Beach, California, facing additional charges and prison time to accompany his sentence of twenty-five years in prison for the murder of Jack Tupper.

On May 16, 1989, Howard "Buddy" Jacobson died from bone cancer at the Erie County Medical Center in Buffalo, New York. He had been undergoing treatment for cancer at the center since 1987, while still serving a sentence of twenty-five years to life in prison for second-degree murder in the brutal death of Jack Tupper.

The Sex Slave Killings

On September 11, 1978, Rhonda Scheffler, seventeen, and Kippi Vaught, sixteen, were lured from a shopping mall in Sacramento, California, by an innocent looking young woman named Charlene Williams Gallego. The teenagers did not know they were being led to the slaughter. They were abducted by Charlene and her sex-crazed husband, Gerald Gallego, and taken in the couple's van to a field where they were sexually assaulted, bludgeoned, and shot to death. The killings were motivated by Gerald Gallego's "sex slave" fantasies with his wife, Charlene, a willing accomplice.

In 1979, the serial murdering couple struck again on Father's Day in Reno, Nevada. After luring fourteen-year-old Brenda Judd and thirteen-year-old Sandra Kay Colley from the Washoe County Fair, the Gallegos sexually assaulted and murdered the teenagers, burying their bodies in the desert.

Between 1978 and 1980, Gerald and Charlene Gallego abducted and killed ten people in three Western states. Their last two victims were Sacramento, California, college sweethearts—Craig Miller and Mary Beth Sowers—who were abducted at gunpoint on November 2, 1980. The murder spree came to an end on November 17, 1980, when FBI agents arrested the pair of fugitives in Omaha, Nebraska.

The twenty-four-year-old Charlene Gallego plea-bargained to testify against Gerald, ten years her senior, in exchange for giving details about the serial murders and avoiding the death penalty. In separate trials in California and Nevada in 1982 and 1984, respectively, Gerald Gallego was convicted of murder and sentenced to death. After serving nearly seventeen years in prison in Nevada, Charlene Gallego was released in July 1997.

On July 18, 2002, Gerald Gallego died of cancer while on death row in Nevada's state penitentiary, having successfully avoided execution through a series of appeals for nearly two decades. *See also* Adult Victims, Sowers, Mary Elizabeth; PAIR AND GROUP KILLERS, Gallego, Gerald.

THE 1980s

The 1980s decade began with the murder-suicide of model-actress Dorothy Stratten and her estranged husband Paul Snider and the killing of former Beatle John Lennon. Other noteworthy murders included the pipe bomb homicides of tobacco heiress Margaret Benson and her son Scott Benson, the shooting deaths of Jose and Mary Menendez by their two sons, and the murder of an eight month's pregnant Carol Stuart.

The Murder of Playmate Dorothy Stratten

On August 14, 1980, celebrity, pornography, and jealousy led to the sensational murder-suicide of Dorothy Stratten and Paul Snider in Los Angeles, California. Twenty-year-old *Playboy* model and actress Stratten was lured to the Los Angeles apartment of her estranged husband, Snider, where he raped and tortured her before shooting her in the face with a 12-gauge shotgun. He then took his own life.

Born in 1977 as Dorothy Ruth Hoogstratten in Vancouver, British Columbia, Stratten met Snider when she was seventeen. Nine years older, Snider—a hustler and opportunist—saw promise in the attractive, shapely young woman. The two began going steady and shortly thereafter, Snider convinced Stratten to take nude pictures to send to *Playboy* magazine for a playmate contest celebrating their twenty-fifth anniversary. Two weeks later, *Playboy* publisher Hugh Hefner invited Stratten to come to his mansion in Los Angeles, where she began living.

Snider, sensing his golden goose was slipping away, also moved to Los Angeles and convinced Stratten to marry him in 1979. In August of that year, Stratten was chosen as *Playboy's* "Playmate of the Year," with her photo layout to be published in the June 1980 issue of the magazine. Things became rocky between the couple with Snider being fiercely jealous and possessive. Stratten had begun having an affair with producer/actor Peter Bogdanovich while trying to embark on an acting career. She soon began living with Bogdanovich, who was twice her age.

Deciding if he could not have her, no one would, Paul Snider managed to get Dorothy Stratten to come to his apartment on that fateful day, where he brutally took her life and then killed himself. Their nude corpses were discovered the following day. *See also* Adult Victims, Stratten, Dorothy; Celebrity Killers – Men, Snider, Paul.

The Killing of John Lennon

On December 8, 1980, former Beatle John Lennon was gunned down outside of the Dakota apartment building where he lived with his wife, Yoko Ono, in Manhattan, New York. The stunning murder of the forty-year-old singer came after he and Yoko returned home from a recording session. As they neared the entrance to the building, a man named Mark David Chapman—whom Lennon had given his autograph to earlier in the day—approached them and said: "Mr. Lennon." When John Lennon turned to face him, Chapman raised a .38-caliber revolver and shot him four times, mortally wounding the singer. Chapman then put the gun down and removed a book from his coat pocket, *Catcher in the Rye*, by J. D. Salinger. He sat down on the sidewalk and began to read.

Lennon was rushed to Roosevelt Hospital where he died from shock caused by massive blood loss. His untimely death brought an end to an era. Born in 1940, the singer and songwriter was part of the 1960s rock group sensation The Beatles who, along with Paul McCartney, George Harrison, and Ringo Starr, produced such hits as "I Saw Her Standing There" and "The Long and Winding Road." The group, known as the Fab Four, broke up in 1970.

Mark Chapman was arrested without resistance and charged with Lennon's murder. His motives for the murder were apparently an obsession with the singer, substance abuse with LSD, and the chance for notoriety. In 1981, Chapman pleaded guilty to the murder and was sentenced to twenty years to life at Attica State Prison in Upstate New York. He has been denied parole nine times. *See also* Adult Victims, Lennon, John; Celebrity Killers – Men, Chapman, Mark David.

The Pipe Bomb Murders

On July 9, 1985, wealthy widow Margaret Benson and her twenty-one-year-old adopted son, Scott Benson, were killed when two pipe bombs exploded in a van they were in outside the family home in Naples, Florida. Severely injured in the explosion was Mrs. Benson's daughter, Carol Lynn Benson Kendall. Sixty-three-year-old Margaret Benson was heiress to the Lancaster Leaf Tobacco Company fortune. In 1980, following the death of her husband, she and her adult children had taken up residence in an expansive estate in Naples.

The only child of Mrs. Benson to come away from the explosion unscathed was her older son, Steven Wayne Benson, causing authorities to be suspicious in this upper class murder case. On the surface, Steven had appeared to be the perfect, loving son, in contrast to his younger, drug abusing, often violent brother, Scott. However, beneath the façade, investigators learned that he had been stealing from the family's company and Mrs. Benson had been threatening to disinherit him. On the day of the explosion, she had asked her lawyer to perform an audit on the company's books.

The family had been preparing to go somewhere in their Chevrolet Suburban van when the explosion occurred. Steven had conveniently left the vehicle moments before the blast, making no effort to help his family members. He was arrested by authorities on multiple charges, including murder.

On August 7, 1986, following a sensational trial, the thirty-five-year-old murderer was found guilty of two counts of first-degree murder, one count of attempted murder, and six counts of purchasing and constructing explosive materials. Steven Benson was sentenced to two consecutive life terms in prison without the possibility of parole for at least fifty years. He died on July 3, 2015, in a Florida prison. *See also* Familial Killers – Men, Benson, Steven Wayne.

The Murders of Jose and Mary Menendez

On August 20, 1989, multimillionaire businessman Jose Menendez and his wife, Mary Louise "Kitty" Menendez were executed in their mansion in Beverly Hills, California. Jose, a forty-five-year-old Cuban refugee who owned a video distribution company, was shot five times with a 12-gauge shotgun. Mary Louise, forty-seven, was shot ten times. Both victims were shot at close range in the particularly vicious attack.

The sole beneficiaries to the Menendez's fourteen million dollar estate were sons, twenty-two-year-old Lyle Menendez and nineteen-year-old Erik Menendez. The two had called in the double homicide to 911. Both had soon cashed in their parents' $400,000 life insurance policies and resumed their lives lavishly while authorities investigated the crime.

Soon the unthinkable became apparent: Lyle and Erik Menendez were not innocent victims but cold-blooded murderers in a tragic case of greed and parricide. In March 1990, police seized tapes a psychologist had secretly recorded in which both Menendez brothers allegedly confessed to the murders. Six months after the murders of Jose and Mary Menendez, their sons were arrested and charged with their deaths.

In 1994, Lyle and Erik Menendez were tried together by different juries. In their defense, both claimed the killings were the result of years of physical, sexual, and psychological abuse by their parents. Neither jury was able to reach a verdict and both ended in mistrials. In their second trial, this time with one jury, Lyle and Erik Menendez were convicted of first-degree murder in the brutal deaths of their parents and sentenced to life in prison with no chance of ever being paroled. In February 1998, an appellate court denied the two convicted killers' petition for a new trial. *See also* Familial Killers – Men, Menendez, Lyle.

The Murder of Carol Stuart

On October 23, 1989, thirty-year-old tax lawyer Carol Stuart was shot in the head and her thirty-year-old husband, Charles Stuart, was shot in the abdomen. The crime occurred while they sat in their car in Boston, Massachusetts' inner city Mission Hill district. Carol was seven months pregnant and the couple had just left a childbirth class at Boston's Bingham and Women's Hospital. Charles Stuart managed to use his cell phone to report the crime to police and help them locate him and his mortally wounded wife.

The shocking crime would tap into racial stereotypes and fears, nearly tearing the country apart. According to Charles Stuart, they were the victims of a black gunman. Law enforcement investigators nationwide—and particularly in Mission Hill's predominantly black public housing projects—searched for the killer, interviewing thousands of possible suspects. While African Americans cried foul, Stuart's story seemed believable to most white Americans.

With Carol Stuart near death, her baby was delivered by Cesarean section prematurely before she died from her head wound on October 24, 1989. Her infant son, Christopher Stuart, died seventeen days later from complications. Meanwhile, Charles Stuart was recuperating from his injuries as the search for a killer continued.

The police thought they had their double murderer when, nineteen days after the crime, they arrested Willie Bennett, a thirty-nine-year-old African American suspected in a robbery. Though he could not positively identify the suspect, Stuart indicated that Bennett looked like the man who had robbed and shot him and his wife.

The case against Bennett and Stuart's story began to unravel when authorities learned that Charles Stuart was having an affair with a twenty-two-year-old college student and co-worker, and stood to benefit financially from his wife's death through her substantial life insurance.

On January 3, 1990, Stuart's brother, Matthew Stuart, told police that Stuart had given him items that had allegedly been stolen that night—including his wife's diamond ring—along with a .38-caliber revolver believed to be the murder weapon.

On January 4, 1990, before police could make an arrest for the murder of Carol Stuart, Charles Stuart committed suicide by jumping off a bridge into the Mystic River 145 feet below. His death ended a disturbing murder case in which the killer played the race card and nearly succeeded. *See also* Adult Victims, Stuart, Carol; Intimate Killers – Men, Stuart, Charles.

THE 1990s

In the last decade of the 20th century, deadly terrorism took center stage with the bombing of the World Trade Center in New York and the Alfred P. Murrah Federal Building in Oklahoma. Also of note were Susan Smith's filicide killings, the murders of Gregory Smart, Nicole Simpson and Ron Goldman, and JonBenet Ramsey, the strange case of the sleepwalker killer, and a mass killing at Columbine High School in Colorado.

The Murder of Gregory Smart

On May 1, 1990, twenty-four-year-old insurance salesman Gregory Smart was shot to death execution style in an apparent robbery-homicide. The murder occurred in the condominium he shared with his twenty-two-year-old wife, Pamela Smart, in Derry, New Hampshire. The newlyweds had been married for less than a year and, on the surface, seemed like a happy and contented couple. Authorities soon learned that Greg

Smart's murder was orchestrated by his wife, who was motivated by infidelity and greed. The shocking crime made national headlines.

Pamela Smart, who had a college degree in communications, worked for the Winnacunnet High School as a media director. It was there that she met fifteen-year-old student William "Billy" Flynn, who was one of the students that assisted her in the production of educational videos. Smart began to have an affair with the teenager, seducing him with sexy photographs of herself and the steamy theatrical movie "9 1/2 Weeks." She also befriended shy student, fifteen-year-old Cecilia Price. Both teens began to spend time at Smart's condo while her husband was on the road.

It was during this time that Pamela Smart concocted the plan of having her husband—whom she suspected was cheating on her—killed and collecting the insurance money from his death. She manipulated Flynn into carrying out the deadly plan.

With promises of continuing their affair, Billy Flynn called on three teenage friends—Patrick Randall, Vance Lattime, and Raymond Fowler—to help commit the murder of Gregory Smart. A month after the homicide, the three youths were arrested and the true story came out about the Smart-Flynn affair and the murder plot.

Pamela Smart had already begun to make use of her late husband's $140,000 life insurance payout when she implicated herself in the crime to Cecilia Price, who was wearing a wire. Smart was arrested and charged with conspiracy to commit murder in the death of Gregory Smart.

The murder case and trial of Pamela Smart drew unprecedented media coverage in New Hampshire and attracted interest worldwide. On March 22, 1991, Smart was found guilty and sentenced to life in prison with no possibility of parole. In exchange for cooperating in Smart's conviction, three of her accomplices were given twenty-eight years to life behind bars, with a fourth, Raymond Fowler, receiving a sentence of fifteen to thirty years in prison. Cecilia Price was not charged in the murder plot. In 2003, Raymond Fowler was paroled and in 2005, Vance Lattime was paroled. William Flynn and Patrick Randall were both released on parole in June 2015 and will remain on lifetime parole.

Pamela Smart, who has maintained her innocence, has unsuccessfully appealed her conviction on the state and federal levels. In 1996, Smart was badly beaten by two other inmates at the Bedford Hills Correctional Facility and had to have a metal plate put in the side of her face. Smart pressed charges against the inmates, who were found guilty of second-degree assault and sent to other prisons. *See also* Adult Victims, Smart, Gregory; PAIR AND GROUP KILLERS, Smart, Pamela.

The Bombing of the World Trade Center

Around noon on February 26, 1993, a truck carrying a 1,200-pound bomb exploded in the underground parking garage of the World Trade Center in New York City. The blast killed six people, injured more than one thousand others, and caused half a million dollars in damage. The foreign terrorist attack was one of the worst on U.S. soil in history.

Authorities determined that the mastermind behind the deadly explosion was a Kuwaiti-born Palestinian by the name of Ramzi Yousef. The twenty-nine-year-old Yousef—who arrived in New York on September 11,

1992, using a fake passport—fled the country the day of the blast on a plane bound for Pakistan. Reputed to be one of the most feared men alive, he had been linked to a number of planned terrorist attacks against U.S. airlines. The bombing was believed to be in retaliation for the United States support of Israel. As a result of the explosion, Yousef became perhaps the world's most wanted fugitive with a two million dollar bounty on his capture. Also wanted were Yousef's accomplices in the crime, including Eyad Ismoil, a twenty-six-year-old fellow Islamic extremist who was believed to have driven the explosive filled truck into the center's underground garage.

In 1995, Yousef was arrested in Pakistan and Ismoil in Jordan. Both were put on trial in federal court in the United States. On November 13, 1997, they were convicted of murder and conspiracy charges in the World Trade Center bombing. Ramzi Yousef and Eyad Ismoil were each sentenced to 240 years in prison. In March 1994, four other men—Mohammed Salameh, Ahmad Ajaj, Mahmud Abouhalima, and Nidal Ajaj—were convicted on conspiracy charges for their roles in the deadly terrorist attack. In May 1997, Abouhalima's brother, Mohammed Abouhalima, was convicted of helping him to escape after the bomb attack. *See also* Terrorist Killers – Men, Yousef, Ramzi.

The Murders of Nicole Brown Simpson and Ronald Goldman

On the night of June 12, 1994, Nicole Brown Simpson and Ronald Goldman were viciously stabbed and slashed to death outside of Nicole's posh townhouse in Brentwood near Los Angeles, California.

The especially brutal attack and its shocking aftermath captured the nation's attention like never before—launching a new age of media coverage, strained race relations, and police scrutiny.

Nicole Brown Simpson, was a thirty-five-year-old, white, attractive blonde and former waitress. She was married to African American former Heisman Award winner and pro football player, Orenthal James (O. J.) Simpson before the couple divorced in 1992. They had two children. Her friend, Ron Goldman, was a twenty-five-year-old aspiring actor and waiter at the Mezzaluna restaurant in Brentwood. The nature of their violent deaths and circumstantial evidence pointed the finger at O. J. Simpson, with whom Nicole had an abusive relationship with and continued to see off and on before reportedly ending their relationship for good a week and a half before the murders.

On June 17, 1994, the forty-seven-year-old Simpson was arrested and charged with the double slaying after leading the police—while the entire country watched on live television—on a high speed chase of his Ford Bronco while he threatened to commit suicide by shooting himself.

The ex-football star's widely publicized trial began on January 24, 1995. In spite of strong DNA evidence against Simpson, incriminating photographs of him wearing Bruno Magli shoes similar to those identified in bloody footprints at the scene of the crime, and testimony that indicated Nicole Simpson was a battered wife—the prosecution's case was tainted by questionable presentation of evidence, sloppy police work, and a racist lead investigator. Detective Mark Fuhrman's negative views toward African Americans called into question the credibility of a bloody glove he found containing Simpson's and the murder victims' DNA.

On October 3, 1995, O. J. Simpson was acquitted by a jury of nine African Americans, two whites, and one Hispanic in the deaths of Nicole Brown Simpson and Ronald Goldman. The country was at once torn over the verdict. Whites mostly felt it was a miscarriage of justice and the African Americans saw it as vindication and righting wrongs of the past toward minorities by the criminal justice system.

Simpson's troubles were not over with the criminal trial. On February 4, 1997, a civil trial jury found him liable in the killings of his ex-wife and Goldman. Total damages of $33.5 million were awarded to Nicole Simpson's children and Goldman's parents. In October 2008, Simpson was convicted in Nevada for kidnapping, armed robbery, and related charges, and sentenced to thirty-three years behind bars. At his parole hearing in July 2017, he was granted parole. After serving nine years, O. J. Simpson was released from prison on October 1, 2017. *See also* Adult Victims – Simpson, Nicole Brown.

The Susan Smith Case of Filicide

On October 19, 1994, in a horrible case of filicide that collectively grieved the country and played on its racial prejudices, Susan Vaughan Smith drowned her two young sons in a lake in Union, South Carolina. Similar to the previous decade when Charles Stuart murdered his pregnant wife before eventually committing suicide, the twenty-three-year-old mother used the race card to throw authorities off in the disappearance of her three-year-old and fourteen-month-old boys.

According to Smith, who was estranged from her husband and involved with another man, her sons had been abducted by an African American carjacker. This sent authorities scrambling to try and find the children and the suspect, both of which led to sightings across the country and the flaring up of racial hostilities. All the while, a convincing Smith pleaded before the cameras to the kidnapper to return her children safely.

It was nine days after the disappearance of her young offspring that Susan Smith, under pressure, confessed that there was no abductor. She had killed her own children by drowning them. Investigators soon located Smith's car at the bottom of a lake. Strapped in their car seats in the back were her two young sons. Susan Smith was arrested and charged with a double homicide.

Smith had a history of mental illness and had been sexually abused by her stepfather. Allegedly, she killed her sons to free her from responsibility in order to be with her boyfriend. She was ruled competent to stand trial, in spite of being on suicide watch.

In 1995, Susan Smith was convicted of first-degree murder in the deaths of her two children. She was spared the death penalty and received a sentence of life in prison.

In September 2000, the twenty-nine-year-old Smith became embroiled in a prison sex scandal. She admitted to having sexual relations with two guards at the Women's Correctional Institution in South Carolina, contracting a sexually transmitted disease in the process. Both guards were disciplined and Smith was transferred to Leath Correctional Institution in

Greenwood County. *See also* Familial Killers – Women, Smith, Susan Vaughan.

The Oklahoma City Bombing of the Alfred P. Murrah Federal Building

On April 19, 1995, a massive bomb inside a Ryder rental truck exploded outside the Alfred P. Murrah Federal Building in Oklahoma City, Oklahoma, leaving 168 people dead and hundreds injured in the country's worst act of terrorism and mass murder. The bomb tore through the north side of the nine story building, demolished half of it, and created an opening twenty feet wide and eight feet deep.

It was only ninety minutes after the devastating explosion that Timothy J. McVeigh was pulled over and arrested by an Oklahoma Highway Patrol officer for driving without a license plate. The twenty-seven-year-old veteran of the Gulf War became a suspect in the bombing and was charged with the crime shortly before he was due to be released on April 21, 1995.

Terry Nichols, an Army friend of McVeigh's, turned himself in shortly after learning that he was wanted by authorities for questioning. The forty-year-old Nichols was later charged with helping McVeigh to make the bomb, using ammonium nitrate and fuel oil. McVeigh's motive in masterminding and carrying out the deadly domestic act of terrorism was apparently in response to the government's role in the Branch Davidian compound siege and fatal fire that killed fifty-eight members of the cult in Waco, Texas, in 1993.

McVeigh's trial began on April 25, 1997, in Denver, Colorado. On June 2, 1997, a federal jury found Timothy McVeigh guilty of murder, conspiracy, and weapons charges in causing the deaths of 168 people. He was sentenced to death by lethal injection.

On December 23, 1997, Terry Nichols was convicted in federal court of involuntary manslaughter and conspiracy, and was acquitted of murder and weapons violations. He received a life sentence of imprisonment.

A fellow military friend of McVeigh's, Michael Fortier, pled guilty to failure to notify authorities of the bomb plot and other offenses. On May 27, 1998, he received a twelve year sentence in federal prison. In January 2006, he was released for good behavior and was granted protection under the federal witness protection program.

On October 12, 2000, Timothy McVeigh was denied an appeal for a new trial. McVeigh was executed on June 11, 2001, at the U.S. Federal Penitentiary located in Terre Haute, Indiana. In the process, he became the first federal inmate to be put to death since Victor Feguer, who was executed in Iowa in March 1963 by the federal government for the kidnap and murder of physician Edward Bartels.

Following his federal conviction, multiple murder charges were brought against Terry Nichols by the Oklahoma County district attorney, with plans to seek the death penalty. On May 26, 2004, Nichols was convicted on all counts. However, during the penalty phase, the jury deadlocked on the death penalty and Nichols received a sentence of 161 consecutive life terms in prison with no chance for parole. *See also* Terrorist Killers – Men, McVeigh, Timothy J.

The Murder of JonBenet Ramsey

On December 26, 1996, six-year-old JonBenet Ramsey was found brutally murdered in the basement of her parents' home in Boulder, Colorado. The young beauty queen contestant and winner of the Little Miss Colorado and National Tiny Miss Beauty titles, among others, had been bound, beaten, strangled, and possibly sexually assaulted in a crime that stunned the nation.

JonBenet's mother, Patsy Ramsey, discovered a three-page ransom note on a back staircase in the house. The note demanded $118,000 for the girl's return. Some eight hours later, JonBenet's body was located by her father in the basement. He removed duct tape from her mouth and brought her upstairs. There was a white cord wrapped around the victim's neck.

With the crime scene compromised by allowing the Ramseys to move around freely, other tainted evidence, and sloppy police and prosecutor's office investigations, John and Patsy Ramsey became the chief suspects in the murder of their daughter. Two older half-siblings had been cleared of the crime. John Ramsey, former president of a computer services company, and Patsy Ramsey, Miss West Virginia in 1977, contributed to the umbrella of suspicion by a lack of cooperation in the investigation. Further damaging to Patsy Ramsey was that based on handwriting samples, she could not be ruled out as the person who wrote the ransom note.

On September 15, 1998, a grand jury was convened to hear evidence in the JonBenet Ramsey murder case. More than a year later—on October 13, 1999—the district attorney made the announcement that no indictment would be issued due to insufficient evidence.

In spite of this, the Ramseys have remained under a cloud of suspicion. In May 2000, the couple announced that each had passed a lie detector test denying any role in their daughter's death. However, Boulder law enforcement officials quickly rejected its validity, given the fact that the FBI had not administered the tests.

In August 2000, Boulder investigators were finally able to thoroughly interview John and Patsy Ramsey over a two-day period. They were neither implicated nor exonerated in the death of JonBenet Ramsey until July 9, 2008, when the Boulder district attorney's office officially cleared the couple of any wrongdoing based on new DNA evidence and testing procedures. Unfortunately, Patsy Ramsey had died in June 2006 from ovarian cancer while still considered a suspect to many in her daughter's death.

In August 2006, John Mark Karr, a forty-one-year-old former school teacher, confessed to murdering JonBenet. However, his DNA did not match that found on the victim and prosecutors declined to file murder charges against Karr. The mysterious murder of JonBenet Ramsey remains unsolved. *See also* Child Victims, Ramsey, JonBenet.

The Case of the Sleepwalker Killer

On January 16, 1997, Yarmila Falater was viciously stabbed to death and drowned in the family swimming pool outside her home in Phoenix, Arizona. Arrested for the murder was her husband of twenty years and the father of her two children, Scott Falater. The bizarre case drew national interest and debate when Falater, a forty-two-year-old Mormon and electrical engineer, claimed he had been sleepwalking when he committed the murder. Yarmila had been stabbed forty-four times with a hunting knife before she was pushed into the swimming pool and her head held under water.

On the surface, the Falaters seemed like a church-going, close-knit, happy family. Having met in high school, Yarmila Klesken and Scott Falater married in a civil ceremony in 1976. While he found work in engineering, Yarmila was employed in a medical laboratory. She stopped working after the birth of their second child. When the family moved to Arizona in 1987, Yarmila returned to work as a preschool aid.

According to Scott Falater, he had no memories of the homicidal rage that took his wife's life that night. He did recall being under tremendous stress at work prior to the homicide and apparently had some history of sleepwalking. However, the authorities noted that the husband "sleepwalker killer" managed to hide crucial evidence, change into pajamas, and bandage his hand that had been cut in the assault—all while allegedly in a sleepwalking state.

On June 24, 1999, a jury rejected Falater's sleepwalking defense and convicted him of first-degree murder in the death of his wife, Yarmila Falater. On January 10, 2000, Scott Falater was sentenced to life in prison without the possibility of parole. *See also* Adult Victims, Falater, Yarmila; Intimate Killers – Men, Falater, Scott.

The Mass Murder at Columbine High School

On the morning of April 20, 1999, two teenagers armed with semiautomatic weapons and wearing long black trench coats went on a murderous rampage through Columbine High School in Littleton, Colorado.

They killed thirteen people and wounded twenty-five others before shooting themselves to death. At the time, it was one of the worst cases of deadly school violence in U.S. history.

The mass murderers were identified as Columbine students, Eric Harris, eighteen, and Dylan Klebold, seventeen. The two killers—who belonged to a small group of student outcasts known as the "Trench Coat Mafia"—began their murder spree in the cafeteria and carried on in the corridors and classrooms, firing away with deadly precision, before finishing their assault in the school library.

The massacre, which had clear racial overtones, though the killers and most victims were white, could have been much worse. As part of their diabolical plan, Harris and Klebold constructed and planted at least thirty bombs throughout the school—including on their own bodies—fully intending to take as many lives as possible. Had all detonated successfully, it is estimated that the death toll could have gone as high as three hundred people. According to writings found in Harris's journal, he had hoped to kill at least five hundred people. The mentally disturbed homicidal pair further had plans of hijacking a plane and crashing it into New York City as the ultimate in death and destruction.

Although law enforcement authorities were able to go after those who illegally supplied some of the weapons to the two young killers, their suicides put them beyond the reach of the criminal justice system, leaving more questions than answers. It was, to most, a wake-up call on the increasing level of school violence in the U.S. beginning in the late 1990s, and the availability of firearms to juveniles and young adults. As school administrators, law enforcement, and lawmakers grappled with the issues of deadly school violence and gun control, the massacre at Columbine High would sadly be repeated by similar tragedies on school campuses in the first two decades of the 21st century. *See also* SCHOOL KILLINGS, Harris, Eric.

PART II

A CENTURY OF MURDERERS

SECTION 1 – MEN KILLERS

BANDITS, OUTLAWS, AND ORGANIZED CRIME KILLERS - MEN

Abbandando, Frank. A professional killer in the 1920s and 1930s, Frank Abbandando was nicknamed "The Dasher." As a hired gun, Abbandando worked for Murder, Inc.—a group of cold-blooded killers for hire by crime syndicates. He served as chief lieutenant to Harry "Happy" Maione, a racketeer living in Ocean Hill, New York. Over a ten-year period, Abbandando is thought to have killed as many as forty people at his employer's orders, averaging $500 per hit. He and Maione were arrested with the help of an informant and former boss of Murder, Inc., Abe "Kid Twist" Reles, and charged with murdering loan shark George "Whitey" Rudnick in Brownsville, New York, on May 25, 1937. Abbandando and Maione were both convicted of first-degree murder for killing Rudnick. The verdicts were overturned on appeal, but in a retrial the two were found guilty again and sentenced to death.

On February 19, 1942, Frank Abbandando died in the electric chair at Sing Sing. *See also* Maione, Harry.

Anastasia, Albert. Born in Italy in 1902 as Umberto Anastasia, Albert Anastasia was thought to be one of the most merciless killers of Murder, Inc.—the Brooklyn, New York, based killer squad for the organized crime syndicate. Working for mob bosses such as Louis Buchalter and Joe Adonis, Anastasia—who became known as "The Executioner"—helped establish Murder, Inc. and recruited many of its ruthless killers starting in the late 1920s. Anastasia personally killed dozens of members of the mob. As the leader of Murder, Inc., he oversaw the murders of hundreds of others, if not thousands. After informants fingered him in a number of mob-related homicides, Anastasia went into hiding. In 1942, he joined the Army as a move to prevent him from being deported, becoming a sergeant. Anastasia became a naturalized U.S. citizen in 1943 and continued his murderous ways and control of gambling, prostitution, and narcotics rackets. On October 25, 1957, Albert Anastasia was gunned down in a barber shop at the Park Sheraton Hotel in New York. Though his killers were never apprehended, his death was thought to have been ordered by Mafia chieftain, Vito "Don Vitone" Genovese. *See also* PAIR AND GROUP KILLERS, Murder, Incorporated.

"Baby Face" Nelson *see* PAIR AND GROUP KILLERS, Nelson, George

Barker, Frederick *see* PAIR AND GROUP KILLERS

Barker-Karpis Gang *see* PAIR AND GROUP KILLERS, Barker, Frederick

Barrow, Clyde *see* PAIR AND GROUP KILLERS

Belcastro, James *see* PAIR AND GROUP KILLERS, Black Hand

Black Hand *see* PAIR AND GROUP KILLERS

Buchalter, Louis "Lepke." Born in 1897, Louis "Lepke" Buchalter was one of the most powerful organized crime figures in the early years of the syndicate in the United States. He began his career as a young thief on New York's Lower East Side and worked his way into a pushcart extortion racket, labor violence, and trafficking of narcotics. Buchalter was reputed to have personally been responsible for dozens of murders of mobsters or others who threatened his hold on power or freedom through the syndicate's killer squad, Murder, Inc. After being fingered by Abe Reles for the murder of candy store owner Joseph Rosen, Buchalter sought to avoid the death penalty by turning himself in to the FBI Director J. Edgar Hoover on August 24, 1939. He was convicted for narcotics violations and sentenced to fourteen years in prison at Leavenworth. However, in 1940, Buchalter was put on trial in New York for the murder of Rosen. He was convicted in 1941 and sentenced to death. Even while in custody, Buchalter reportedly ordered hits on a number of his enemies including Reles. On March 4, 1944, Louis Buchalter was executed in the electric chair at Sing Sing prison—becoming the first mob leader to die from a legal execution. *See also* PAIR AND GROUP KILLERS, Murder, Incorporated.

"Bugsy" Siegel *see* Siegel, Benjamin

Burke, Fred. Born in 1885 in Kansas, Fred Burke—nicknamed "Killer"—was involved in many payroll and bank robberies, killing an estimated twenty people during his violent career. His murderous early trademark was impersonating police and relying on submachine guns in perpetrating robberies of banks. He became a hired hit man for Al Capone in the late 1920s and was believed to have participated in the 1929 St. Valentine's Day Massacre. On March 26 1931, Burke was arrested in Missouri and extradited to Michigan for the murder of a police officer, Charles Skelly. Fred Burke was convicted of the murder and sentenced to life in prison where he died on July 10, 1940. *See also*, Capone, Alphonse.

Campione, Frank *see* PAIR AND GROUP KILLERS, Black Hand

Capone, Alphonse. This notorious gangster and killer has captured the imagination of both the American and international public perhaps more than any other organized crime figure. Born in Brooklyn, New York in 1899, Alphonse Capone was also known as Al Capone and "Scarface" Al (a name given to him because of the facial scars he accumulated early in his career while working as a bartender and bouncer). He also had several other aliases. Capone rose through the ranks of crime syndicates in New York and Chicago during the 1910s and 1920s, killing hundreds of people along the way. It was in Chicago that Capone, who was married and had a son, made his mark as a mobster and murderer. Under the tutelage of gangster Johnny Torrio, by the age of twenty-five Scarface Al had earned millions, achieving notoriety as a bootlegger, pimp, and partner in crime. In spite of a violent track record as a hit man—and later as an organized crime boss who personally killed those who got in his way and ordered the deaths of competitors and others—authorities were unable to convict Capone for murder. His downfall came when he was charged with income tax evasion in 1931. Al Capone was convicted and sentenced to eleven years in prison and fined $50,000. In 1934, he was among the first "Public Enemies" to be sent to prison at Alcatraz. Diagnosed with advanced syphilis and paresis of the brain, Capone was released from prison on November 19, 1939. While battling pneumonia, he suffered a massive brain hemorrhage and died on January 25, 1947.

Cardinelli, Sam *see* PAIR AND GROUP KILLERS, Black Hand

"The Dasher" *see* Abbandando, Frank

DiGiovannis, Joseph *see* PAIR AND GROUP KILLERS, Black Hand

DiGiovannis, Peter *see* PAIR AND GROUP KILLERS, Black Hand

Dillinger, John Herbert. On January 15, 1934, John Dillinger shot and killed patrolman William O'Malley during the course of a robbery of the First National Bank in East Chicago, Illinois. Dillinger was born in 1903 in Indianapolis, Indiana, and made headlines across the country during the Depression as an outlaw. He committed countless bank robberies, survived shootouts with the police and FBI, eluded authorities, and escaped from custody twice. Following his capture in Tucson, Arizona, on January 25, 1934, for the O'Malley murder and bank robbery, Dillinger used a wooden pistol to break out of jail on March 3, 1934. He became the country's first Public Enemy Number One on June 22, 1934, as federal and local authorities intensified their efforts to recapture him. On July 22, 1934, in an ambush, Dillinger was killed by law enforcement as he stepped outside the Biograph Theater on North Lincoln Avenue in Chicago. *See also* The 1930s – The Life and Death of Public Enemy Number One, John Dillinger.

"The Enforcer" *see* Nitti, Frank

"The Executioner" *see* Anastasia, Albert

Floyd, Charles Arthur. Born in 1904 in Adairsville, Georgia, Charles Arthur Floyd, nicknamed "Pretty Boy" Floyd, gained national attention during the 1920s and 1930s as a bank robber and killer. He is believed to have committed at least ten murders and robbed as many as forty banks. While the infamous outlaw was seen by some as a Robin Hood type character during his day, Floyd may be most remembered for his participation in the Kansas City Massacre on June 17, 1933, that took place in the Union Square parking lot— killing five men, including three law enforcement officers. Floyd was identified as one of the submachine gun armed killers who were attempting to free a fellow robber, Frank Nash, who had been recaptured after escaping from prison. Nash was killed during the massacre. On October 22, 1934, FBI agents gunned down thirty-year-old Charles Floyd while he was hiding out on a farm near Clarkson, Ohio. *See also* The 1930s – The Kansas City Massacre.

Giancana, Sam. Born in Chicago in 1908 as Salvatore Giancana, Sam Giancana was a leader of the Chicago mob in the 1950s and 1960s. His early years as a criminal included auto theft, robbery, and rape as part of a teenage gang prior to working for Al Capone as a hit man. Before the age of twenty, he is believed to have committed dozens of murders and been involved in the infamous St. Valentine's Day Massacre. Giancana's organized crime activities stretched to Las Vegas, Mexico, and Cuba—where he was possibly part of a CIA conspiracy to overthrow Cuban leader Fidel Castro. Amongst Giancana's powerful political and entertainment friends and acquaintances were John F.

Kennedy and Frank Sinatra. On June 19, 1975—after being ordered to testify before a Senate committee investigating the CIA and his possible relationship with it—Sam Giancana was shot to death by an unknown assailant in the kitchen of his home in Oak Park, Illinois. The CIA denied they played any role in the murder of the sixty-seven-year-old mobster. *See also* The 1920s – The St. Valentine's Day Massacre.

Gotti, John. Born in 1940, John Gotti became one of the most powerful organized crime figures in New York during the 1980s, after seizing control of the Carlos Gambino Mafia family, which ran most of the rackets. Gotti gained and maintained his power through violence, reportedly being involved in ten murders. Though he spent some time in prison in his earlier years in working as a racketeer and killer, John Gotti was adept at evading the arms of the law for years—acquitted in three trials of various charges and gaining a reputation of being untouchable. That changed when the FBI finally made a case against Gotti that he could not beat. On April 2, 1992, John Gotti was convicted on fourteen counts against him—including the murders of reputed Gambino family underbosses Paul Castellano and Thomas Bilotti—and sentenced to life in prison with no chance for parole. On June 24, 1992, he arrived at the federal prison in Marion, Illinois, to begin serving his time. On June 10, 2002, John Gotti died of throat cancer while being treated at the United States Medical Center for Federal Prisoners located in Springfield, Missouri.

Joey. Born in 1932, an organized crime hit man using the undercover name "Joey" confessed to murdering thirty-eight people in his 1973 autobiography. All of his victims were said to be part of the underworld, with thirty-five of them contract murders. Along with being a serial organized crime killer, Joey also participated in other mob activities including narcotics smuggling, bootlegging, book making, and producing porn films. He claimed to have only been sixteen when he killed his first victim. Later, his own pregnant wife was a victim of a gangland slaying—leaving him bitter and eventually causing him to avenge her death by killing the attackers. Though estimating to have made approximately four million dollars as a mob hit man, Joey has somehow avoided justice in paying for his violent crimes. He has reportedly been questioned by the authorities in as many as seventeen murder cases, come before seven grand juries, and been put on trial three times. To date, he has not been convicted of any homicide.

Karpis, Alvin. Born in Montreal, Canada, in 1908 as Francis Alvin Karpaviecz, Alvin Karpis was the co-leader of the infamous Barker-Karpis gang that included Fred Barker, Arthur Barker, and their mother, Kate "Ma" Barker. The gang participated in burglaries, mail, bank, and train robberies, kidnappings, and murder. The gang is blamed for at least ten murders between 1931 and 1936 and the kidnappings for ransom of two businessmen, William A. Hamm Jr. and Edward G. Bremer. Karpis himself was identified as delivering the fatal bullets in the murder of a sheriff in a West Plains, Missouri, clothing store on December 18, 1931. On May 1, 1936, Karpis was taken into custody in New Orleans by FBI Director J. Edgar Hoover. He pleaded guilty to kidnapping and was sentenced to life imprisonment. On January 14, 1969, Alvin Karpis was paroled and deported to Canada. He died in Spain from a drug overdose on August 26, 1979. *See also* PAIR AND GROUP KILLERS, Barker, Frederick.

"Kid Twist" *see* Reles, Abraham

"Killer" *see* Burke, Fred

Lansky, Meyer. Born in 1902 in Russia as Maier Suchowljansky, Meyer Lansky and his family immigrated to America, living in New York's Lower East Side. In the 1920s, Lansky, "Lucky" Luciano, and Bugsy Siegel became leaders of the newly formed national crime syndicate. In New York, Lansky and Siegel ran the Bugs and Meyer Mob and contracted out professional hit men to other gangs. These paid killers would later be called Murder, Inc. Meyer Lansky and company were also involved in gambling and bootlegging activities as well as hijackings. In the 1930s, he took up residence in Miami and became a force in gambling operations in Florida and Cuba. In spite of being linked to a number of murders and other violent crimes, he was only prosecuted for tax evasion, unsuccessfully. On January 15, 1983, Meyer Lansky died of a heart attack at eighty-one-years of age. *See also* Luciano, Charles; Siegel, Benjamin; PAIR AND GROUP KILLERS, Murder, Incorporated.

Legenza, Walter *see* Mais, Robert Howard

Luciano, Charles. Born in Italy in 1897 as Salvatore Lucania, Charles "Lucky" Luciano helped establish organized crime syndicates in the United States during the early 1930s. He began his crime career on the Lower East Side of Manhattan as a thief, narcotics dealer, pimp, and messenger for the Five Points Gang. He worked for mobster Johnny Torrio and befriended future mob leaders such as Al Capone and Bugsy Siegel. In 1931, Luciano—en route to becoming the most powerful organized crime figure in the country running prostitution, bootlegging, and narcotics smuggling rackets—orchestrated the murders of mob bosses Joe Masseria and Salvatore Maranzano. Luciano was convicted on prostitution and extortion charges and sentenced to thirty to fifty years in prison. He was pardoned in 1946 and deported to Sicily, moving to Cuba a year later. In June 1947, Luciano ordered the murder of Bugsy Siegel, whom he had loaned millions of unpaid mob money to toward the construction of a Las Vegas hotel and casino. At the age of sixty-four, Charles Luciano died of a heart attack in Naples, Italy, on January 26, 1962. *See also* Lansky, Meyer; Siegel, Benjamin; PAIR AND GROUP KILLERS, Murder, Incorporated.

Mais, Robert Howard. Born in 1906, Robert Howard Mais was a co-leader of the Tri-State Gang, along with Walter Legenza. During the 1930s, the Tri-State Gang committed murders, hijackings, and payroll and bank robberies in some eastern states. On June 1, 1934, Mais and Legenza were arrested by police in Baltimore, Maryland, and charged with the murder of a bank messenger. Both were extradited to Virginia where they were convicted and sentenced to death. With the help of a smuggled gun, the two killers broke out of jail on September 29, 1934, reestablishing their gang and criminal activities. In January 1935, FBI agents recaptured Mais and Legenza in New York City. On February 2, 1935, Robert Mais and Walter Legenza were executed in Virginia's electric chair.

Murder, Incorporated *see* PAIR AND GROUP KILLERS

Nitti, Frank. Born in Italy in 1889, Frank Nitti became a bootlegger in Chicago under mobster Johnny Torrio in 1920. By 1925, he was a prominent member of Al Capone's syndicate. Known as "The Enforcer," Nitti was said to have been involved in the planning of the St. Valentine's Day Massacre in 1929. He and his associates also murdered a number of mob rivals in a battle for control of the Chicago mob after Capone was imprisoned for income tax evasion in 1931. By the mid 1930s, Nitti succeeded in taking over leadership of Capone's organized crime empire. A continuing racketeer in the post-Prohibition Era, in 1943 Nitti was indicted for extortion, for which he had previously served time behind bars. Fearing imprisonment again and reportedly stricken with cancer, Frank Nitti committed suicide in Chicago on March 19, 1943, shooting himself to death. *See also* Capone, Alphonse; The 1920s – The St. Valentine's Day Massacre.

"Pittsburgh Phil" *see* Strauss, Harry

"Pretty Boy" Floyd *see* Floyd, Charles Arthur

Public Enemy Number One *see* Dillinger, John

Reles, Abraham. Born in 1907, Abraham Reles, also known as Abe and "Kid Twist," was a Brooklyn mobster and killer for hire. In the 1930s, Reles was in charge of the street operations for Murder, Inc., the assassination branch of the syndicate. He was thought to have personally been a party to at least thirty homicides. In spite of a lengthy arrest record, Reles was never convicted of any of the murders he allegedly committed. In 1940, he became a police informant. The information he provided to the authorities helped solve dozens of gangland murders and led to a number of murder convictions of mob members, while encouraging other informants to come forward. On November 12, 1941—while in protective custody and heavily guarded at the Half Moon Hotel on Coney Island—Abe Reles mysteriously fell from a sixth story window to his death on the pavement below. While an official investigation never solved the case, it was two decades later that mob boss Charles "Lucky" Luciano alleged that Reles had been the victim of a syndicate hit carried out by crooked police who had been guarding him. *See also* PAIR AND GROUP KILLERS, Murder, Incorporated.

Saietta, Ignazio *see* PAIR AND GROUP KILLERS, Black Hand

"Scarface" *see* Capone, Alphonse

Siegel, Benjamin. Born in Brooklyn in 1906, Benjamin Siegel began his criminal career as a small time extortionist and thief before moving into illegal gambling operations and becoming a hit man for such mobsters as Meyer Lansky and Charles "Lucky" Luciano. Under the tutelage of Lansky, Siegel established Murder, Inc.—a gang of Jewish hired killers who worked for the crime syndicates to eliminate rival or uncooperative mobsters. Siegel acquired the nickname of "Bugsy" due to his temper and reckless behavior as a gangland killer for hire. During the 1920s and 1930s, Bugsy Siegel is believed to have participated in at least a dozen murders. His main claim to fame may have been his role in bringing organized crime to Las Vegas, Nevada. Using his own money and syndicate money, Siegel built the first grand gambling casino and hotel on the Las Vegas Strip—the Flamingo Hotel. When the mob investment failed to pay off in quick dividends, a hit was put out on him. On June 20, 1947, the forty-one-year-old Siegel was shot to death at the Beverly Hills, California, mansion of his longtime girlfriend and syndicate courier, Virginia Hill. *See also,* Lansky, Meyer; Luciano, Charles; PAIR AND GROUP KILLERS, Murder, Incorporated.

Strauss, Harry. Born in 1908 in Brooklyn, New York, Harry Strauss was one of the most deadly and ruthless killers of the organized crime hit squad, Murder, Inc. During the 1930s, Strauss—who was nicknamed "Pittsburgh Phil"—was estimated to have murdered more than one hundred people. Some believe he may have killed as many as five hundred. Strauss was proficient in multiple ways of murdering his targets including using a gun, rope, and ice pick. The paid assassin and ladies' man managed to escape prosecution in spite of numerous arrests, until fellow Murder, Inc. hit man Abraham Reles turned informant in 1940 and fingered him as a killer. Strauss was indicted for the May 10, 1939, murder of gambler and racketeer Irving "Puggy" Feinstein. A jury convicted him of first-degree murder and sentenced Strauss to death. On June 12, 1941, Harry Strauss was executed in the electric chair at Sing Sing prison. *See also* PAIR AND GROUP KILLERS, Murder, Incorporated.

CELEBRITY KILLERS - MEN

Chapman, Mark David. On December 8, 1980, Mark David Chapman shot to death former Beatle John Lennon as he and his wife, Yoko Ono, were about to enter the Dakota apartment building where they lived in New York City. The twenty-five-year-old Chapman had sought and succeeded in getting the singer's autograph earlier in the day. Armed with a .38-caliber revolver, Chapman fired five shots at Lennon upon his return home from a recording session. Four hit the mark, mortally wounding the singer and songwriter who gained fame as a member of the British group The Beatles. Lennon died at Roosevelt Hospital from shock brought on by massive hemorrhaging. He was forty years old. Chapman was arrested without incident and charged with murder. In 1981, he pled guilty to a crime motivated by jealousy and fame and was sentenced to twenty years to life in prison. He has been denied parole nine times. *See also* The 1980s – The Killing of John Lennon; Adult Victims, Lennon, John.

Cunanan, Andrew *see* Serial Killers - Men

Gay, Marvin P., Sr. On April 1, 1984, Marvin P. Gay Sr. shot to death his son, singer Marvin Gaye, during a scuffle at the family home in Los Angeles, California. Born in 1939 as Marvin Pentz Gay Jr., the forty-four-year-old Gaye was one of Motown Records' top solo and duet artists during the 1960s and 1970s. He recorded such classics as "Pride and Joy" and "If I Could Build My Whole World Around You." He later won two Grammy awards. Marvin Gay Sr.—an ordained minister with whom the singer had a long time stormy relationship—fatally shot him at point-blank range following a physical and verbal altercation that included Gaye's mother. Gay was arrested and eventually pleaded no contest to voluntary manslaughter. He was sentenced to five years' probation. Marvin Gay Sr. died on October 17, 1998, at the age of eighty-four. *See also* Adult Victims, Gaye, Marvin.

Rathbun, Charles. On November 16, 1995, Charles Rathbun sexually assaulted and murdered twenty-seven-year-old model and former Los Angeles Raiders cheerleader Linda Sobek in a remote area in the San Gabriel Mountains near Los Angeles, California. The thirty-eight-year-old freelance photographer lured Sobek to the scene under the guise of a photo shoot for a magazine where he violently sodomized then strangled her. Rathbun was charged with murder. He led authorities to the shallow grave where he had buried Sobek in the Los Angeles National Forest. He attempted to commit suicide before his arrest and while in jail. On November 1, 1996, a jury found Charles Rathbun guilty of first-degree murder in the death of Linda Sobek. He was also convicted of anal rape and sentenced to life in prison with no chance of parole. *See also* Adult Victims, Sobek, Linda.

Snider, Paul. On August 14, 1980, Paul Snider murdered his *Playboy* model-actress wife, Dorothy Stratten. Snider, twenty-nine, lured his estranged wife to his Los Angeles, California, apartment where he raped and tortured her before shooting her in the face with a 12-gauge shotgun. Snider was jealous and vindictive and killed the twenty-year-old Stratten when she told him she planned to divorce him. After he murdered his wife, Paul Snider committed suicide. *See also* The 1980s – The Murder of Playmate Dorothy Stratten; Adult Victims, Stratten, Dorothy.

CHILD KILLERS - MEN

Bishop, Arthur Gary *see* Serial Killers – Men

Dahmer, Jeffrey L. *see* Serial Killers – Men

Davis, Richard Allen. On October 1, 1993, Richard Allen Davis, a twice-convicted kidnapper, took twelve-year-old Polly Klaas at knife-point from her home in Petaluma, California, and killed her. A nationwide search for the missing girl ensued before her body was found thirty miles away in December 1993. Davis, thirty-nine, was arrested and charged with the kidnapping and murder of Polly Klaas. On June 19, 1996, Richard Allen Davis was found guilty and sentenced to death on September 26, 1996. He is currently on death row at San Quentin prison. *See also* Child Victims, Klaas, Polly Hannah.

Dodd, Westley Allan *see* Serial Killers – Men

Evans, Donald Leroy *see* Serial Killers – Men

Fish, Albert *see* Serial Killers – Men

Frank, Leo. On April 26, 1913, Mary Phagan was murdered at the National Pencil Factory in Atlanta,

Georgia. The thirteen-year-old's body was found beaten and strangled in the basement of the factory where she worked as a pencil maker. Arrested for her murder was Leo Frank, a twenty-seven-year-old Jewish man who was the factory superintendent. Frank was convicted of murdering Phagan on August 25, 1913, and sentenced to death. Under pressure from those who believed Frank's trial was a sham, his sentence was commuted to life in prison on June 21, 1915. A lynch mob thought otherwise, forcibly removing Frank from the Milledgeville state prison on the morning of August 17, 1915. He was taken to a site in Mary Phagan's hometown of Marietta, Georgia, hooded, and hung from an oak tree. His killers were never brought to justice. *See also* The 1910s – The Murder of Mary Phagan; Child Victims, Phagan, Mary.

Gacy, John Wayne *see* Serial Killers – Men

Gallego, Gerald Armond *see* PAIR AND GROUP KILLERS

Hauptmann, Bruno Richard. On March 1, 1932, twenty-month-old Charles Augustus Lindbergh Jr. was kidnapped from the second story nursery of the Lindbergh home close to Hopewell, New Jersey. After a series of ransom notes and a payoff, the decomposed body of the missing child was found on May 12, 1932, nearly five miles from the Lindbergh home. Richard Bruno Hauptmann was arrested on September 19, 1934, after ransom notes were traced to him and he fit the description of the suspect. The thirty-five-year-old illegal German immigrant and carpenter was indicted for extortion and murder in October 1934. On February 13, 1935, he was convicted of first-degree murder in the death of Charles Lindbergh Jr. and sentenced to death. Hauptmann was put to death in

New Jersey's electric chair on April 3, 1936. *See also* The 1930s – The Lindbergh Baby Kidnapping and Murder; Child Victims, Lindbergh, Charles Augustus, Jr.

LaMarca, Angelo. On July 4, 1956, Angelo LaMarca kidnapped one-month-old Peter Weinberger from his home in Long Island, New York. The truck driver and taxi dispatcher made ransom demands of $2,000 for the boy's return. Through handwriting analysis of the ransom note, the FBI was able to identify LaMarca as the kidnapper. He was arrested on August 23, 1956. After confessing to the abduction, he told authorities where to locate the infant. Peter Weinberger's decomposed remains were found in heavy brush near a highway exit. LaMarca faced state charges for kidnapping and murder. He was convicted and received the death penalty on December 14, 1956. Following failed appeals, Angelo LaMarca was put to death in the electric chair at Sing Sing prison on August 7, 1958. *See also* The 1950s – The Kidnapping and Murder of Peter Weinberger; Child Victims, Weinberger, Peter.

Leopold, Nathan *see* PAIR AND GROUP KILLERS

Loeb, Richard *see* PAIR AND GROUP KILLERS, Leopold, Nathan

Mullin, Herbert *see* Serial Killers – Men

Panzram, Carl *see* Serial Killers – Men

Shawcross, Arthur J. *see* Serial Killers – Men

Timmendequas, Jesse K. On July 29, 1994, Jesse Timmendequas brutally murdered seven-year-old Megan Kanka in Hamilton Township, New Jersey. The thirty-six-year-old twice-convicted sex offender lived across the street from the Kanka family. Timmendequas lured Megan to his home, where he raped and strangled her before leaving her body in a nearby park. On May 31, 1997, Timmendequas was convicted of the kidnapping, aggravated sexual assault, and murder of Megan Kanka. He was sentenced to death on June 20, 1997. In August 1999, he filed an appeal for a new trial that was turned down by the Supreme Court. The Kanka's helped to change New Jersey law regarding sex offender notification, resulting in the passage of Megan's Law in October 1994, which required public notification when a sex offender is released into the community. A federal sex offender notification law was enacted in May 1996. Timmendequas was on New Jersey's Death Row until December 17, 2007, when the New Jersey legislature abolished the state's death penalty. His sentence was commuted to life in prison without parole. *See also* Child Victims, Kanka, Megan.

Williams, Wayne *see* Serial Killers — Men

FAMILIAL KILLERS - MEN

Amityville Horror Killer *see* DeFeo, Ronald Butch, Jr.

Benson, Steven Wayne. On July 9, 1985, thirty-four-year-old tobacco heir Steven Benson planted two pipe bombs beneath the family's van outside their home in Naples, Florida. The explosion killed his mother, Margaret Benson, his twenty-one-year-old brother, Scott, and severely injured his sister, Carol Lynn Benson Kendall. The sixty-three-year-old Margaret Benson was a widow and heiress to the Lancaster Leaf Tobacco Company family fortune. When her husband died, it was Steven who assumed control in managing the family's business interests. However, once it was suspected that he was stealing money from the company, Mrs. Benson threatened to disinherit her son. She was preparing to have the company books audited when the blast took place. Steven Benson was arrested for the family crime and went to trial in 1986. He was convicted of two counts of murder in the first degree, attempted murder, and six counts of purchasing materials and building explosives. Benson received a sentence of two consecutive life terms with no possibility of parole for fifty years. On July 3, 2015, he died in a Florida prison. *See also* The 1980s – The Pipe Bomb Murders.

DeFeo, Ronald Butch, Jr. On November 13, 1974, Ronald Butch DeFeo Jr., armed with a .35-caliber rifle, murdered six members of his family in Amityville, New York. In a case that was the inspiration for a novel called *The Amityville Horror*, and later a movie by the same name, the twenty-three-year-old DeFeo claimed he was possessed by Satan when he murdered his parents and siblings in their beds. At the time of the massacre, DeFeo was on probation and under surveillance as a drug user. He was convicted in 1975 for the murders and sentenced to six consecutive twenty-five-year life sentences, or a 150-year prison term. In appealing the conviction, DeFeo claimed that his eighteen-year-old sister, Dawn, had killed the family members and he fatally wounded her in a fit of rage. The appeal was rejected by the state Supreme Court as unbelievable.

Falater, Scott *see* Intimate Killers - Men

Gilbert, Roswell *see* Intimate Killers - Men

Graham, Jack Gilbert *see* Mass Murderers - Men

Grentz, Tom. On January 3, 1996, eighty-seven-year-old Tom Grentz used a .25-caliber gun to shoot his eighty-five-year-old sister, Eleanor Simpson, and himself. The murder-suicide took place in the house they shared in Baltimore, Maryland. Both Grentz and Simpson were seriously ill. He had emphysema and heart problems and his sister had recently suffered a stroke and fractured her hip, requiring Tom's assistance to get around. After calling the police during the crime, Tom Grentz died at the scene. Eleanor Simpson was pronounced dead shortly after arriving at the hospital.

MacDonald, Jeffrey. On February 17, 1970, twenty-six-year-old Jeffrey MacDonald bludgeoned and stabbed his wife, Colette, and their two daughters, Kimberley and Kristen, in their Fort Bragg home in Wilmington, North Carolina. MacDonald, an Army doctor, claimed drug-crazed hippies committed the murders. An official investigation, though controversial, indicated otherwise. The former Green Beret went on trial for the murders in 1979. He was convicted of the murder of his wife and two children and sentenced to three life sentences. The shocking crime was the basis for several books and a TV miniseries. Jeffrey MacDonald has filed numerous appeals, going all the way up to the U.S. Supreme Court, and they have all been rejected. *See also* The 1970s – The Fort Bragg Murder Case.

Menendez, Lyle, and **Erik Menendez.** On August 20, 1989, in a shocking and brutal crime of family homicide and privilege, Jose Menendez and his wife, Mary Louise "Kitty" Menendez, were murdered in their Beverly Hills, California, home by their sons, Lyle and Erik Menendez. Jose, a forty-five-year-old entertainment executive, was shot five times with a 12-gauge shotgun and Mary Louise, forty-seven, was shot ten times. Both were shot at close range. Lyle, twenty-two, and Erik, nineteen, the sole beneficiaries of their parents' multimillion dollar estate and life insurance, were arrested six months later and charged with their deaths. This came after law enforcement authorities obtained a psychologist's secretly recorded tapes in which the Menendez boys allegedly confessed to the murders. In 1994, Erik and Lyle Menendez were tried together by two different juries. They defended their actions by claiming the killings were "self-defense," motivated by years of physical, sexual, and emotional abuse by their parents. Both juries were unable to reach a verdict, ending in a mistrial. In a 1996 retrial by a single jury, the Menendez brothers were convicted of first-degree murder in the deaths of their parents and sentenced to life in prison without the possibility of parole. In February 1998, an appellate court denied Lyle and Erik Menendez a new trial. *See also* The 1980s – The Murders of Jose and Mary Menendez.

Ruppert, James. On March 30, 1975, James Ruppert gunned down eleven family members during an Easter Sunday dinner in Hamilton, Ohio. The victims included the forty-year-old Ruppert's mother. He received a life sentence at the Allen Correctional Institution in Lima. In June 1995, the mass murderer's parole request was rejected and he was ordered to serve a minimum of forty more years in prison.

Simmons, Ronald Gene. On December 28, 1987, Ronald Gene Simmons ended a shooting spree that included the murder of fourteen family members, by shooting to death two co-workers and wounding four others in Russellville, Arkansas. The family victims died mostly in their beds, some who were found in shallow graves outside the home of the killer. Simmons was convicted of sixteen murders and sentenced to death. After waiving all appeals and pleading for a swift execution to end his suffering, Simmons was put to death by lethal injection in June 1990.

Stuart, Charles *see* Intimate Killers - Men

Xiong, Kao. On December 4, 1999, Kao Xiong used a high-powered rifle and shotgun to kill five of his seven children, aged one to seven, before fatally shooting himself. The incident took place in their one bedroom apartment in Del Paso Heights, just north of Sacramento, California. Two older children managed to escape the attack. Xiong—who had spent fifteen years in a refugee camp in Thailand—and his family had come to the United States from Laos seven years earlier. He had allegedly had an argument with his wife prior to the murders.

INTIMATE KILLERS - MEN

Falater, Scott. On January 16, 1997, Scott Falater viciously attacked his wife, preschool aid Yarmila Falater, stabbing her forty-four times and then holding her head under water in the family's swimming pool outside their home in Phoenix, Arizona. The couple had been married for twenty years and had two children. Falater, a forty-two-year-old Mormon and Motorola engineer, claimed that he was sleepwalking during the commission of the murder and had no memory of it. However, law enforcement authorities found that he had tried to conceal evidence at the time of the killing. He was charged with the murder of his wife. Falater had an apparent history of sleepwalking and was under a great deal of stress at work—possible triggers for his homicidal rage. A jury thought otherwise and on June 24, 1999, found the "sleepwalker killer" guilty of murder in the first degree. On January 10, 2000, Scott Falater was sentenced to spend the rest of his life in prison without the possibility of parole. *See* *also* The 1990s – The Case of the Sleepwalker Killer; Adult Victims, Falater, Yarmila.

Gilbert, Roswell. On March 4, 1985, seventy-six-year-old Roswell Gilbert shot to death his seventy-three-year-old wife, Emily, in their Fort Lauderdale, Florida, condo. The couple had been married for more than fifty years. Emily, who suffered from Alzheimer's disease and was in constant pain, was completely dependent on Roswell, a retired engineer. He was convicted of first-degree murder and sentenced to twenty-five years in prison without the possibility of parole. With the mercy killing nature of the crime receiving attention in the media, on August 2, 1990, Roswell Gilbert was granted clemency by the governor of Florida and released from prison at age eighty-one. He died in September 1994 at the age of eighty-five.

Stuart, Charles. On October 23, 1989, Charles Stuart—a thirty-two-year-old manager of a furrier—used his car cell phone to report that he and his pregnant wife, Carol Stuart, had just been shot in their car in the Mission Hill area of Boston, Massachusetts. Stuart claimed that the gunman and robber was an African American man. Carol Stuart, a thirty-year-old tax lawyer who was seven months pregnant, was mortally wounded and died the following day. Her infant son, Christopher Stuart, was delivered by Cesarean section and died seventeen days later due to complications. While authorities searched for a suspect matching Stuart's description, they learned that he was having an affair with a young college student and stood to gain financially from his wife's death through her life insurance. On January 3, 1990, Stuart's brother, Matthew Stuart, confessed to authorities that Charles had given him the alleged murder weapon and other personal effects that had supposedly been stolen. On January 4, 1990, as police closed in on Charles Stuart to make an arrest for the murder of Carol Stuart, he killed himself by jumping 145 feet off a bridge into the Mystic River. *See also* The 1980s – The Murder of Carol Stuart; Adult Victims, Stuart, Carol.

MASS MURDERERS - MEN

Allaway, Edward Charles *see* SCHOOL KILLINGS

Amityville Horror Killer *see* Familial Killers – Men, DeFeo, Ronald Butch, Jr.

Ashbrook, Larry Gene. On September 15, 1999, a gunman wearing black, screaming profanities and mocking religion, burst into the Wedgewood Baptist Church in Fort Worth, Texas, and opened fire, killing eight. Identified as forty-seven-year-old Larry Gene Ashbrook, the unemployed man—described as a loner, temperamental, and paranoid—shot fourteen people before fatally shooting himself. The killings, which occurred during a rally attracting hundreds of teenagers from several local churches, were called the worst mass murder in the city's history.

Barton, Mark Orrin. On July 29, 1999, day trader Mark Orrin Barton entered two brokerage firms in Atlanta, Georgia, killing nine people and wounding twelve before fleeing the scene. The shootings were apparently spurred on by heavy losses the forty-four-year-old Barton had recently sustained in the stock market. The killing spree began when the former chemist bludgeoned to death his estranged wife and their two young children to save them from "a lifetime of pain." Barton shot and killed himself in his van five hours later after being surrounded by police.

Brown, Carl Robert. On August 20, 1982, Carl Robert Brown entered a Miami welding and machine shop and unloaded a 12-gauge shotgun, killing eight employees. The fifty-one-year-old history teacher was reportedly upset over the bill for work done there on his lawn mower engine. Called Miami's worst massacre, Brown calmly left the crime scene on a bicycle. Pursued by two men who had chased him from the shop, he was run over and killed after reportedly aiming his shotgun at the car they were in. Brown, estranged from his wife and son, was known to have psychiatric problems.

Burke, David. On December 7, 1987, David Burke, a vengeful former employee of the parent company of Pacific Southwest Airlines, boarded Flight 1771 and shot the pilots in flight, causing the jet to crash into a muddy hillside in California. All forty-three people on board were killed. Burke, who was fired from his job as a ticket agent for the airline, sought revenge against the man responsible for his dismissal who was on the flight. Six shots were reportedly fired, four inside the cockpit, before it went down. As a result of the Pacific Southwest Airlines mass murder-suicide, the U.S. Department of Transportation issued new federal rules requiring all employees of airlines and airports to pass through the same security checkpoints with metal detectors and baggage x-ray equipment as passengers.

Cowan, Frederick *see* HATE CRIME KILLERS

Essex, Mark Robert James *see* HATE CRIME KILLERS

Farley, Richard Wade. On February 16, 1988, a man obsessed with a female co-worker at a Silicon Valley defense plant shot to death seven and wounded four more at the company's offices in Sunnyvale, California. Identified as Richard Wade Farley, a thirty-nine-year-old software development engineer technician, the gunman had been spurned by the female object of his obsession, one of his victims. Following a six-hour standoff, Farley surrendered to police and was charged with seven counts of murder, three counts of attempted murder, and other crimes. In December 1991, a judge sentenced Richard Farley to death in the gas chamber. He is currently on death row at San Quentin prison.

Ferri, Gian Luigi. On July 1, 1993, Gian Luigi Ferri entered a law firm in a San Francisco high-rise equipped with a .45-caliber handgun and two semiautomatic TEC-9 pistols. He killed eight people and wounded four others. The fifty-five-year-old mortgage broker, who had a longstanding grievance with the firm, then committed suicide with a gunshot to the head.

Gonzalez, Julio. On March 25, 1990, eighty-seven people lost their lives in a fire at a social club in the Bronx in New York City—one of the country's worst fatal fires and mass murders. Confessing to setting the fire was Julio Gonzalez, a thirty-five-year-old Cuban émigré. The fire was set by Gonzalez following an argument with his girlfriend who was at the Happy Land Social Club—a place frequented mostly by Latinos to listen to music, dance, and drink alcoholic beverages. Vowing to "shut the place down," Gonzalez bought one dollar's worth of gasoline at a nearby gas station and returned to the club where he splashed the gas inside the entrance, set fire to it with a match, and fled the scene. Most of the eighty-seven victims were Honduran immigrants. Gonzalez was convicted in the summer of 1991 on 174 counts of murder (two for each of his eighty-seven victims) and sentenced to twenty-five years to life in prison.

Happy Land had been operating in spite of being in violation of building and fire regulations. As a result of the fire, New York City established a Social Club Task Force to investigate unlicensed premises and after hours and illegal social clubs.

On September 13, 2016, Julio Gonzalez died of a heart attack in prison.

Graham, Jack Gilbert. In 1955, a madman named Jack Gilbert Graham sent his visiting mother off on an airplane from Denver carrying a gift-wrapped bomb. The bomb exploded shortly after takeoff, killing all forty-four people. Graham, born in 1932, was married with two young children. He was a smalltime con who hated his mother and her interference in his life. He also hoped to collect on her life insurance. His gift to her was, in fact, fourteen pounds of dynamite along with a timer. Jack Graham was tried and convicted of the mass murder and sentenced to death. He was executed in the gas chamber on January 11, 1957. *See also* The 1950s – The Deadly Explosion Aboard Flight 629.

Harris, Eric *see* The 1990s – The Mass Murder at Columbine High School; SCHOOL KILLINGS

Hennard, George. On October 16, 1991, after ramming a pickup truck through the window of a Luby's Cafeteria in Killeen, Texas, George Hennard opened fire on the lunchtime patrons, killing twenty-three people and injuring nineteen others. Thirty-five-year-old Hennard, described as a loner with a hatred of women, committed suicide in the bathroom of the restaurant with a gunshot to the head. Among his possessions, authorities recovered a movie ticket to "The Fisher King," a dark tale that included a massacre at a New York restaurant.

Hickock, Richard Eugene *see* PAIR AND GROUP KILLERS, Smith, Perry Edward

Huberty, James Oliver. On July 18, 1984, James Oliver Huberty entered a McDonald's restaurant in San Ysidro, California, armed with three weapons including an Uzi, and opened fire, killing twenty. The shooting, called at the time the worst single day mass murder in United States history, came after the forty-one-year-old unemployed security guard had gotten into a fight with his wife. He followed her and his daughter to the restaurant, where he went into his homicidal rage. Huberty, described by a psychiatrist as fitting the profile of a "Soldier of Fortune" killer, was known to be a loner, heavily into drug use, and violent, while stockpiling an arsenal of weapons. He became the twenty-first victim of the McDonald's mass slaying when a police sniper killed him.

Ismoil, Eyad *see* The 1990s – The Bombing of the World Trade Center; Terrorist Killers - Men, Yousef, Ramzi

Kehoe, Andrew *see* SCHOOL KILLINGS

King, Alvin Lee III. On June 22, 1980, Alvin Lee King III stormed into the First Baptist Church in Dangerfield, Texas, and opened fire on the congregation, killing five. Seeking vengeance upon those he believed had condemned him, the murder spree came after King was accused of molesting his nineteen-year-old-daughter and a day before he was due to appear in court. After fleeing the church, King attempted suicide but survived a gunshot to the head. While awaiting trial, he ripped a towel in half and hung himself on January 19, 1982.

MacDonald, Jeffrey *see* Familial Killers - Men

McVeigh, Timothy J. *see* The 1990s – The Oklahoma City Bombing of The Alfred P. Murrah Federal Building; Terrorist Killers – Men

Mullin, Herbert. Herbert Mullin grew up in Santa Cruz, California. When his best friend was killed in a car accident in 1965, Mullin became mentally unbalanced. He set up a shrine to his dead friend in his bedroom and broke up with his girlfriend, claiming he was gay. His family then put him in a mental hospital and he was diagnosed a year later as a paranoid schizophrenic. Mullin began doing drugs and hearing voices, and was in an out of mental institutions for two years. On October 13, 1972, he claimed a "voice" told him to kill an old vagrant with a baseball bat. Eleven days later he stabbed a college student, cut open her body, and dug her entrails out with his hands so the vultures could eat them. Mullin bought a gun in December 1972 and claimed that people were begging him to kill them. He shot five people in one day. On February 6, 1973, Mullin shot and killed four teenage boys who were camping in Santa Cruz. Then he shot a man to death while he worked in his garden. A neighbor saw Mullin do it and called the police. He was arrested and confessed to thirteen murders. At his trial in 1973, a jury decided he was legally sane even though he had been diagnosed with paranoid schizophrenia. He was indicted for ten murders and found guilty of two counts of first-degree murder and eight counts of second-degree murder. He was sentenced to life in prison and is currently serving his time at Mule Creek State Prison in California.

Nichols, Terry *see* The 1990s – The Oklahoma City Bombing of The Alfred P. Murrah Federal Building; Terrorist Killers – Men, McVeigh, Timothy J.

Pough, James Edwards. On June 18, 1990, James Edwards Pough walked into a General Motors Acceptance Corporation office in Jacksonville, Florida, with a .30-caliber rifle and started shooting, killing eight. Three others were wounded, though one would die later, before Pough fatally shot himself. The forty-two-year-old day laborer was angry about having his car repossessed earlier in the year by the auto loan company. Prior to the mass killing, called the worst in Florida history at the time, Pough had shot and killed two others in separate incidents.

Purdy, Patrick Edward *see* SCHOOL KILLINGS

Ruppert, James *see* Familial Killers - Men

Sherrill, Patrick Henry. On August 21, 1986, part-time postal worker Patrick Henry Sherrill entered the post office in Edmond, Oklahoma. Carrying several guns and ammunition, he opened fire, killing fourteen fellow employees and wounding six more. The forty-four-year-old gunman, described as a loner with pent-up anger, was about to be terminated when he went on the shooting rampage. It ended when Sherrill shot himself to death.

Silka, Michael. On May 20, 1984, Michael Silka went on a deadly three-hour shooting rampage in Manley Hot Springs, Alaska, killing eight people and dumping their bodies into the Tanana River. The bearded, twenty-five-year-old drifter was wanted by authorities for questioning about a murder in Fairbanks.

Silka was shot to death by state police while trying to escape upriver, but not before killing a state trooper who was pursuing him in a helicopter, making his total victim count nine.

Simmons, Ronald Gene *see* Familial Killers - Men

Smith, Perry Edward *see* PAIR AND GROUP KILLERS

Smith, Roland *see* HATE CRIME KILLERS

Torre, Humberto de la. In September 1982, Humberto de la Torre set fire to the Dorothy Mae apartment building in Los Angeles, killing twenty-five people. The nineteen-year-old gang member's mass murder and arson followed an argument he had with his uncle, the manager of the downtown hotel. Six of the victims had the same surname as Torre. He was arrested on December 23, 1982, in Texas, where he had fled, and charged with twenty-five counts of murder. On June 28, 1985, after pleading guilty to first-degree murder in the arson slayings, Humberto de la Torre was sentenced to 625 years to life behind bars.

Unruh, Howard. On September 5, 1949, armed with a German Luger, Howard Unruh went on a killing spree in his neighborhood in Camden, New Jersey, taking thirteen lives and wounding three others. The World War II veteran, described by a psychiatrist as a schizophrenic, was ruled insane and sent to the Trenton State Psychiatric Hospital. In 1980, having never been tried for his crimes, a judge ordered that the thirteen murder indictments against Unruh be dropped. After sixty years of confinement, Unruh died in October 2009 at the age of eighty-eight in a nursing home in Trenton, New Jersey. *See also* The 1940s – The Mass Killing By Howard Unruh.

Uyesugi, Byran Koji. On November 2, 1999, Byran Koji Uyesugi, a fifteen-year Xerox employee went berserk at a Xerox Corporation building in Honolulu, Hawaii. He shot and killed seven before fleeing the murder scene in a company van. The forty-year-old disgruntled Xerox repairman was surrounded by police for several hours in the van before surrendering in what was called the worst mass murder in Hawaiian history. Uyesugi was charged with one count of first-degree murder and seven counts of murder in the second degree, carrying a mandatory sentence of life imprisonment without the possibility of parole. He was convicted on June 13, 2000, on all counts and sentenced to life in prison without parole.

Westbecker, Joseph. On September 14, 1989, Joseph Westbecker, a mentally ill employee of a printing plant in Louisville, Kentucky, went on a shooting spree there. He killed seven and wounded thirteen others, before taking his own life. The forty-seven-year-old Westbecker, who was on permanent disability and receiving treatment for mental disorders, entered the plant carrying an AK-47 and two MAC-11 semiautomatic weapons in pursuit of the massacre.

Whitman, Charles Joseph *see* SCHOOL KILLINGS

Xiong, Kao *see* Familial Killers – Men

Yousef, Ramzi *see* The 1990s – The Bombing of the World Trade Center; Terrorist Killers – Men

POLITICALLY MOTIVATED
KILLERS - MEN

Czolgosz, Leon. On September 6, 1901, Leon Czolgosz—a twenty-eight-year-old anarchist—assassinated President William McKinley at the Pan-American Exposition in Buffalo, New York. Czolgosz, a blacksmith from Cleveland, Ohio, carefully planned the assassination. He shot the President twice, fatally wounding him, as he was being greeted at a reception at the Exposition's Temple of Music. The killer was swiftly apprehended and taken into custody. Czolgosz went on trial on September 23, 1901, and was found guilty of first-degree murder in the death of William McKinley. On October 29, 1901, Leon Czolgosz became the fiftieth person to be put to death in the electric chair in New York. *See also* The 1900s – The Assassination of President William McKinley; Adult Victims, McKinley, William.

Oswald, Lee Harvey. On November 22, 1963, ex-Marine Lee Harvey Oswald took aim with a rifle through the Texas School Book Depository in Dallas and shot to death forty-six-year-old President John F. Kennedy as he rode in an automobile procession through Dealey Plaza. Born in New Orleans in 1939, Oswald had worked at the depository for just five weeks before the assassination, making Kennedy the fourth president to die at the hands of an assassin. Oswald fled the scene of the crime and later shot to death policeman J. D. Tippit, before he was arrested at the Texas Theater and charged with the two homicides.

Declaring that he was a patsy, Oswald was gunned down on November 24, 1963, in the basement of the Dallas city jail en route to being transferred to the county jail. Millions watched on television as Dallas nightclub owner Jack Ruby shot and killed Oswald, preventing a trial and unraveling a possible conspiracy. On March 14, 1964, Ruby—who had a string of arrests for weapons charges and other offenses—was convicted of murder with malice and given a death sentence. In October 1966, an appeals court reversed the conviction. Before there was a second trial, Jack Ruby, suffering from terminal lung cancer, died from a blood clot on January 3, 1967, at the age of fifty-six. *See also* The 1960s – The Assassination of President John F. Kennedy; Adult Victims, Kennedy, John Fitzgerald; Politically Motivated Killers – Men, Ruby, Jack.

Ruby, Jack. Born in 1911 as Jacob Rubenstein, Jack Ruby gained infamy on November 24, 1963, when he entered the basement of the Dallas city jail and shot to death Lee Harvey Oswald, the man suspected of assassinating President John F. Kennedy two days earlier. The fifty-two-year-old operator of a Dallas nightclub called the Carousel Club, had a history of weapons related arrests and violence. He dismissed the notion of a conspiracy before the murder that was seen by millions of television viewers. On March 14, 1964, Ruby was charged with and convicted of murdering Oswald and sentenced to death. In October 1966, the Texas Court of Criminal Appeals overturned the conviction for improper testimony and the need for a change of venue. Ruby was diagnosed with terminal lung cancer before a second trial could get underway. He died from a blood clot on January 3, 1967. Until the end, he insisted that he played no part in a conspiracy to assassinate Kennedy or Oswald but shot Oswald as an impulsive act borne out of patriotism and grief over the President's death. *See also* Politically Motivated Killers – Men, Oswald, Lee Harvey.

Sirhan, Bashara Sirhan. On June 5, 1968, Sirhan Bashara Sirhan, a Palestinian immigrant, shot to death Senator Robert F. Kennedy at the Ambassador Hotel in Los Angeles, California. The twenty-five-year-old shooter was apparently protesting the American sale of fifty fighter jets to Israel and its control over the Palestinians. The forty-two-year-old senator from New York was the brother of the late President John F. Kennedy, under whom he had served as the Attorney General. Sirhan was quickly captured after the assassination and charged with murder. His trial opened in Los Angeles on January 7, 1969. After fifteen weeks of testimony and three days of deliberation, Sirhan Sirhan was found guilty of the murder of Robert Kennedy and sentenced to death on April 17, 1969. The sentence was commuted to life when the Supreme Court abolished the death penalty in 1972. Despite conspiracy theorists and Sirhan's memory lapse about the shooting, he remains the sole person convicted and imprisoned for the death of Robert Kennedy. He has been denied parole numerous times. *See also* The 1960s – The Assassination of Robert F. Kennedy; Adult Victims, Kennedy, Robert Francis.

White, Dan. On November 27, 1978, Dan White, an embittered former San Francisco city supervisor armed with a .38-caliber revolver, entered City Hall and shot to death San Francisco Mayor George Moscone and City Supervisor Harvey Milk. White, a thirty-nine-year-old ex-police officer and fireman, was upset over losing his seat on the board of supervisors, having recently resigned after opposing the enactment of a gay civil rights ordinance. The forty-seven-year-old Milk was the first openly gay person to win election to the board and had become a close political ally to the forty-nine-year-old mayor Moscone. On May 21, 1979, after what became known as a "Twinkie Defense," in which White blamed the murders on eating too much junk food such as Twinkies, causing a "diminished capacity," he was found guilty of manslaughter in the deaths of Moscone and Milk. Dan White was sentenced to seven years in prison and paroled in January 1984. He committed suicide on October 21, 1985. *See also* Adult Victims, Milk, Harvey; Moscone, George.

Zangara, Guiseppe. On February 15, 1933, Guiseppe Zangara, armed with a .32-caliber revolver, fired five shots toward President-elect Franklin D. Roosevelt, who sat in the back of a convertible during a parade in Miami, Florida. While Roosevelt escaped injury, the mayor of Chicago, Anton Joseph Cermak, was fatally wounded. Born in 1900, the thirty-two-year-old assassin was a naturalized Italian citizen and bricklayer. Three weeks later, the fifty-nine-year-old Cermak died. He had been Chicago's mayor since 1931 and was instrumental in helping Roosevelt win the

Democratic nomination. On March 10, 1933, Zangara pleaded guilty to murder in state court and was sentenced to die for his crime. In what was one of the fastest execution dates in the American 20th century, Guiseppe Zangara was electrocuted ten days later on March 20, 1933. *See also* Adult Victims, Cermak, Anton Joseph.

SERIAL KILLERS - MEN

Angelo, Richard. Twenty-three-year-old Richard Angelo was a registered nurse at Good Samaritan Hospital on Long Island, New York, who desperately wanted to be a hero. He felt if he "rescued" enough dying patients, he would become a valued employee of the hospital. He tried his first heroic experiment in September 1987 with a patient who was in intensive care. After he injected something into his IV tube, the patient died, and Angelo's experiment failed. Though we have no way of knowing how many times his experiment did work, we do know he was unsuccessful at least three more times, as three more patients died from September to October 1987. Finally a patient who had been injected by Angelo got sick and called for a nurse. He told the hospital authorities about a bearded man with a white coat, which led to Angelo's arrest. He was arrested in November 1987 and confessed to murder. He was found guilty in 1989 of two counts of second-degree murder, one count of manslaughter, and one count of criminally negligent homicide. Richard Angelo received the maximum sentence of sixty-one years to life.

Atlanta Child Murders *see* Williams, Wayne

Ball, Joe. The landlord of a 1930s Texas roadhouse called The Sociable Inn, forty-year-old Joe Ball was implicated in the murders of at least five waitresses he employed, several of which were pregnant at the time of death. On September 24, 1938, under the weight of questioning by police, the burly Ball committed suicide with a gunshot to the head. Known as "Alligator Joe," some of the victims were reportedly dismembered and fed to the five live alligators Ball kept out in the back of The Sociable Inn.

Berdella, Robert. Proprietor of a Kansas City, Missouri, store called Bob's Bizarre Bazaar that specialized in the macabre, Robert Berdella's real life was even more frightening. In April 1988, Kansas City police raided his home after a tip from a young man would-be victim of the serial killer. There, they discovered explicit photographs of male victims of torture and human skulls buried in the backyard. During interrogation, Berdella confessed to sexually assaulting, imprisoning, torturing, murdering, and dismembering six men between January 1984 and August 1987. After pleading guilty to the murders on December 19, 1988, Berdella was sentenced to six concurrent life sentences in prison where he died of a heart attack in 1992.

Berkowitz, David. Starting in the summer of 1976, a postal worker and former auxiliary policeman began a reign of murder and terror in New York City that lasted thirteen months. David Berkowitz, called "The .44 Killer" and self-identified as "Son of Sam" used a .44-

caliber pistol to randomly shoot females and males in Queens and the Bronx—killing six and wounding seven others. Police arrested the twenty-four-year-old resident of Yonkers, a New York suburb, after linking his vehicle to a parking ticket and finding a .44-caliber gun on the front seat. Berkowitz, a victim of parental rejection and adoption, pleaded insanity while blaming his killing spree on voices in his head and his neighbors' black Labrador. He was found fit enough to stand trial and on August 23, 1977, was convicted of murder and sentenced to 365 years in prison. He has been denied parole numerous times.

Bianchi, Kenneth *see* PAIR AND GROUP KILLERS

Bishop, Arthur Gary. In Salt Lake City, Utah, in 1983, police went to the home of Roger Downs, an accountant, to investigate the disappearance of a thirteen-year-old boy who was supposed to have gone on a camping trip with Downs. Police discovered that his real name was Arthur Gary Bishop. He confessed to killing five boys, one of them the missing thirteen-year-old. Bishop, thirty-three, a Big Brother to fatherless boys, admitted to killing boys aged four to thirteen over four years. The victims had all been raped before they were murdered. Bishop was arrested on July 23, 1983, and charged with first-degree murder. On March 19, 1984, he was convicted of five counts of murder and sentenced to die. After four years of appeals, he decided he was ready to die and stopped the appeals process. He died of lethal injection on June 10, 1988.

Bladel, Rudy. A series of shooting deaths of men around freight yards in Michigan and Indiana between August 3, 1963, and January 1, 1978, led law enforcement authorities to Rudy Bladel. An ex-railman, he had been laid off in 1959 and imprisoned in 1971 following a conviction for assaulting another railman. A shotgun he owned was tied to three railway murders that occurred on New Year's Day 1978 in Jackson, Michigan. Rudy Bladel confessed to the murders then retracted the confession, but he was found guilty and received three concurrent life sentences. The conviction was overturned on a technicality. A second trial ended with the same verdict, this time with no possibility of parole added to the sentence. Four other earlier murders of freight workers were also attributed to Bladel. He died of thyroid cancer in prison on November 15, 2006.

Bolber, Morris *see* PAIR AND GROUP KILLERS

Bonin, William. During the late 1970s, William Bonin is believed to have raped and murdered as many as twenty-one young men in California. A truck driver and Vietnam veteran from Downey, California, Bonin was dubbed the "Freeway Killer," as he picked up teenage male hitchhikers along California freeways and raped and strangled them. Similar to other sexual serial killers, Bonin was a physically and sexually abused child. He was also a manic depressive and suffered from brain damage that may have contributed to his violent tendencies. Bonin was convicted of murdering fourteen people and sentenced to death in 1982 and 1983. On February 23, 1996, William Bonin was executed, becoming the first prisoner to die by lethal injection in California. After his death, it was discovered that he had illegally received almost $80,000 in Social Security disability benefits while a prisoner on death row.

"Boston Strangler" *see* De Salvo, Albert

Briggen, Joseph. Pig farmer Joseph Briggen boasted of his prize-winning herd in Sierra Morena,

California, in the early part of the 20th century. Few could argue that Briggen's healthy, plump Berkshire pigs were amongst the most sought after in the state at auctions. Only when a hired hand found severed fingers in his quarters did the deadly secrets of Briggen's ranch and successful herd emerge. When police searched the ranch and surrounding Sierra Morena, they discovered the human remains of at least twelve people, including bones and a skull in the pigpen. Briggen used human flesh as part of his Berkshire's diet and as a means to keep from paying workers their just do. In August 1902, Joseph Briggen was convicted of murder and given a life sentence behind bars. He died in prison a few months later.

Brudos, Jerry. A married electronics technician in Portland, Oregon, Jerry Brudos had a bizarre shoe fetish that started when he was an infant and escalated to murder in 1968. He would pick up women, rape them, bludgeon or strangle them, and then take them to his garage where he would hang them on a hook and sexually assault and mutilate them. He would save various body parts in the freezer he kept in the garage and dump their weighted bodies in the nearby river. Young women disappearing from the Oregon State University campus caused alarm among the students. Police were told about a man frequently seen hanging around the campus trying to pick up a date. When he was seen again on May 25, 1969, police arrested the twenty-eight-year-old Brudos. While in custody, he told police his horrific tale of the rape, murder, and mutilation of four young women. He also confessed to photographing the suffering and death of his victims. Charged with murder, Brudos pleaded insanity but was found legally sane by seven psychiatrists. He was convicted of murder and sentenced to life in the Oregon State Prison in 1969. He died of liver cancer in prison on March 28, 2006.

Bundy, Theodore Robert. Between 1974 and 1978, serial killer Theodore "Ted" Bundy is thought to have sexually assaulted and murdered as many as forty females in five states. Believed by many criminologists to be the prototype sexual serial murderer, Bundy was charming, well educated, active in politics, and both elusive and an escape artist. On August 16, 1975, the twenty-nine-year-old Bundy was arrested in Utah in connection with the disappearance of several young women, and eventually convicted and imprisoned for kidnapping. Extradited to Colorado to face murder charges, he escaped while awaiting trial in 1977 and was quickly captured. He escaped again six months later and made his way to Florida where he raped and brutally murdered more women. On February 15, 1978, Ted Bundy was captured again and soon confessed to killing more than a hundred women, though he later recanted the confession. On June 25, 1979, he went to trial in Florida and was found guilty of the sexual murders of sorority sisters and sentenced to death. While on death row, Bundy cooperated with law enforcement officials and psychiatrists in helping them to profile serial killers. On January 24, 1989, Theodore Bundy was executed in the electric chair at Florida's Starke State Prison.

Buono, Angelo *see* PAIR AND GROUP KILLERS, Bianchi, Kenneth

"Butcher of Kingsbury Run." In the 1930s this unknown killer brutally murdered approximately twelve people in Cleveland, Ohio. The victims, both male and female, were all decapitated and mutilated, as if by a butcher. The murders stopped just as quickly as they started. There were plenty of rumors and speculation about the identity of the killer, but the police were never able to capture the elusive butcher.

"Cannibal Killer" *see* Fish, Albert

Carpenter, David J. Known as Marin County, California's "Trailside Killer," David Carpenter was responsible for the murder of at least eight people from 1979 to 1981. His victims were all shot or stabbed. When one of his victims was shot, but not fatally, they were able to identify him. He already had a record for armed robbery and sexual assault. David Carpenter was arrested in 1981 for two murders and on July 6, 1984, he was convicted and sentenced to death. On May 10, 1988, a San Diego jury convicted him of five murders and sentenced him to death. He currently resides on San Quentin's death row and is the oldest inmate there at age eighty-eight.

"Casanova Killer" *see* Knowles, Paul John

Chase, Richard. Mentally unstable starting early in his life, Richard Chase was admitted to psychiatric hospitals twice. He had been torturing small animals, killing them, and drinking their blood. In Sacramento, California, in December 1977 he bought a pistol and killed a stranger on the street just to see what it would be like. On January 23, 1978, he entered the home of Theresa Wallin and shot her. He then disemboweled her, spread her intestines around the room, and wiped her blood on his face. She had been three months pregnant at the time. Craving blood again, Chase broke into another house on January 27. He shot Evelyn Miroth, twenty-seven, in the head and then shot her six-year-old son, and her boyfriend. He also shot her twenty-two-month-old nephew who was asleep in his playpen. Chase then mutilated Evelyn's body and sodomized her. He was in the process of mutilating the baby when a visitor to the house interrupted him. He took the infant with him. The baby was found two months later in a vacant lot where he had thrown it. Police were tipped off by one of Chase's neighbors who was uneasy about his weird behavior. They paid a visit to his apartment and found traces of human tissue. After his arrest, it was determined he could not be tried in Sacramento as he was too hated by the community. He was tried in San Jose in 1979. On May 8, 1979, he was found guilty and sentenced to death. On December 26, 1980, Chase was found dead in his cell. Coroners determined that he had overdosed on his medication and committed suicide.

Clark, Douglas D. *see* PAIR AND GROUP KILLERS

"Co-ed Killer" *see* Kemper, Edmund III

Cole, Carroll Edward. Hating "loose women" because they reminded him of his mother, Carroll Edward Cole told police that he felt he murdered thirty-five women because he was killing her through them. He strangled his first victim in his car in San Diego, California, in 1971. He was questioned but not charged. In 1977 in Las Vegas, Cole strangled another woman in a parking lot. In San Diego in the summer of 1979, he strangled yet another woman. Both of the last two victims were nude and had been sexually assaulted after their murder. Back in Las Vegas in the fall of 1979, he strangled a woman in her hotel room. On November 11, 1980, he strangled a woman in her home in Dallas, Texas. On the following night, Cole strangled his next victim in a parking lot. Near the end of November 1980, he strangled a woman in her apartment. While he was killing her, neighbors had called the police to complain about all the noise coming from her apartment. Police found the body and questioned Cole but then released him. Later, he was arrested again and confessed to the murders. Carroll Edward Cole was tried in April 1981 in Dallas for three murders there. He claimed to be insane and said that in a nine-year period he killed thirty-five women in five states. He also claimed to have eaten part of one of his Oklahoma victims before cutting her up and dumping her in a garbage can. He was convicted and sentenced to three life terms, two to be served consecutively. After the Texas trial, Nevada authorities charged him with two murders. He was extradited to Las Vegas to stand trial for the two murders. He pleaded guilty and told the judge he did not want a jury trial because they would be too lenient. The judge agreed and sentenced him to death. He waived his appeals and was executed in Carson City, Nevada, by lethal injection on December 6, 1985.

Coleman, Alton *see* PAIR AND GROUP KILLERS

Collins, John Norman. From July 1967 to July 1969, John Norman Collins was killing young women in the Ypsilanti, Michigan, area. The murders were referred to as the "Michigan Murders." Collins killed his first victim on July 10, 1967. An Eastern Michigan University student, she was stabbed to death and her hands and feet had been cut off. On July 6, 1968, his next victim, also an E.M.U. student, was found in Ann Arbor with forty-seven stab wounds. Friends police she had been seen with twenty-one-year-old John Collins. He told police he had been with his mother and they assumed it was a case of mistaken identity. The third victim, also a student at E.M.U., was found in a cemetery on March 21, 1969. She had been shot and strangled. On March 26, the body of a sixteen-year-old girl was found. She had been brutally beaten and her head smashed with a club. Three weeks later, the body of a strangled thirteen-year-old girl was found. Three young boys found victim number six in a field. She had been shot in the head, stabbed all over, her throat slashed. The seventh victim, a student at E.M.U., was found on July 26, 1969. She had been beaten, strangled, and sexually abused. Finally, the police had a lead. The victim had been seen in town with a man identified as John Norman Collins. He was arrested and denied murdering the girl. Police found hair clippings and blood that matched the victim. On August 19, 1970, he was convicted of murder and sentenced to life in prison with no parole.

Copeland, Ray *see* PAIR AND GROUP KILLERS

Corll, Dean *see* PAIR AND GROUP KILLERS

Corona, Juan Vallejo. In the 1950s, Juan Vallejo Corona came to California from Mexico as a migrant worker to pick fruit. In ten years he developed his own labor contracting business where he would hire out Mexican migrants to California fruit growers. He was respected in the community of Yuba City, California, as a hard and honest worker. In 1971, police acted on an anonymous tip to search his home and bunkhouse. They found the remains of twenty-five men—drifters and migrants—in shallow graves. They had all been stabbed to death and their heads were hacked with a machete, which police found at the scene. Police also found a ledger that Corona used to record his victims' names, dates of arrival, and dates of "departure." He was indicted on twenty-five murder charges. He was found guilty on all counts and sentenced to twenty-five life terms. Ten years after his conviction, Corona won a retrial, claiming his now dead brother, Natividad, had committed the murders. The trial took place in Hayward, California, and cost the taxpayers five million dollars. The trial was more like a circus with nine hundred exhibits and over two hundred witnesses. In the end, the jury found Juan Corona guilty and he returned to prison to serve his twenty-five life sentences. He has been denied parole numerous times.

Corwin, Daniel Lee. A resident of Temple, Texas, Daniel Lee Corwin had a history of sexual assaults that started when he was a teenager. While he was serving a ninety-nine year sentence for attempted capital murder, he confessed to killing three women. Corwin abducted his first victim in February 1987 while she walked near her home. She was raped, stabbed, and strangled. His second victim was abducted from her job in July 1987. She was found two days later having been raped, stabbed, and strangled. His third victim was washing her car in October 1987 at a car wash when he tried to abduct her. When she tried to resist, he fatally stabbed her while her three-year-old daughter watched from inside the car. His next victim, for whom he was currently serving the ninety-nine year sentence, was a student he abducted at knifepoint. He took off all her clothes, raped her, tied her to a tree, and slit her throat, leaving her for dead. She was able to free herself and flag down a passing motorist. Corwin pleaded guilty to attempted capital murder and received the ninety-nine year sentence. Two years later, after he confessed to the three murders, he was tried under a new "serial murder law" for all three victims at the same time. In March 1990, Daniel Lee Corwin was convicted and sentenced to death. He was executed by lethal injection on December 7, 1998.

Cunanan, Andrew Phillip. Between April and July 1997, gay hustler Andrew Cunanan, twenty-seven, murdered five men. On April 27, 1997, Andrew Trail, twenty-eight, was killed in Minneapolis, Minnesota. Cunanan viciously bludgeoned Trail to death with a claw hammer. On May 2, 1997, he shot and killed his former lover, David Madson, thirty-three, leaving his body by a lake in Minnesota. On May 4, 1997, he brutally tortured, bludgeoned, and murdered seventy-two-year-old Lee Miglin in Chicago, Illinois. His fourth victim, forty-five-year-old cemetery caretaker, William Reese, was found shot to death on May 9, 1997, in Pennsville, New Jersey. Cunanan's final victim was fifty-one-year-old Italian designer Gianni Versace, who was shot to death in front of his Miami Beach, Florida, mansion on July 15, 1997. The FBI launched one of the largest manhunts in the nation to capture the elusive serial murderer. Cunanan had been holed up in a houseboat not far from Versace's mansion. After surrounding the houseboat on July 23, 1997, police went in and discovered the killer's body. He had shot himself in the head. Though there were many rumors and much speculation, it was never determined why Andrew Cunanan went on his killing rampage. *See also* Adult Victims, Versace, Gianni.

Dahmer, Jeffrey L. He lured young, mostly minority, boys to his apartment in Milwaukee, Wisconsin, where he would then do the unthinkable. Thirty-one-year-old Jeffrey Dahmer was arrested on July 24, 1991, after one of his potential victims escaped and alerted police. When the police searched his putrid apartment, they found severed heads, torsos wedged in a barrel, and several pieces of male genitalia in a pot on the stove. There were scraps of bodies and limbs spread about and the smell was horrific. He confessed to seventeen murders—sixteen in Wisconsin and one in Ohio—and said that he would drug, strangle, and gradually dismember his victims while taking photos and videos along the way. He told police that he cooked and ate parts of his victims so he could experience their bodies and get closer to them. He was found legally sane to stand trial and in February 1992 was found guilty and sentenced to fifteen consecutive life terms, as Wisconsin does not have the death penalty. On May 1, 1992, Jeffrey Dahmer was convicted of the Ohio murder and sentenced to a sixteenth life sentence in Akron, Ohio. He was returned to Wisconsin to serve out his sentences. On November 28, 1994, while cleaning a shower with wife-killer Jesse Anderson, they were both beaten to death. Christopher Scarver, serving a life term for murder, was charged with killing the two men with a metal club.

De Salvo, Albert. From June 1962 to January 1964, Albert De Salvo killed thirteen women in Boston, Massachusetts. Dubbed the "Boston Strangler," he grew to be a modern legend of sorts. He would pose as a workman to gain entry to his victims' homes. He would then rape them and strangle them, usually with a piece of their clothing. Some of the victims were also bitten, bludgeoned, and stabbed. On October 27, 1964, he entered a woman's apartment by posing as a detective. He tied her to the bed, sexually assaulted her, and left, telling her he was sorry. The woman described him to the police who identified him as Albert De Salvo. When his picture was made public, dozens of women came forward claiming that he had sexually assaulted them. However, he was not suspected of being the Boston Strangler. In 1965, while he was being held on rape charges, he confessed to the crimes. Unfortunately, there was no direct evidence to link him to the murders other than his detailed knowledge of them. He plea bargained and stood trial for some earlier crimes not connected with the Boston Stranger. Albert De Salvo never went to trial for the murders, but was convicted of robbery and sexual offenses and sentenced to life in prison. On November 26, 1973, he was found dead in his cell at age forty-two. He had been stabbed in the heart.

Dodd, Westley Allan. In September and October 1989, child sexual serial killer Westley Allan Dodd murdered three young boys and attempted to abduct another in Washington and Oregon. Dodd, a career criminal with a history of mental illness, child molestation, and sexual perversion, stabbed to death his first two victims and strangled the third. His downfall came after attempting to kidnap a boy outside a Vancouver, Washington, theater. Westley Dodd was arrested and charged in Washington state with three counts of first-degree murder and attempted kidnapping. In January 1990, Dodd changed his plea to guilty of all charges and demanded that he be put to death for his heinous crimes. On July 15, 1990, a jury gave Dodd the death penalty. He chose hanging as his method of execution. On January 5, 1993, Westley Allan Dodd became the first person in the United States to go to the gallows since 1965.

Evans, Donald Leroy. A convicted rapist from Texas, Donald Leroy Evans was arrested in Louisiana in August 1991. The thirty-four-year-old confessed to the kidnap and murder of ten-year-old Beatrice Routh in Mississippi. He then confessed to more than eighty murders, telling police he had killed over a ten-year period in seventeen states. Evans eventually told police his confession to eighty murders was just a hoax to get attention and gain notoriety. In 1993, he was sentenced to death in Mississippi for killing Routh. In July 1995, he pleaded guilty in Florida to killing Ira Smith in 1985. He was given a life sentence and sent back to death row at the Mississippi State Penitentiary. On January 5, 1999, Donald Leroy Evans was fatally stabbed by fellow death row inmate Jimmie Mack.

Fernandez, Raymond Martinez *see* PAIR AND GROUP KILLERS

Fish, Albert. Hamilton "Albert" Fish was born in 1870 in Washington, D.C. Orphaned at the age of five after the death of his father, Fish became a habitual runaway and bed-wetter en route to a life of religious obsession, child molestation, sexual perversions, and serial murder. After his wife left him, Fish's sadomasochistic and homicidal tendencies came to the surface. He engaged in self-flagellation, burning, and inserting needles into his body as well as child sexual abuse, coprolagnia, cannibalism, and murder. His undoing came when he sent a confession letter to the parents of a twelve-year-old girl he murdered and dismembered. Authorities traced the letter to Fish, who was living in a rundown boarding house in New York. The "Cannibal Killer" confessed to the murder as well as several other murders of children. In all, Fish is believed to have molested well over one hundred young females and murdering from seven to fifteen of them. Despite defense attempts to portray him as insane, early in 1935 a jury found Albert Fish sane and guilty of murder and sentenced him to death. On January 16, 1936, Fish was electrocuted at Sing Sing Prison.

"Freeway Killer" *see* Bonin, William

Gacy, John Wayne. A convicted sex offender, John Wayne Gacy appeared to be reformed. He was a successful building contractor, involved in the community and politics, and would dress up as Pogo the Clown to entertain hospitalized children. But all was not what it seemed. Beneath the facade was a serial killer. From 1972 to 1978 he murdered thirty-three boys and young men in the Chicago, Illinois, area. He would take the victims to his house, often telling them he was a plainclothes policeman. Once there, he would handcuff, rape, and torture them repeatedly. Finally, he would strangle them while achieving sexual gratification. In December 1978, police were investigating a missing boy who had gone to see Gacy about a job. When they learned he had a convicted sex offender record in Iowa, they got a warrant to search his house. In the crawlspace under his house they found the bodies of twenty-nine boys. He had also apparently thrown four bodies in the river. Dubbed the "Killer Clown," he was tried and convicted on March 12, 1980, after the jury disregarded his plea of insanity. John Gacy was executed by lethal injection in 1994 at age fifty-two.

Gallego, Gerald Armond *see* PAIR AND GROUP KILLERS

Glatman, Harvey Murray. In Los Angeles, California, Harvey Glatman ran a TV repair shop and also enjoyed photography as a hobby. He posed as a professional photographer and used a variety of aliases, taking out ads in the paper for models to photograph. Glatman hired his first model on August 1, 1957. When she arrived, he raped her and tied her to the bed while he took pictures. He then killed her and buried her in the desert. His next victim was a woman he met through a dating service. On their first date in March 1958, he took her to the desert, raped her, and took pictures before he killed her. His next victim was a stripper and part-time model. He tied her up and raped her in her home. Then he drove her to the desert where he raped her again and killed her. Glatman's next would-be victim was also a model whom he took to the desert to photograph on October 27, 1958. He pulled out a gun and accidentally shot her in the leg. She grabbed the gun and held it on him until a police officer came to the rescue. When police searched his house, they found numerous photos of his victims—taken before and after he killed them. He was convicted of murder in November 1958 in San Diego and sentenced to death. Refusing to appeal, Harvey Glatman was executed on September 18, 1959 in the gas chamber. *See also* The 1950s – The Model and the Lonely Hearts Murders.

Glaze, Billy (Jesse Sitting Crow). A Native American drifter, Billy Glaze, calling himself Jesse Sitting Crow, had been heard saying that all Native American women should be raped and killed. In April 1987 in Minneapolis, Minnesota, he killed his first victim—a Native American prostitute. He raped, strangled, and beat her face with a pipe. His next victim was also a Native American prostitute. She was killed by suffocation when Glaze stomped heavily on her chest. He also sexually assaulted her with a tree branch that he left by her body. His third victim, again a Native American prostitute, was raped and then beaten to death with a rock. Police investigating the murders were told of Glaze's statement regarding Native American women and he was arrested and charged with the murders. In jail while waiting for his trial to begin, he wrote a confession to another prisoner. In February 1989, Billy Glaze was convicted and received three life sentences to be served consecutively. He died of lung cancer on December 22, 2015.

Gohl, Billy. In the early 1900s in Aberdeen, Washington, someone was killing sailors. Billy Gohl was the union official at the office of the Sailors' Union of the Pacific. Sailors would go there after arriving at the port to collect their mail and leave their pay so they wouldn't lose it all while enjoying their port stay. Gohl was friendly and would casually find out if they had friends or family there or were just passing through. He was also able to learn how much cash and valuables they had. Those who had no family and were just passing through were killed. Gohl dropped the corpses down a chute in the building that went directly to the river. The bodies would eventually wash out to sea. In 1912, a sailor's body washed ashore. It was proven that he was last seen in Gohl's office. In 1913, he was charged and convicted for only two of his suspected forty-one or more murders. Billy Gohl received a sentence of life in prison, where he died in 1928.

"Gorilla Murderer" *see* Nelson, Earle Leonard

"Green River Killer" *see* Ridgway, Gary Leon

Greenwood, Vaughn Orrin. Called the "Skid Row Slasher," Vaughn Orrin Greenwood was killing vagrants in Los Angeles and Hollywood, California. From December 1974 to January 1975 nine bodies of vagrants were found in the Los Angeles and Hollywood area. They had all been killed the same way—their throats were cut open, salt was spread around the bodies, and their shoes were removed and pointed toward the victims' feet. On February 3, 1975, police arrested thirty-one-year-old Vaughn Greenwood, an African American, for trying to murder two men in Hollywood. In January 1976, he was charged with nine counts of murder. He was found guilty and sentenced to life in prison on January 19, 1977.

Hansen, Robert. In 1980 and 1981 bodies began showing up that had been buried in shallow graves in Anchorage, Alaska. Two of the victims were topless barmaids. All four of the victims had been killed with a high-powered rifle. At the same time, police were investigating a teenage prostitute's story that she was kidnapped, tortured, and raped by Robert Hansen, a well-known Anchorage resident. They searched his house and found a rifle, which was later proven to have been used in two of the murders. Police also found a map showing the graves of twenty women. Hansen confessed to killing seventeen women after he tortured and sexually abused them. He told them that he sometimes let the naked girls run away in the open country so he could track them down and shoot them like an animal. On February 28, 1981, Robert Hansen pleaded guilty to four murders and one count of murder and rape. He was sentenced to life in prison without the possibility of parole. He died on August 21, 2014.

"Happy Face Killer" *see* Jesperson, Keith Hunter

Heidnik, Gary. Born in 1943 in Pennsylvania, Gary Heidnik had several jobs including soldier, nurse, landlord, minister, and stock investor. In the early 1960s he was in the Army for two years before being discharged with a mental disability. He then tried to commit suicide several times, ending up in and out of mental institutions. He founded his own church and also started investing in stocks. With an IQ of 130, he made a half a million dollars playing the stock market. Heidnik blamed is mental problems on LSD experiments while in the Army, but it is believed that his alcoholic mother and her strict husband were to blame. He married a Filipino woman in 1985. When he abused her and forced her to watch him have sex with prostitutes, she left him. In 1986, he began hearing "voices" that told him to acquire a harem of ten women to make him the father of numerous offspring. Heidnik preferred African American women who were mentally disabled. He even served time in prison in the 1970s for kidnapping, raping, and sodomizing such a woman in front of a mental institution. Near the end of 1986, he kidnapped six women and kept them in the basement of his house. For four months, he tortured them, kept them naked and chained, beat them, and raped them. When one of the women escaped and told the police, they went to Heidnik's house on March 25, 1987. They found the women in the basement along with a human arm in his freezer and a roasted human rib on the stove. He had killed one of his prisoners, cut her up with a saw, put her flesh in a food processor, mixed it with dog food, and forced the other women to eat it. He had also electrocuted one of the victims while she lay in chains in a water filled pit. Heidnik was tried and convicted of two counts of first-degree murder and eighteen other counts of various crimes. Sentenced to death, Gary Heidnik was executed by lethal injection on July 6, 1999.

Henley, Elmer Wayne, Jr. *see* PAIR AND GROUP KILLERS, Corll, Dean

"Hillside Strangler" *see* PAIR AND GROUP KILLERS, Bianchi, Kenneth

Jesperson, Keith Hunter. Serial killer Keith Hunter Jesperson confessed to the strangulation and murder of eight women in five states over a five-year period in the early 1990s. The Canadian long-haul trucker was dubbed the "Happy Face Killer" by the press after sending letters to newspapers with a smiling face at the top of the page. Jesperson's first murder was the strangulation death of a twenty-three-year-old Portland prostitute named Taunja Bennett on January 23, 1990. In a bizarre turn of events, a fifty-seven-year-old grandmother, Laverne Pavlinac, implicated herself and her abusive boyfriend, thirty-nine-year-old John Sosnovske, in the Bennett murder. In spite of attempting to retract her confession, Pavlinac was convicted of the murder in January 1991 and sent to prison. Sosnovske had pleaded guilty in February 1990 to Bennett's murder to avoid the death penalty. The two would remain in prison for five years until the forty-year-old Jesperson confessed to the murder and that of several other women after being arrested in March 1995. He pleaded guilty to Bennett's murder on November 2, 1995, and later pleaded guilty to two other murders, receiving a life sentence in the Oregon State Prison.

Kemper, Edmund III. Raised by his mother who severely disciplined and demeaned him, Edmund Kemper hated her. He enjoyed killing and dismembering animals, keeping some of the pieces in his closet. Kemper had been sent to live with his grandparents and, at age fifteen, shot and killed them in 1963. He told police he wanted to know what it would be like to shoot his grandmother. After the shooting, he was put in a mental hospital for six years. When he was released, he went back to live with his mother in Santa Cruz, California. Three years later, from May 1972 to February 1973, he killed six females. Dubbed the "Co-ed Killer," Kemper liked to pick up young co-ed female hitchhikers. He would shoot or stab them to death, then put them in the trunk and head to his house. While his mother was gone, he would bring the bodies inside and sexually abuse the corpses. Sometimes he would cut off their head or cook and eat their flesh. On the day before Easter 1973, he killed his mother while she slept. He bashed her head with a hammer and decapitated her. Then, perhaps for all the years of verbal abuse, he cut out her larynx and shredded it in the garbage disposal to silence her forever. After the murder, Kemper invited his mother's friend over for dinner. When she arrived, he hit her on the head with a brick, strangled and decapitated her, and had sex with her corpse before driving off in her car. He drove to Colorado and called the Santa Cruz police to confess. It took three calls to convince them he was telling the truth. Edmund Kemper III was judged legally sane and went on trial in Santa Cruz in April 1973. He was convicted of eight murders and received a life sentence. Kemper remains incarcerated at the California Medical Facility in Vacaville, California.

"Killer Clown" *see* Gacy, John Wayne

Knowles, Paul John. Described by many as charming, Paul John Knowles was a man who was able to get people to trust him. Dubbed the "Casanova Killer" by the press, he killed at least eighteen people from July to November 1974 in several states. On November 8, 1974, he met a British journalist named Sandy Fawkes at a bar in Atlanta, Georgia. They spent six days together and were almost inseparable. He had told her that he was a killer, hoping she would write a book about him. Fawkes broke off the relationship out of fear. Knowles told her that within a year he would be dead. On November 16, 1974, he killed two more people, one of them a police officer. He stole the patrol car and was arrested when he ran off the road at a roadblock. On November 17, Paul Knowles tried to escape and went for the sheriff's gun and an FBI agent shot and killed him. Sandy Fawkes eventually wrote a book about him.

Kraft, Randy. A sadistic killer, Randy Kraft tortured and murdered the men he had sex with. From 1972 to 1983, he killed at least sixteen men in Southern California. All of his victims were drugged, sexually assaulted, and strangled. Kraft also castrated his victims—some still alive during the mutilation. On May 14, 1983, he was stopped while driving erratically. The officers found a dead Marine in the car and Kraft was arrested. He was tried in Orange County, California, on sixteen counts of murder, nine counts of sexual mutilation, and three counts of sodomy. Randy Kraft was convicted on all counts on November 29, 1989, and sentenced to death. He is currently on death row at San Quentin State Prison.

Lake, Leonard *see* PAIR AND GROUP KILLERS, Ng, Charles Chitat

Lucas, Henry Lee. In 1960, at age twenty-four, Henry Lee Lucas stabbed his seventy-four-year-old mother to death after they had a fight. Put in a psychiatric hospital, he was released ten years later and went on a seventeen-year murder spree. Eventually Lucas met Ottis Toole in Florida in 1976. Together they murdered several people along Florida's highways.

Lucas showed an interest in Toole's ten-year-old niece, Becky Powell. They became common-law husband and wife a few years later. When they got in an argument while camping, Becky slapped him. Infuriated, he got his knife and stabbed his fourteen-year-old wife in the heart. Lucas carved up her body and buried the pieces. Three weeks later, he killed and mutilated an elderly woman that had befriended him. Arrested for handgun possession, he began to confess to murder. Claiming to have killed at least 200 people in virtually every state in America, Henry Lee Lucas was arrested in Texas on May 9, 1983. After his arrest, he changed his story and the number of his victims many times. He had eleven murder convictions, one death sentence, six life terms, two seventy-five year sentences, and one sixty-year sentence from the states that have tried him. In June 1999, while on death row in Texas, Henry Lee Lucas had his death sentence commuted to life in prison. Ottis Toole died of cirrhosis of the liver in 1996 while serving his sentence and Lucas died of heart failure in prison on March 13, 2001.

Majors, Orville Lynn. As a nurse, this serial killer targeted elderly victims with lethal injections. During a thirteen-month span between 1993 and 1995, Orville Lynn Majors is believed to have murdered dozens of senior citizens at Vermillion County Hospital in Clinton, Indiana, by injecting them with potassium chloride, epinephrine, or both drugs. Authorities charged the thirty-eight-year-old Majors with six of the deaths, though they noted he may have been responsible for the deaths of as many as 130 of 147 patients who died while he was present. On October 17, 1999, Majors was convicted on five of the murder counts, the sixth ended in a mistrial. Orville Majors was sentenced to a maximum term of 360 years in prison on November 15, 1999. He died of natural causes on September 24, 2017.

Marlow, James Gregory *see* PAIR AND GROUP KILLERS, Coffman, Cynthia

"Michigan Murders" *see* Collins, John Norman

Miller, Donald Gene. Stark fear arrived at the East Lansing, Michigan, campus of Michigan State University when Donald Gene Miller sexually assaulted and murdered four young women and attempted to rape and murder a teenage girl between January 1977 and August 1978. The twenty-two-year-old Miller was a graduate of the university's School of Criminal Justice and worked as a security guard before becoming a serial killer. His murder victims included ex-fiancée and college coed, Martha Sue Young, twenty; another student, Wendy Bush, twenty-one; and two other local women. After being arrested on two counts of attempted murder, Donald Miller confessed to murdering the four women and, in 1979, received three concurrent terms of thirty to fifty years of imprisonment. In July of that year, he led authorities to the skeletal remains of Young and another one of his victims. In 1998, Miller was given an additional term of twenty to forty years behind bars for harboring a concealed weapon in his cell.

Neelley, Alvin *see* PAIR AND GROUP KILLERS

Nelson, Earle Leonard. An abnormal looking man with protruding lips, receding forehead, and huge hands, Earle Nelson was dubbed the "Gorilla Murderer." Born in Philadelphia, Pennsylvania, in 1897, he was raised by his very strict and devoutly religious aunt after his mother died of syphilis when he was almost one. When he was ten, he had a severe head injury that caused him to have mental and physical problems. Because sex was forbidden as "bad" by his aunt, and due to his mental and physical problems, Nelson began to take an abnormal interest in women. From February 1926 to June 1927, he killed at least twenty-two women who were boardinghouse landladies. All were strangled and then raped. Nelson killed women in nine states and stayed ahead of the police by constantly moving and changing his name. On June 8, 1927, he went to Winnipeg, Canada, where he killed two more females—one a fourteen-year-old girl. He was finally recognized by someone who saw him on a wanted poster. He was tried and convicted in Winnipeg in November 1927. Earle Nelson was hanged on January 13, 1928.

Ng, Charles Chitat *see* PAIR AND GROUP KILLERS

"Night Stalker" *see* Ramirez, Richard

Panzram, Carl. Born in Minnesota in 1891, Carl Panzram was "bad" starting at a very early age. Arrested at age eight for being drunk and disorderly, he graduated to burglary, arson, assault, sodomy, and murder. Panzram traveled around the United States robbing, assaulting, and killing people. Most of his victims were young men and boys. He proudly claimed that he killed more than twenty-one people and sodomized more than 1,000 men and boys. In 1920, he stole money, bought a yacht, and hired ten sailors to fix it up. When it was ready to sail, he invited them on board, drugged them, and then raped them. He then shot them and threw them overboard. As a merchant seaman in West Africa, Panzram shot six Africans who he said he had hired to go crocodile hunting. He fed the six men to the crocodiles. He was arrested in

Washington, D.C., on August 16, 1928, for burglary and got a twenty-five year sentence at Fort Leavenworth Prison. Shortly after that, he killed a fellow inmate and received a death sentence. Carl Panzram was hanged on September 5, 1930.

Petrillo, Herman *see* PAIR AND GROUP KILLERS, Bolber, Morris

Petrillo, Paul *see* PAIR AND GROUP KILLERS, Bolber, Morris

Ramirez, Richard. From June 1984 to August 1985, the "Night Stalker" Richard Ramirez, a Satan worshiper, murdered at least thirteen people in the Los Angeles, California, area. He would enter homes at night through an open window or unlocked door and strangle or shoot any males before focusing on the women and children. Ramirez would brutally rape and mutilate them all in the name of Satan. The FBI found a smudged print on a getaway car that led them to Ramirez, who had been previously arrested for theft. The next day his picture appeared in the morning newspaper. In August 1985, a crowd of people at a shopping center saw a man trying to grab a woman from her car while the husband hit the assailant. The crowd recognized the man from the photo in the paper and began to attack him. When police arrived, Ramirez was bruised and bleeding. He was convicted in 1989 of twelve first-degree murders, one second-degree murder, and thirty charges of rape and burglary and sentenced to death. While serving his time on death row at San Quentin State Prison, Richard Ramirez died of cancer on June 7, 2013.

Resendiz, Angel Maturino. Using various aliases, including Rafael Resendiz-Ramirez, Resendiz, known as the "Rail Killer," is suspected of killing as many as twenty-four people living near railroad tracks in the United States and Mexico. Between 1997 and 1999, nine deaths in Texas, Kentucky, and Florida were blamed on the elusive thirty-nine-year-old Mexican drifter. Following a nationwide manhunt in which Resendiz was part of the FBI's Ten Most Wanted Fugitives list, the serial killer turned himself in at a border checkpoint in El Paso, Texas, on July 13, 1999. On December 17, 1998, Resendiz was put on trial in Texas for the brutal rape, bludgeoning, and murder of thirty-nine-year-old Houston doctor Claudia Benton, who was found murdered in her home. In May 2000, Maturino Resendiz was found guilty of capital murder and sentenced to death after the jury rejected defense arguments that he was insane. He was executed by lethal injection in Huntsville, Texas, on June 27, 2006.

Ridgway, Gary Leon. Referred to as the "Green River Killer," Gary Ridgway is believed to have murdered up to forty-nine women in Seattle, Washington's Green River area between 1982 and 1984. Most of the victims were young prostitutes, runaways, or hitchhikers. A Green River Task Force was formed to try to apprehend the killer, spending as much as $15 million, with little success. According to an FBI profile, the then unknown serial killer was described as white, middle-aged, a heavy smoker and drinker, with a deep hatred for women. Various bona fide suspects emerged over the years, including an ex-con and former law student named William J. Stevens II. Stevens, who was known to have had over thirty aliases, was arrested in 1989 and then released. Another suspect was Donald Leroy Evans, a confessed serial killer from Texas who was arrested in August 1991. Ridgway, an early suspect, was arrested in November 2001 when DNA evidence linked him to the murders. On December 18, 2003, after plea bargaining to spare him from a death sentence, Gary Ridgway was sentenced to forty-eight sentences of life in prison without the possibility of parole and a life sentence—all to be carried out consecutively at the Walla Walla State Penitentiary in Washington.

Schaefer, John Gerard. An ex-policeman, sadistic sexual serial killer John Gerard Schaefer is believed to have raped, tortured, mutilated, and murdered as many as thirty young women in Florida during the 1970s. Some of his victims he left tied to trees while he went to work, before completing the assault and murder later. Schaefer was finally arrested, tried, and convicted of first-degree murder in the deaths of two teenage females. On December 3, 1995, while in the Florida State Prison, John Schaefer was found dead in his cell, the victim of multiple stab wounds.

Shawcross, Arthur J. A vicious serial killer of children and prostitutes, Arthur Shawcross murdered at least thirteen people in the 1970s and 1980s while practicing pedophilia, cannibalism, and torture. Believed by criminologists to be the worst example of a dangerous and deadly sexual predator, Shawcross often tortured, mutilated, dismembered, and ate the people he killed. His first two victims were children he murdered in Watertown, New York. He pleaded guilty to manslaughter and served nine years behind bars before being paroled in 1988 to Rochester, New York. During a twenty-month stretch, Shawcross hunted and sadistically murdered eleven women before he was captured again. In February 1991, a jury convicted him on all counts and sentenced him to 250 years in prison. He died of cardiac arrest on November 10, 2008.

"Skid Row Slasher" *see* Greenwood, Vaughn Orrin
"Son of Sam" *see* Berkowitz, David
"Southside Slayer" *see* Spencer, Timothy W.

Speck, Richard. Over the years, Richard Speck had developed a growing urge to kill women. A merchant seaman, the twenty-four-year-old Speck was in Chicago, Illinois, waiting to be shipped out. On July 13, 1966, after spending the day watching nursing students sunbathing near their residence by the South Chicago Community Hospital, he acted on his urge to kill. At around eleven that night, he went to the nursing residence. Armed with a gun, he was let in by a young nurse. He gathered the six women, tied them up, and put them in a room. They didn't resist, as he had told them he wasn't going to hurt them, but just needed some money to go to New Orleans. Then he methodically took the women, sometimes two at a time, to another room where he stabbed and strangled them. One of the women, Corazon Amuro, untied herself and hid while the others were too fearful to move. When Speck got to what he thought was his last victim, he raped her, mutilated her anus, and strangled her. He then left the house certain there were no survivors. Amuro, terrified, went to the police, gave them a description, and told them he had said he was going to New Orleans. They captured Speck in New Orleans and took him back to Chicago. Tried and convicted, he was sentenced to death. After the death penalty was ruled unconstitutional, Richard Speck was re-sentenced to 400 years in prison. He died of a heart attack in 1991 after serving nineteen years.

Spencer, Timothy W. Known as the "Southside Slayer," Timothy Spencer raped and murdered four women in Richmond, Virginia, in 1987. The four women were all found raped and strangled in their homes from September to December 1987. Police arrested Spencer, an African American, in January 1988 and charged him with the last murder. Through DNA evidence, he was also linked to two of the other murders. There was not enough evidence to link him to the fourth murder. It was also discovered through DNA that he had murdered a woman in January 1984—a crime that another man had already served five years of a thirty-year sentence for. Spencer's first trial was in July 1988 for one count of murder. It was the first Virginia case in which DNA evidence was used. Spencer was convicted and sentenced to life in prison. He then went on trial for two other victims and was found guilty on two counts of rape and murder and sentenced to death. Timothy Spencer was executed on April 27, 1994.

Stephani, Paul Michael. Minnesota serial killer Paul Michael Stephani confessed to murdering three women and seriously wounding another between 1981 and 1982. Dubbed the "Weepy-Voiced Killer" because of his tearful phone confessions of his crimes to police, the fifty-three-year-old Stephani was arrested in 1982 following the vicious attack on a woman named Denise Williams. He was tried and convicted in 1982 of the murder of Barbara Simons, who was stabbed more than 100 times, and sentenced to forty years behind bars. He was also sentenced to another eighteen years in prison for the attack on Williams. Paul Stephani died of skin cancer on June 12, 1998, at age fifty-three.

"The .44 Killer" *see* Berkowitz, David

"Trailside Killer" *see* Carpenter, David J.

"Vampire of Sacramento" *see* Chase, Richard

"Weepy-Voiced Killer" *see* Stephani, Paul Michael

Wilder, Christopher. A native Australian, Christopher Wilder was a wealthy playboy with a speedboat, expensive cars, and a high-priced waterfront home. He earned his money through real estate investments and the two contracting companies he co-founded in Florida. For unknown reasons other than a woman had refused to marry him, the thirty-eight-year-old Wilder suddenly went on a killing spree. He killed his first victim in February 1984 in Florida. He went on to murder several women all over the United States. Wilder's victims were raped and tortured with an electric prod before he stabbed them to death. One of his victims escaped, though he had already sealed her eyes shut with glue. In April 1984, he shot a woman, stole her car, and drove off. Two policemen identified the stolen car at a gas station in New Hampshire. When they approached him, Wilder picked up his gun and killed himself.

Williams, Wayne. From July 1979 to May 1981, twenty-seven African American children were killed in Atlanta, Georgia. Dubbed the "Atlanta Child Murders" by the press, the city of Atlanta was living in fear for its young African American children. The city got a break on May 22, 1981, when someone saw a man getting into a car near the Chattahoochee River after they heard a loud splash and called the police. Police questioned the driver, Wayne Williams, a young African American man. They had no evidence to hold him, but kept him under surveillance. Two days later, they recovered a body from the river that contained dog hairs matching dog hair taken from Williams' car. They also found the same matching hair on at least ten other victims. Wayne Williams was put on trial at the end of 1981 and charged with two counts of murder. In February 1982, he was convicted on both counts and sentenced to two life sentences. There is still speculation that Wayne Williams was not responsible for murdering all of the victims and it is possible that one day the case of the "Atlanta Child Killings" may be re-opened.

Yates, Robert Lee, Jr. Between 1990 and 1998, serial killer Robert Lee Yates Jr. is believed to have murdered as many as seventeen women in the state of Washington. The forty-eight-year-old Army veteran, husband, and father of five, shot to death his victims— mostly prostitutes, drug users, or homeless women living on the streets in Tacoma and Spokane. Their bodies were discarded in remote areas. Dubbed by some foreign presses as the "notorious Washington Ripper," Yates, who worked at a Kaiser Aluminum smelting plant, typically cruised red-light districts in his white Corvette in search of prey. The sexual serial murderer was charged on April 19, 2000, with the murder of a sixteen-year-old prostitute, Jennifer Joseph. Authorities used DNA and other evidence to link Yates to at least twelve of the murders. On October 26, 2000, after pleading guilty to murdering thirteen women in order to avoid the death penalty, Robert Yates was sentenced to 408 years in prison. In 2001, Yates was charged in Pierce County with the murders of two additional women. He was convicted in October 2002 and sentenced to death by lethal injection. Yates is currently on death row at the Washington State Penitentiary.

Young, Robert *see* PAIR AND GROUP KILLERS

"Zodiac Killer." This unknown California serial killer is believed to have murdered from five to forty-nine people between December 1968 and sometime in 1974, scribbling zodiac signs near some of his victims.

The killer was described by a gunshot victim survivor as between twenty-five and thirty years old, stocky, with a round face, wavy red or brown hair, and thrived on publicity. Newspapers received letters from the alleged killer, boasting of the murders and signed with the zodiac symbol. His M.O. also included phoning police departments to report the murders using a "gruff" voice. There is no indication that the Zodiac Killer has ever been apprehended, though some believe he has continued his killing ways.

TERRORIST KILLERS - MEN

McVeigh, Timothy J., and **Terry Nichols**. On April 19, 1995, Timothy J. McVeigh and Terry Nichols launched the worst terrorist attack and mass murder in U.S. history when a bomb inside a Ryder rental truck blew up the Alfred P. Murrah Federal Building in Oklahoma City, Oklahoma. The explosion killed 168 people and injured hundreds of others. McVeigh, a bitter Gulf War veteran, was the mastermind behind the attack. He blamed the federal government for the Branch Davidian compound assault that killed fifty-eight cult members in Waco, Texas, two years earlier and the death of a white separatist's wife in Ruby Ridge, Idaho, in 1992. McVeigh and Nichols constructed the bomb using fertilizer and gas, and carried out their violent attack on the government and the American public.

McVeigh was taken into custody an hour and a half after the bombing on a weapon's charge before being charged with the mass murder and related offenses. On

June 2, 1997, a federal jury found Timothy McVeigh guilty of murder, conspiracy, and weapons charges, sentencing him to death by lethal injection. McVeigh was executed on June 11, 2001. On December 23, 1997, a federal jury convicted Terry Nichols of involuntary manslaughter and conspiracy and he was sentenced to life in prison. Following his federal conviction, multiple murder charges were brought against Terry Nichols by the Oklahoma County district attorney. On May 26, 2004, Nichols was convicted on all counts. During the penalty phase, the jury deadlocked on the death penalty and Nichols received a sentence of 161 consecutive life terms in prison with no chance for parole. *See also* The 1990s – The Oklahoma City Bombing of the Alfred P. Murrah Federal Building.

Yousef, Ramzi, and **Eyad Ismoil**. On February 26, 1993, a truck bomb exploded in the underground parking garage of the World Trade Center in New York, killing six people and injuring more than a thousand, causing $500 million in damage. Ramzi Yousef, a twenty-nine-year-old Palestinian Arab, was accused of being the mastermind of the deadly explosion, including building the bomb, which at the time was called "the worst terrorist attack" in U.S. history. Yousef was arrested in Pakistan in February 1995. Also arrested in 1995 in Jordan was his accomplice, Eyad Ismoil, twenty-six. He was accused of being the driver of the van that carried the bomb into the garage and setting it off. Yousef and Ismoil were convicted in federal court in November 1997 on murder and conspiracy charges and sentenced to 240 years in prison. Earlier, five other men were convicted and imprisoned for their roles in the conspiracy by Islamic extremists as a form of protest for the United

States' support of Israel. *See also* The 1990s – The Bombing of the World Trade Center.

OTHER KILLERS - MEN

Babarin, Sergei. On April 16, 1999, seventy-one-year-old Sergei Babarin went on a shooting rampage at the Mormon Family History Library in Salt Lake City, Utah. He killed two people and wounded four others before being shot and killed by police. Babarin, a Russian immigrant, had been taking medication for schizophrenia and had a history of violence, having been previously arrested for assault and possession of a concealed weapon. The library is considered the world's largest center for genealogical research. In collecting records for 170 years for the "baptism of the dead," the Mormon Church believes these baptisms allow the dead an opportunity in the afterlife to join the church.

Bryant, Billie Austin. On January 8, 1969, bank robber Billie Austin Bryant shot and killed two FBI agents in Washington, D.C. The fugitive was placed on the FBI's "Ten Most Wanted Fugitives" list for two hours before his capture in an attic of an apartment building. Bryant confessed to the murder of Special

Agents Woodriffe and Palmisano, though he claimed it was self-defense. On March 5, 1969, he was indicted by a federal grand jury and charged with two counts of first-degree murder and two counts of killing a federal officer. On April 14, 1969, Bryant was found guilty of armed robbery in Maryland State Court and given a twenty year sentence. After being convicted on two counts of first-degree murder in October 1969, Billie Bryant was sentenced on November 3, 1969, to two consecutive life sentences with no possibility of ever being released on parole. His is serving his time at the Federal Penitentiary in Atlanta, Georgia.

Kevorkian, Jack. On September 17, 1998, Dr. Jack Kevorkian videotaped himself injecting a lethal dose of drugs into Thomas Youk, a fifty-three-year-old suffering from Lou Gehrig's disease. The seventy-one-year-old retired pathologist and strong advocate of assisted suicide turned the tape over to the CBS news program "60 Minutes." On November 25, 1998, Kevorkian was arrested in Oakland County, Michigan, and charged with homicide, assisted suicide, and the delivery of a controlled substance. Admitting to participating in the deaths of over 130 terminally ill people, Kevorkian had previously been tried four times on charges of assisted suicide, resulting in three acquittals and one mistrial. On March 26, 1999, the man some referred to as "Dr. Death" was found guilty of second-degree murder and delivery of a controlled substance. Dr. Jack Kevorkian was sentenced to ten to twenty-five years in prison. On June 1, 2007, he was released on parole. He died on June 3, 2011, at age eighty-three. *See also* Adult Victims, Youk, Thomas.

Markhasev, Mikail. On January 16, 1997, Mikail Markhasev shot and killed Ennis Cosby during a robbery attempt on a road near Bel Air, California. The twenty-seven-year-old Cosby was the only son of comedian Bill Cosby. Markhasev, a nineteen-year-old Ukrainian, had a history of gang connections and was a racist as well, based on a confession he made to the murder verbally and in letters. He was arrested two months after the crime that occurred when Cosby was changing a flat tire. On July 7, 1998, Mikail Markhasev was convicted of murder, attempted robbery, and the use of a firearm during an attempted robbery. He was sentenced to life without parole, plus ten years.

Scott, David Lynn III. Following a string of violent crimes between September 1992 and January 1993 in Riverside, California, that included murder, attempted murder, and rape, David Lynn Scott III was finally brought to justice. Called the "Ninja Prowler," the twenty-seven-year-old Scott patterned his reign of terror from Japan's feudal ninja warriors. Donning black garb and armed with a sword and gun, Scott murdered thirty-eight-year-old Riverside librarian Brenda Gail Kenny in her apartment. He was arrested in January 1993 and charged with Kenny's rape and murder, the rape of two other women, the attempted murder of two men, and additional crimes. Despite a troubled childhood that included being diagnosed as a psychotic and a mother who was a prostitute, Scott was convicted on fifteen counts, including murder, on January 8, 1998. After a botched escape attempt prior to sentencing, a jury recommended that David Scott be put to death. On March 23, 1998, Scott unsuccessfully attempted to commit suicide by slashing his arm with a razor. He is currently on death row at San Quentin.

Smith, Dennis Keith. Relying on the use of DNA evidence, the rapist-murderer of a woman was convicted in spite of the absence of the victim's body. Vancouver, Washington, resident Dennis Keith Smith, thirty-five, an already convicted murderer for strangling his sister in 1982, was charged with the rape, kidnap, and murder of Carolyn Ruth Killaby, thirty-four, who vanished on November 11, 1995, after leaving a restaurant with Smith. DNA evidence taken from Smith's pickup truck was linked to Killaby. On May 12, 1998, a jury returned guilty verdicts against Smith for first-degree aggravated murder for attempting to conceal a crime, felony murder, kidnapping, and the rape of Carolyn Killaby. He was sentenced to life in prison without the possibility of parole. Smith hanged himself at the Washington State Penitentiary in 2004.

SECTION 2 – WOMEN KILLERS

BLACK WIDOW KILLERS - WOMEN

Allen, Shirley Goude. Born in 1941 in St. Louis, Missouri, Shirley Goude Allen was once referred to as a "pathological liar," which served her well through six marriages—at least two of which ended in the murder of a husband and a third in attempted murder. Collecting insurance payments was this Black Widow's motivation for killing. Her methods of carrying out her crimes included various means of poisoning, such as rat poison and the use of ethylene glycol, commonly found in antifreeze. It was only after toxicology tests were performed on husband number six, Lloyd Allen, that the poisonous nature of his death was confirmed and his widow the chief suspect. Five days later, in November 1982, Shirley Allen was arrested and charged with first-degree murder. She was convicted and sentenced to life in prison on July 6, 1984, with at least fifty years to be spent behind bars. Allen died in prison in July 2000.

Archer-Gilligan, Amy. In the early 1900s, a Black Widow serial murderess named Amy Archer-Gilligan took the lives of five of her husbands and several elderly nursing home patients. Born in 1869, she preyed on well-to-do senior citizens who stayed in the private nursing home that she opened in Windsor, Connecticut, at the age of thirty-two. Archer-Gillian married five elderly residents between 1901 and 1914, purchasing sizeable life insurance policies on each, and then poisoning them. In addition, she managed to coerce several female patients into making her a beneficiary in their wills before poisoning them. Only when an autopsy was done on her last victim at the request of relatives did authorities uncover her poisoning scheme and link her to eight other deaths, noting that she had collected life insurance benefits for each of them. Following her arrest, Amy Archer-Gilligan was put on trial for murder and sentenced to life in prison. She was ultimately committed to a state asylum where she died in 1928.

Barfield, Margie Velma. This North Carolina Black Widow killer also used various forms of poison to murder her six victims, which included two husbands, her fiancé, and her mother. Margie Velma Barfield was thirty-seven, the mother of two, and addicted to prescription drugs to fight depression and deal with a tumultuous marriage when she began her killing spree by setting her husband on fire in his bed. Regarded by authorities as an accidental death at the time, Barfield mixed drug addiction and writing bad checks with more murders, including her second husband, Jennings Barfield, and an elderly woman that she worked for as a live-in maid. It was only after an autopsy had been performed on Barfield's last victim—

her lover—that they learned he died from arsenic poisoning. She was arrested and confessed to his murder and the others. During her trial, she blamed the deaths on her drug problem. She was convicted of murder and sentenced to death. In 1984, Margie Barfield died by lethal injection, becoming the first woman to be executed in the United States since 1976.

Beets, Betty Lou. This Black Widow barmaid was born in Texas in 1937, married five times, and had six children who inherited her disrespect for the law and violent tendencies. Betty Lou Beets murdered two of her husbands, Doyle Barker and James Beets, the latter a Dallas Fire Department captain, and attempted to murder a third. In at least one case she was aided and abetted by her daughter, Shirley Stegner. Profit from life insurance and a pension appeared to be the motive for killing the men. Police received help from an informant who led them to the area around Beets's mobile home where the skeletal remains of the two husbands were found on June 8, 1985. Beets was arrested and charged with capital murder in the shooting deaths of Doyle Barker and James Beets. Her daughter, Shirley, was charged with murder in Barker's death and testified against her mother. In October 1985, Beets was found guilty of murder and sentenced to death. The Texas Court of Criminal Appeals overturned the conviction on November 12, 1987, but reversed its decision on September 21, 1988. In June 1989, the U.S. Supreme Court rejected hearing the case of Betty Lou Beets. She was executed on February 24, 2000.

Birch, Pearl Choate. Unlike most Black Widows, Pearl Choate Birch set her sights on aging, wealthy victims before insurance policies even needed to be cashed in. Born in 1907, the Texas nurse stood over six feet tall and weighed about 250 pounds during the height of her private nursing of elderly millionaires. During the 1950s she married six such men in their nineties, each of whom died shortly thereafter. Most of the deaths aroused little suspicion, under the circumstances. However, the sixth victim was shot four times and Choate said it was self-defense. A jury of her peers felt otherwise and she was convicted of murder. She was released from prison on good behavior in 1963. Around that time she met and married her last husband, A. Otis Birch, a ninety-five-year-old California millionaire. After his death in March 1966, Pearl Choate Birch was once again suspected of murder, but authorities were unable to prove it.

Buenoano, Judias (Judy). Between 1971 and 1980 the Texas born Judias Buenoano murdered her husband, boyfriend, son, and attempted to kill her fiancé. She poisoned each victim with arsenic so she could collect on their insurance policies. Described as a classic Black Widow serial killer, Buenoano, who was twenty-eight when the killings began, was also an arsonist who benefited from a number of fraudulent insurance claims. She was tried and found guilty of murder and a number of other charges before being sentenced to death in 1985. On March 30, 1998, fifty-nine-year-old Judy Buenoano, was executed in Florida's electric chair, becoming the first woman put to death in the state since 1848.

Creighton, Mary Frances *see* PAIR AND GROUP KILLERS

Doss, Nanny Hazel. A notorious Black Widow and family murderess was Nanny Hazel Doss. Dubbed the "Giggling Grandma" by the press because of a habit of giggling while discussing her murderous offenses, she was twenty when she began her serial killing in 1925 and forty-nine when it ended. In all, she murdered at least ten people in the South including four husbands, two sisters, her mother, two of her children, and a grandchild. All the victims died from poisoning with money acquired from life insurance and family savings the primary motivation. Her last victim was her fourth husband, Samuel Doss, whose name she adopted. The post-mortem on Doss indicated that he had been poisoned by arsenic. Nanny Doss confessed to this and nine other murders. She was found guilty of the crimes in court and sentenced to life in prison in 1955. Ten years later, while still incarcerated, Doss died of leukemia.

Gates, Anne. A former nurse, Anne Gates is believed to have murdered two husbands between 1978 and 1987 in Indiana and Louisiana, respectively. Like other Black Widows, insurance money was her primary motive for the killings. After the brutal death of her estranged elderly second husband, Raymond Gates, law enforcement investigators took a close look at the thirty-eight-year-old Anne Gates. Upon questioning, she was arrested on December 9, 1987, and indicted for first-degree murder in May 1988. She pled no contest to manslaughter and received a ten-year prison term in 1989. Because she was not technically found guilty of murder, Anne Gates actually inherited $25,000 from the estate of her late husband. The convicted murderess became the chief beneficiary of his death.

Gburek, Tillie. Black Widow Tillie Gburek began her murdering ways when she was nearly fifty, actually predicting the deaths of her mates to them before carrying them out. Between 1914 and 1921, Gburek used arsenic to murder four husbands and a neighbor to profit from life insurance policies and the assets of the victims. Her uncannily accurate ability to foretell these deaths caught the attention of law enforcement. They discovered that her fifth husband was dying of arsenic poisoning that was being mixed with his food. Tillie Gburek was arrested and the bodies of her previous victims exhumed. They too had died of poisoning. Gburek went to trial in 1921 and received a life sentence with no chance of parole. She died in prison on November 20, 1936.

Gibbs, Janie Lou. This Christian fundamentalist from Georgia had a darker side as a Black Widow and family murderer. From 1965 to 1967, Janie Lou Gibbs murdered her husband and four children with arsenic. Her motive was collecting on insurance policies, a portion of which she would donate to her church. An autopsy performed on her last victim revealed the presence of arsenic and led to discovering the same poisoning of her other victims. Janie Lou Gibbs was arrested in 1967 and confessed to the five murders that she was charged with. She received a sentence of five life terms. She died in a nursing home on February 7, 2010.

Gunness, Belle. Born as Brynhild Paulsdatter Størseth in 1859, Belle Gunness achieved infamy as a Black Widow and gold digger. Dubbed "Lady Bluebeard," she emigrated from Norway at twenty-one years of age and settled in Chicago three years later. It was there that she began her murderous ways at the age of thirty-seven, driven by profit from insurance settlements or robbery of the deceased. Between 1896 and 1908, Gunness is believed to have murdered anywhere from sixteen to forty-nine people. These included two husbands, several of her children, and at least two suitors. Following the death of her second husband, Gunness used some of her insurance money to move to a farmhouse in La Porte, Indiana. There she placed "lonely hearts" and employment classified ads to attract her future victims.

In April 1908, a fire leveled her farm. Investigators uncovered the dismembered remains of adults and children, including human bone fragments in the hog pen. Among the remains was a headless body presumed to be Belle Gunness, identified by her dental bridge. However, her handyman, Ray Lamphere, insisted that she had faked her death at the expense of another woman. He was charged with arson and multiple counts of murder, but found not guilty of the homicides. Gunness was reportedly seen in various parts of the country until 1935. *See also* The 1900s – The Gunness Farmhouse Fire.

Hahn, Anna Marie *see* Serial Killers – Women

Kinne, Sharon. Following a long line of murder-for-profit female killers, Sharon Kinne was also willing to kill anyone who stood in her way. Between March 1960 and September 1964, authorities believe that she shot to death her husband, the wife of her lover, and another man she picked up while on the run in Mexico City. At the age of twenty, Kinne was indicted for the murder of Patricia Jones in September 1960. She was acquitted when ballistics tests failed to support her .22-caliber pistol as the murder weapon. She was brought to trial soon after to face murder charges in the death of her husband, James Kinne. She was convicted of murder in January 1962 and sentenced to life in prison. This was overturned on appeal and a second trial ended in a mistrial. There was a hung jury in Kinne's third trial. Before a fourth trial could get underway in October 1964, she fled to Mexico with a boyfriend. She ended up in a motel room with another man whom she shot to death. In spite of claiming self-defense, Kinne was convicted in a Mexican court and sentenced to thirteen years in prison, following a failed appeal. Sharon Kinne apparently escaped from the Iztapalapa Women's Prison on December 7, 1969, and hasn't been seen since. She continues to face murder charges in the United States.

Martin, Rhonda Bell. Born in 1907, this Black Widow from Alabama was involved in serial murder throughout much of her adult life. Rhonda Bell Martin took the lives of at least seven people in spouse and familial homicides, including three husbands, three of her children, and her mother. The victims all died from arsenic poisoning, with life insurance money her motivation. Martin's fifth husband survived the poisonous attempt on his life, but was left with permanent paralysis as a result of being fed arsenic with his meals. Similar to other Black Widow killers, an autopsy on a victim that revealed the poisoning led to her downfall. She was arrested and charged with committing multiple murders. Convicted, Rhonda Bell Martin was sentenced to death. In 1957, she was put to death in the electric chair.

Monahan, Annie. It was early in the 20th century that Black Widow Annie Monahan murdered her three husbands and her niece in New Haven, Connecticut. The murders occurred between 1906 and 1917. Arsenic was her weapon and insurance money her motivation. After beating the charges of murdering her niece due to insufficient evidence, the death of her third husband and former brother-in-law, John Monahan, in

December 1917 proved to be her undoing. Arrested and charged with murder a second time, Annie Monahan was found guilty on February 13, 1919. She received a sentence of life in prison, where she eventually died.

Moore, Blanche Taylor. Born as Blanche Kiser in 1933 in North Carolina, this Black Widow was believed to be among the few who killed not only for insurance profit but also for revenge. From 1966 to 1989, Blanche Taylor Moore murdered her husband, a lover, her father, and mother-in-law. A victim of childhood sexual abuse, forced prostitution, and her father's alcoholism, Moore got her revenge by poisoning to death her abusive father. A few years later, her despised elderly mother-in-law had a similar fate. Her husband and her lover were the next victims of arsenic poisoning by her hand. Only when her second husband, the Reverend Dwight Moore, nearly died due to a lethal amount of arsenic in his system, did police begin to put together the murderous crimes of Blanche Taylor Moore by exhuming the bodies of her previous victims. She went on trial in October 1990 for the murder of her lover, Raymond Reid, and was found guilty. She was sentenced to death by lethal injection on November 16, 1990. A movie made in the 1980s about Blanche Taylor Moore's life starring Elizabeth Montgomery was called "Black Widow." She currently resides on death row at the North Carolina Correctional Institution for Women.

Peete, Louise. Born in Louisiana, the former Lofie Louise Preslar has been called one of history's worst examples of the Black Widow serial killer. After her first husband committed suicide because he was despondent over her infidelity, Louise Peete turned to prostitution, thievery, and murder for profit as a way of life. In the early part of the 20th century, suicide and homicide seemed to follow her. Three of her husbands took their own lives and another died by her hand. Louise Peete was convicted in California of murdering one of her lovers in January 1921. She received a life sentence, but was paroled in 1933. More murders followed, including that of social worker Margaret Logan, to whom Peete had been paroled and named as the sole beneficiary in her insurance policy. Charged with and convicted of Logan's murder, Peete was sentenced to death. On April 11, 1947, she was executed in the gas chamber at San Quentin.

Quinn, Jane. This Black Widow used poison and bullets to take the lives of three husbands and her mother between 1901 and 1911. The last victim—husband number three—was John Miller. He was shot to death in the couple's Chicago apartment on November 2, 1911. Following an inquest, Jane Quinn was arrested and charged with murder. With the evidence substantiated, she was convicted and sentenced to life in prison.

Rearden, Virginia. This cold-blooded killer may be the quintessential Black Widow in that she used virtually any means necessary—including arson and murder—to collect life and fire insurance. Born in 1932, Virginia Rearden had a long history of collecting on fire insurance for suspicious fires in houses and other property she was associated with. However, she was equally resilient when it came to profiting on life insurance policies, as she was suspected of killing her second husband and a three-year-old girl. The beginning of the end of her crime spree came with the apparent accidental death of a young woman, Deana

Wild, who fell from a cliff in Big Sur, California, on April 2, 1987. Rearden, her husband, and son had been at the scene. Authorities eventually learned that Rearden had taken out an insurance policy on the victim one day before her death. An autopsy further revealed that Wild had been drugged, causing disorientation. Rearden and her now ex-husband, Billy Joe McGinnis, were charged with first-degree murder. While McGinnis died prior to his trial, Virginia Rearden was convicted of murder and sentenced to life in prison without the possibility of parole on March 30, 1992. Her bizarre story was the subject of two made-for-television movies.

Smart, Pamela *see* PAIR AND GROUP KILLERS

Trueblood, Lydia. This Black Widow, like others, was motivated by the financial benefits of insurance in choosing and murdering her victims in Idaho and Montana. Between 1915 and 1919, Lydia Trueblood murdered four husbands, her brother-in-law, and a child. All died of poisoning. After the suspicious death of Edward Meyer, her fourth husband, a post-mortem found arsenic in his system. Though suspected of his death, Trueblood remained free to marry a fifth husband in California. Before he could be killed, authorities had gathered enough evidence against her in the Meyer death to arrest her for murder. She was brought back to Idaho to stand trial in 1921. Trueblood was convicted of murder and sentenced to life in prison where she died of natural causes. *See also* The 1910s – Black Widow Murderess Lydia Trueblood.

Vermilyea, Louise. Similar to other Black Widows, Chicago born Louise Vermilyea was motivated by collecting on insurance policies and acquiring other assets of her victims. However, she targeted not only husbands but also others she was close to or acquainted with. From 1893 to 1911, Vermilyea murdered ten people, including two spouses, three of her children, a stepchild, and four acquaintances that stayed at or ate meals in the boardinghouse she operated. The method of death for all the victims was arsenic poisoning. She was arrested in 1911 and indicted for the murders of all ten people. Before her trial could begin, she laced her own meals with arsenic and, as a result, became permanently paralyzed in December 1911. Consequently, Vermilyea was never tried for the lives she took.

CARETAKER KILLERS - WOMEN

Jones, Genene. At thirty-two, Genene Jones was a licensed vocational nurse in Texas. She had worked at several hospitals in the San Antonio area from 1977 to 1982. Jones worked for a doctor in private practice in early 1982, but was fired in September of that year when they found a bottle of succinylincholine in her purse with needle marks in it. This was after seven children suffered seizures in August and September at the hands of Jones. In February 1983, a grand jury was investigating the suspicious death of forty-seven children over the past four years at Bexar County Medical Center where Jones had worked during part of that time. On May 26, 1983, she was indicted on two counts of murder in Kerr County, Texas. Jones was charged with injecting lethal amounts of a muscle relaxant and other drugs to deliberately kill fifteen-month-old Chelsea McClellan. Additional charges were also filed against her for causing injury to six children who were injected with drugs. On November 21, 1983,

Jones was indicted in San Antonio for injuring four-week-old Rolando Santos, who almost died. She was also suspected in at least ten infant deaths at the Bexar County Medical Center. Genene Jones was convicted of murder on February 15, 1984, and sentenced to ninety-nine years in prison. On October 24, 1984, she was convicted in San Antonio for injuring Rolando Santos and received a sentence of sixty years to be served concurrently.

Matajke, Dorothy Jean. In Iowa in the 1970s, Dorothy Matajke was a nurse's aide and live-in nurse for the elderly and sick. When several of her patients died, it was assumed it was due to natural causes. In 1973, Matajke was convicted of fraud and sentenced to five years in prison. She escaped and was on the run for six years before being recaptured and sent back to finish her sentence in 1980. Matajke then moved to Little Rock, Arkansas, and moved in with seventy-two-year-old Paul Kinsey and his seventy-one-year-old wife, Opal, on March 24, 1985. When Opal died on April 5, it was assumed she died of her recently diagnosed cancer. When Paul became sick shortly after his wife's death, relatives assumed it was due to grief and loneliness. Matajke then became the nurse to cancer patient Marion Doyle in September 1986. She died nine days later. At the same time, Matajke was still living with and "caring" for Paul Kinsey, whose health continued to decline. He attributed his illness to her and ordered her to move out in October. Three days later he was in critical condition and put in the hospital. Matajke was arrested and charged with forgery and theft for stealing Marion Doyle's money from her bank account. She was later charged with possession of a gun and forgery for checks she wrote on Paul Kinsey's account. When police searched Matajke's house, they found bottles of drugs, tranquilizers, and arsenic. On November 24, 1986, Dorothy Matajke was charged with first-degree murder for the death of Marion Doyle and first-degree battery for poisoning Paul Kinsey. When Kinsey died on February 10, 1987, the charge was changed to first-degree murder. Matajke was convicted in June 1987 for Paul Kinsey's murder and sentenced to life. Two months later, after a plea bargain, she received an additional sixty year sentence for killing Marion Doyle.

Puente, Dorothea Montalvo *see* Serial Killers - Women

Rachals, Terri. Born in 1962, Terri Rachals had an awful childhood. Her mother had a nervous breakdown when she was two so her father gave her up for adoption. Her adoptive mother died in 1973 and Terri claimed she had been repeatedly molested by her adoptive father. She married Roger Rachals in 1980 and had a son four years later. In Albany, Georgia, from October to November 1985, six suspicious deaths and six close calls occurred in Putney Hospital's cardiac unit where Terri worked. Administrators notified police and autopsies revealed the six deaths occurred by an injection of potassium chloride. Police were also suspicious of four other deaths going back to August 1985. Twenty-four-year-old nurse Terri Rachals was brought in for questioning. In March 1986, she confessed to murdering five patients and was indicted on six counts of murder and twenty counts of aggravated assault. Rachals was tried and convicted in September 1986. She was found guilty but mentally ill on one count of aggravated assault and acquitted of all the charges. Terri Rachals was sentenced to seventeen years in prison on October 1, 1986. She was released on April 1, 2003.

Terrell, Bobbie Sue. Born in Illinois, Bobbie Sue Terrell grew up as a shy and overweight girl. She became a registered nurse and then married her first husband Danny Dudley. The marriage was over quickly when their adopted son was hospitalized for a drug overdose. Bobbie Sue's husband blamed her for giving him her schizophrenia medicine and she lost custody of him in the divorce. Alone, her mental and physical health declined quickly. She had numerous physical problems and surgeries. Bobbie Sue committed herself to a state hospital and spent a year there. She moved to St. Petersburg, Florida, in 1984. Still plagued by numerous health problems and more surgeries, she finally got a nursing job as the night shift supervisor at a rest home. Soon the patients began dying under her watch. In November 1984, at least twelve patients died. An investigation was underway and Bobbie Sue was fired. On January 31, 1985, she entered a hospital for psychiatric treatment. Meanwhile, detectives had exhumed the bodies of nine patients in Florida and three other states. During this time, Bobbie Sue married Ron Terrell, a plumber. It wasn't long before he had her committed against her will. On March 17, 1985, she was formally charged with attempted murder and four counts of first-degree murder. At her trial in 1988, Bobbie Sue Terrell pleaded guilty to reduced charges of second-degree murder and was sentenced to sixty-five years in prison. She died in prison on August 27, 2007.

Toppan, Jane. In 1854, Nora Kelly was born in Boston, Massachusetts. Her mother died shortly after and her father went insane and was sent to an asylum. Mr. and Mrs. Toppan adopted Nora Kelly in 1859 and changed her name to Jane Toppan. In 1880, after surviving two attempted suicides, she got a job as a student nurse in Cambridge. Toppan was fired when two patients died mysteriously under her care. For twenty years she worked for numerous New England families to care for the sick and elderly. Not many of her patients were able to survive her care. In July and August 1901, after being hired as the family nurse, Toppan killed the patriarch and his two daughters. An autopsy on one of the daughters revealed lethal doses of morphine. Before she was arrested in New Hampshire on October 29, 1901, Toppan also killed her foster sister with an overdose of morphine. She confessed to thirty-one murders, but authorities felt she may have killed as many as one hundred. During the trial, Toppan testified that it was her goal to kill more helpless people than any other man or woman. Jane Toppan was declared insane and confined for life to the state asylum in Massachusetts. She died there in 1938 at the age of eighty-four.

CELEBRITY KILLERS - WOMEN

Hartman, Brynn. On May 28, 1998, Brynn Hartman shot to death her husband, forty-nine-year-old comic actor Phil Hartman, in their Encino, California, home. The forty-year-old one-time model then took her life. The couple married in 1987 and had two children. Brynn Hartman, who had a long history of drug problems and was said to be temperamental and jealous, had a blood alcohol level of 0.12 percent the day of the crime—well above the level in California for being legally drunk. Toxicology tests also found traces of cocaine and a prescription anti-depressant in her system. *See also* Adult Victims, Hartman, Phil.

Longet, Claudine. On March 21, 1976, former showgirl and actress Claudine Longet shot and killed her lover, champion skier Vladimir "Spider" Sabich, at their home in Aspen, Colorado. The thirty-one-year-old Sabich and thirty-four-year-old Longet were living together with her three children from her marriage to singer Andy Williams. At the time of the murder, the two year Sabich-Longet relationship had shown signs of strain in the resort town where alcohol and drug abuse, promiscuity, and wild parties were the norm. Longet claimed she had accidentally shot Sabich with his .22-caliber pistol. She was charged with reckless manslaughter on April 8, 1976, and pleaded not guilty. On January 14, 1977, a jury convicted Longet of criminally negligent homicide. She was sentenced to thirty days' jail time, put on two years' probation, and fined $250. She was later sued for $1.3 million by Vladimir Sabich's parents. *See also* The 1970s – The Murder of Champion Skier Vladimir Sabich; Adult Victims, Sabich, Vladimir "Spider".

Saldivar, Yolanda. On March 31, 1995, Latina singing sensation, Selena Quintanilla, was shot to death outside a Days Inn motel room in Corpus Christi, Texas, by Yolanda Saldivar, the former president of Selena's fan club. The thirty-four-year-old Saldivar, suspected of embezzling funds from the twenty-three-year-old singer and her family, was apparently about to be fired when the shooting occurred. Saldivar managed to keep law enforcement at bay for ten hours in the motel parking lot as she threatened to commit suicide while sitting in a pickup truck with a gun pointed at her head. She was finally talked into giving up and was arrested and charged with murder. On October 23, 1995, a jury convicted Yolanda Saldivar of first-degree murder and she was sentenced to life in prison. *See also* Adult Victims, Selena.

CHILD KILLERS - WOMEN

Bacher, Johanna *see* Familial Killers – Women

Baniszewski, Gertrude. On October 26, 1965, the tortured corpse of sixteen-year-old Sylvia Likens was found by police at the home of Gertrude Baniszewski in Indianapolis, Indiana. Likens and her fifteen-year-old sister, Jenny, were living with Baniszewski while their parents traveled with a circus through the Midwest. For four months a maniacal Gertrude Baniszewski—who was thirty-six, divorced, and struggling to make ends meet with odd jobs and child support payments— abused, humiliated, and mutilated the Likens sisters. Helping her abuse the girls were neighborhood teenage boys and some of her own children. The torture inflicted upon the girls included being beaten with belts, paddles, and wooden boards, and being burned with cigarettes.

Sylvia Likens took the brunt of the punishment, including being starved, being forced to insert a Coke bottle into her vagina, and made to eat and drink her own excrement and urine. Baniszewski punctuated her sadistic torture by using a heated needle to carve onto Sylvia's stomach the words: "I am a prostitute and proud of it." Sylvia Likens died when Baniszewski slammed her head against a concrete floor to keep her from alerting neighbors of the unbelievable abuse that would stun the nation. In 1966, Gertrude Baniszewski was convicted of murder in the death of Sylvia Likens and sentenced to life in prison. In 1985, she was paroled in spite of public condemnation. Baniszewski died on June 16, 1990. *See also* Child Victims, Likens, Sylvia.

Basuta, Manjit. On March 17, 1998, child killer Manjit Basuta took the life of thirteen-month-old Christopher Evan Oliver Smith while he was in her custody as a day care operator in San Diego, California. The forty-three-year-old Basuta, an Indian woman born and raised in England, operated her day care facility out of her home. She was accused of shaking to death the boy when he did not respond to her demands. Basuta, a wife and mother of three boys, was charged with assaulting a child under eight years old resulting in the child's death. In August 1999, a jury found Manjit Basuta guilty as charged. On October 1, 1999, she was sentenced to twenty-five years to life in prison. In court in April 2002, Basuta pleaded guilty to involuntary manslaughter and had her sentence reduced to eight years. She was paroled in August 2003 and deported to England.

Bearce, Mrs. Leon *see* Familial Killers – Women

Buenoano, Judias *see* Black Widow Killers – Women

Church, Ellen *see* Familial Killers – Women

Collins, Opal Juanita *see* Familial Killers – Women

Cooper, Glenda *see* Familial Killers – Women

Crimmins, Alice *see* Familial Killers – Women

David, Rachal *see* Familial Killers – Women

Dcyzheski, Nellie *see* Familial Killers – Women

Doss, Nanny Hazel *see* Black Widow Killers – Women

Downs, Elizabeth Diane *see* Familial Killers – Women

Edwards, Lillian *see* Familial Killers – Women

Etheridge, Ellen *see* Familial Killers – Women

Eubanks, Susan *see* Familial Killers – Women

Falling, Christine Laverne. Born in 1963 in Florida as Christine Laverne Slaughter, this female multiple murderer had a history of poverty, sickness, aggressive and violent behavior, and animal abuse before she began killing children that she was babysitting. Between 1980 and 1982, Falling murdered at least five children, injured a number of others, and killed an elderly man in different Florida towns. She was nineteen when she began her killing ways by suffocating her victims. On July 2, 1982, following the death of a ten-week-old infant in her care, Falling was brought in for questioning. She confessed to the murder of three children, claiming to hear voices ordering her to do it. Found to be legally sane, Christine Falling received a life sentence in prison with no possibility of parole for twenty-five years. She is currently in custody at the Homestead Correctional Institution in Florida.

Fuller, Edna *see* Familial Killers – Women

Gibbs, Janie Lou *see* Black Widow Killers – Women

Grant, Rosalie *see* Familial Killers – Women

Green, Ann. Born in 1946, this murderess killed two of her children, attempted to kill a third, and may have murdered other children as a nurse. Ann Green is believed to have suffered from Munchausen syndrome by proxy, a rare disorder in which one manufactures or imagines physical ailments in their children, typically bringing the children to doctor's offices or hospitals for treatment. She perpetrated her crimes between 1970 and 1985, starting at the age of twenty-four. During this time, she worked in the pediatric ward at a hospital and was suspected of being involved in the deaths of a number of children under her care who died under suspicious circumstances. After the near-death of her third child, Ann Green was indicted in 1986 on two counts of second-degree murder for her first two children, whose deaths had previously been considered due to natural causes. In October 1988, she was exonerated by the jury due to mental illness caused by severe postpartum depression. She was ordered to undergo psychiatric counseling.

Gunness, Belle *see* Black Widow Killers – Women

Her, Khoua *see* Familial Killers – Women

Hogg, Megan *see* Familial Killers – Women

Hoyt, Waneta E. *see* Familial Killers - Women

Hultberg, Violet *see* Familial Killers – Women

Jackson, Gertrude *see* PAIR AND GROUP KILLERS

Johnson, Martha Ann *see* Familial Killers – Women

Jones, Annie *see* Familial Killers – Women

Jones, Roxanne *see* Familial Killers – Women

Kantarian, Nancy Lee *see* Familial Killers – Women

Kimura, Fumiko *see* Familial Killers – Women

King, Kathleen *see* Familial Killers – Women

Lumbrera, Diana *see* Familial Killers – Women

Martin, Rhonda Bell *see* Black Widow Killers – Women

McAninch, Alma May *see* Familial Killers – Women

MacDonald, Carol *see* Familial Killers – Women

Nollen, Elsie *see* Familial Killers – Women

Pasos, Marie *see* Familial Killers – Women

Rowney, Margaret *see* Familial Killers – Women

Shoaf, Mamie Shey *see* Familial Killers – Women

Sims, Paula Marie *see* Familial Killers – Women

Smith, Susan Vaughan *see* Familial Killers – Women

Tinning, Marybeth *see* Familial Killers – Women

Trueblood, Lydia *see* Black Widow Killers – Women

Tuggle, Debra Sue. Between 1974 and 1982, Debra Sue Tuggle killed her three sons and her fiancé's daughter. This African American woman, born in Arkansas, had a history of mental illness when she suffocated her first two children in 1974. At the time, death had been attributed to SIDS. Her third son died in 1976, also of suffocation, but Tuggle was able to escape prosecution. In 1982, she was suspected of drowning her fiancé's daughter, Tomekia Paxton, and arrested for her murder in March 1984. In September 1984, she was convicted of second-degree murder for her death and sentenced to ten years in prison. She was released in 1994 at the age of thirty-six. Due to insufficient evidence, Debra Sue Tuggle was not tried for the murder of her own children.

Urdanivia, Ruth *see* Familial Killers – Women

Vermilyea, Louise *see* Black Widow Killers – Women

Walkup, Marie *see* Familial Killers – Women
Williamson, Stella *see* Familial Killers – Women
Woods, Martha *see* Familial Killers - Women
Woodward, Louise. A British au pair, Louise Woodward made international headlines when she was charged with killing an infant under her care in Newton, Massachusetts, in 1997. On February 5, eight-month-old Matthew Eappen was rushed to the hospital suffering from brain damage and a fractured skull. He died five days later. The eighteen-year-old Woodward was arrested and charged with violently shaking and slamming the baby, causing his death. On March 5, 1997, she was indicted for first-degree murder. Though insisting she had done nothing that could have caused the death of the baby, a jury convicted Louise Woodward of second-degree murder on October 30, 1997. She was sentenced to life in prison. However, on November 10, 1997, a judge reduced the verdict against Woodward to manslaughter and time served, releasing the nanny after she spent 279 days behind bars. On January 29, 1999, a wrongful death lawsuit against Louise Woodward by the parents of Matthew Eappen was settled out of court, preventing Woodward from profiting from the child's death.

Wright, Jeanne Anne *see* Familial Killers - Women

FAMILIAL KILLERS - WOMEN

Bacher, Johanna. Born Johanna Healey in 1891 in Connecticut, this child killer was already unstable by the time her husband, Henry Bacher, filed for a divorce on the grounds of intolerable cruelty in 1921. She was left with the couple's three young children in Greenwich, but was worried about losing custody of them in court. Johanna purchased rat poison with the intent of killing her children, but after talking with the local police chief she promised not to harm them. Unfortunately, the promise did not hold. On March 26, 1922, Johanna Bacher slit the throats of her three children with a butcher knife and then committed suicide by cutting her own throat. She left behind a suicide note.

Basore, Eleanor. Separated from her husband for several months, Eleanor Basore lived in Fayetteville, Arkansas. She heard about a family reunion scheduled for September 4, 1971, that she was not invited to. Infuriated, she drove twenty miles to the reunion location with a revolver. Upon arrival, Basore shot and killed her husband, his parents, and her brother-in-law. She also wounded her twenty-three-year-old son. Eleanor Basore then put the gun in her mouth and pulled the trigger, killing herself.

Bearce, Mrs. Leon. Mentally unstable, this multiple murderess committed infanticide and child murder in the early 1930s. Born in 1901, Mrs. Leon Bearce was the mother of three, including twins. She and her husband operated a tourist camp close to Glen Falls, New York. The marriage fell apart in early 1931 after Leon found his wife acting a bit too unbalanced. On June 20, 1931, an effort at reconciliation on the campgrounds went awry when Mrs. Leon Bearce slit the throat of her twins and fourteen-year-old daughter, killing them. She was arrested, found to be insane, and committed to an asylum for the remainder of her life.

Bolin, Patricia. Married and the mother of three children, forty-year-old Patricia Bolin appeared to have a perfect life. In 1970 the family moved to the exclusive Ohio suburb of Upper Arlington, where they had built a large custom home. Shortly thereafter, Bolin began drinking heavily. On the afternoon of December 8, 1976, Bolin and her husband Ron were home alone while the children were visiting friends. She retrieved the .22-caliber pistol she had purchased, along with fifty rounds of ammunition. She then shot Ron in the head, neck, and chest, apparently while he was running for the front door. Shortly thereafter, when their twelve-year-old daughter Tamela came home, Bolin met her in the garage, shot her, and then dragged her body into the house. When her nine-year-old son Todd came in, she shot him where he stood. Alicia, age fifteen, was the last to come home. She came through the garage and, upon seeing the blood, ran into the house screaming for her mother. Bolin was waiting for her in the kitchen. She fired the gun, but it was out of bullets. She then ordered her daughter to wait in her room, but Alicia ran to a neighbor's house and called the police. Before they arrived, Bolin had shot and killed herself. Police and relatives were never able to determine what Patricia Bolin's motive was.

Calbeck, Lorene. On May 24, 1956, Lorene Calbeck shot to death her three young daughters as they sat in the family car in Polk County, Florida. The thirty-four-year-old housewife fatally shot each child four times in the chest, brought the bodies home to their trailer park, wrote a suicide note, then shot herself in the chest. She somehow survived. A grand jury chose not to indict her for murder; instead Calbeck was committed to a state mental hospital. Eventually she was judged sane enough to be released to her husband Mark. On January 3, 1989, more than three decades after killing her children, Lorene Calbeck, depressed over her husband's recent death, shot herself in the chest with a .32-caliber gun. She died en route to the hospital.

Campbell, Inez Ethel. Born as Inez Kapphaum in 1921, this self-admitted "crazy" Montana wife and mother went berserk on May 25, 1945, when she murdered four of her six children. The killings took place on a bridge running across the Milk River in Glasgow, Montana. Campbell bludgeoned five of her children—aged three months to seven years—with a hammer, then tossed them into the river where all but one drowned. She then jumped into the river, killing herself. Inez Campbell left a suicide note indicating that she was going mad and could no longer handle it.

Church, Ellen. On May 25, 1959, Ellen Church, wife of nationally recognized microbiologist, Doctor Brooks Church, did the unimaginable in killing two of her children and attempting to kill the other two in the family's home in Denville, New Jersey. Ellen, who somehow believed her children were insane, beat and strangled her two-year-old and six-month-old, then tried to murder her older children with an overdose of sleeping pills. Both survived and Ellen was arrested. She was found to be suffering from schizophrenia and unfit to stand trial. Ellen Church was confined to a state psychiatric institution.

Collins, Opal Juanita. Born in 1931 in Kentucky, Opal Juanita Collins was already twice divorced with two children when in 1953 she met her third husband, Ben Collins Jr. Collins, a World War II veteran, had been paralyzed from the chest down in an automobile accident a few years earlier. The relationship was often marked by violence at the hands of Opal. Ben feared for his safety and that of his parents and three young siblings with whom they lived in Hammond, Indiana. On May 26, 1956, one day after Ben filed for divorce, Opal used his own .22-caliber rifle to shoot to death her husband, his mother, and his two sisters. Opal Collins was arrested and tried for murder. Rejecting her innocent plea by reason of insanity, a jury convicted her. She was sentenced to death in the electric chair on October 26, 1956.

Cooper, Glenda. Born in 1943 as Glenda Benson, this child slayer began to exhibit paranoid delusions and obsessive characteristics shortly after her marriage to James Cooper, a welder, in Schenectady, New York. The couple had three children by the time they moved out to the country to live in Watsonville in 1967. Aside from starting to neglect her children, Cooper showed signs of the same mental illness that landed her mother in an insane asylum in the 1950s. Glenda was put in a mental hospital briefly, but her violent tendencies were not discovered until it was too late. On February 23, 1969, while her husband worked the late night shift, she used a hatchet to kill her three young children and then set the house on fire. Cooper tried to kill herself by slashing her wrists, but changed her mind and fled the burning home. She was arrested and charged with murder. In February 1970, Glenda Cooper was convicted of the murder of her three children and sentenced to three concurrent terms of fifteen years to life.

Crimmins, Alice. This New York child murderess managed to take advantage of the legal system for years in avoiding true justice in the deaths of her two young children. Alice Crimmins was twenty-six, divorced, and described as a "free swinger" when she murdered her four-year-old daughter, Missy, and five-year-old son, Eddie, on July 14, 1965. Eddie had died of strangulation. Investigators believed Crimmins killed the children because they were an inconvenience in her promiscuous lifestyle. She was arrested and charged with Missy's murder and convicted of first-degree manslaughter and sentenced to five to twenty years behind bars. However, an appeals court overturned the verdict and a new trial was ordered for March 1971. This time prosecutors brought charges against Alice Crimmins for both of her children. She was convicted of manslaughter again in Missy's death and first-degree murder in the death of Eddie. This verdict was also thrown out on appeal, but a higher court upheld the conviction and she was sent to prison in May 1971.

While on a work release program in 1976, Alice Crimmons married Anthony Grace, whom she had been romantically involved with at the time of her children's murders. She was paroled in September 1977.

Cunningham, Anna. Anna Cunningham was born in 1878 in Gary, Indiana. She married her husband David, moved to a farm in Valparaiso, and had six children. When her fifteen-year-old son, Charles, accidentally shot and killed a neighbor's son in 1918, the whole family was shocked but Anna took it the hardest. She became violent, and started threatening to murder people close to her. A doctor recommended that she be put in an asylum but her family refused. In July 1918, her fifty-one-year-old husband died suddenly after two weeks of horrible stomach cramps. Cunningham sold the farm and moved the family back to Gary. In December 1920, her eighteen-year-old daughter, Isabelle, died after two weeks of severe cramps and paralysis. Harry, her twenty-four-year-old son, died in October 1921. Charles, age nineteen, died next in September 1922. Walter, thirteen, died in September 1923. All of the children died after suffering from severe stomach cramps. In 1925, Anna's twenty-four-year-old son, David, became seriously ill. He was near death and then hospitalized when he became paralyzed. Doctors were finally able to save him after six weeks of hospital treatment and diagnosed him with arsenic poisoning. While investigating, police found large amounts of arsenic in the home. Cunningham was put in a hospital for observation and tried to strangle herself with torn sheets. Psychiatrists claimed she was suffering from epileptic psychosis. On April 25, 1925, she confessed to poisoning three of her children with arsenic. She denied killing her husband and her son,

Harry, even though large amounts of arsenic were found in their bodies. She claimed she had killed her children out of love and so she would have company in heaven when she got there. Anna Cunningham was ruled sane and competent to stand trial and was convicted of Walter's murder in July 1925. She received a sentence of life in prison.

Curry, Shirley Marie. In 1967, while living in Arkansas, thirty-year-old Shirley Marie Curry was in the middle of a spiteful divorce. She got custody of her three children with the stipulation that they could go live with their father when they turned fourteen. Her daughter, Sabrina, was the first to leave. After she left, Curry refused to speak to her or even acknowledge her. When her son, Richard, turned fourteen, he decided to go too. On July 19, 1974, the day before he was scheduled to move out, Curry went on a killing spree. She shot and killed her two sons at home. Then she drove to her ex-husband's home and shot him and then her daughter. Curry then went to her ex-husband's half-sister's house and shot and killed her. After that, she drove to her sister's ex-husband's house and shot him twice, but not fatally. She was charged with murder on July 22, 1974. Found to be incompetent to stand trial, she was put in a state hospital for four years. When she was finally tried, she was convicted on two counts of murder. Shirley Curry was sentenced to life with no possibility of parole.

David, Rachal. Considered one of Utah's worst mass and family murderers, Rachal David was born in Sweden in 1939 as Margit Brigitta Ericsson. In the 1960s she ended up in Provo, Utah, where she met and married student and follower of the Mormon Church, Charles Bruce Longo. The couple moved to Salt Lake

City and had seven children between 1963 and 1972. After clashing with church leaders, Longo was excommunicated in June 1969 after which he established a cult of devoted followers. In 1970, Longo legally changed his name to Immanuel David and his wife became Rachal David. By 1978, the family had experienced financial ups and downs while living in motels. Meanwhile, the FBI was closing in on Immanuel for possible wire fraud and other violations of the law. On August 1, 1978, he committed suicide by carbon monoxide poisoning in a van. Two days later, Rachal, fearful of being evicted from the Dunes Hotel where they were staying, decided to end it all. She brought her children out onto the eleventh story balcony of their suite—250 feet above the ground— and dropped, pushed, or ordered each to jump off. She followed suit, plunging to her death. Six of the children died. The lone survivor, a fifteen-year-old girl, spent a year in the hospital before being released and placed in a foster home in July 1979.

Dcyzheski, Nellie. Poverty and the real threat of becoming homeless during the Great Depression may have led Nellie Dcyzheski to bludgeon to death her children on May 24, 1933, in Saxonville, Massachusetts. The day before, the Dcyzheski's had been given an eviction notice from their small apartment. Both Nellie, who had tired of her job as a part-time employee at a carpet company, and her husband, Paul, injured after being stabbed, were out of work. With Paul staying the night with in-laws, Nellie used a hammer to beat three of her young children to death. A fourth, age eight, managed to escape the bludgeoning but not the fire Nellie set in the apartment, using kerosene she had purchased earlier. He survived but was left in critical condition. Nellie Dcyzheski was charged with three murders and found incompetent to stand trial. She was committed to a mental institution where she eventually died.

Downs, Elizabeth Diane. On May 19, 1983, in a bid to rekindle a love relationship, Elizabeth Diane Downs murdered her seven-year-old daughter and attempted to kill her two other children in Springfield, Oregon. The crime later inspired a book and a TV miniseries. Downs, a surrogate mother, had claimed she and her children, who were all shot, were victims of a carjacker on a dark, deserted road. Authorities contended that Downs saw her children as obstacles in her love life. On June 17, 1984, Diane Downs was convicted on one count of murder, two counts of attempted murder, and two counts of assault. The twenty-eight-year-old Downs, who was pregnant with her fifth child, was sentenced to life imprisonment plus fifty years. In 1987, she escaped from prison and was recaptured ten days later. After losing a number of state court appeals on her conviction, in February 1999 a federal court also ruled against Diane Downs on her claims that she was improperly convicted. She has been denied parole two times and will be eligible again in 2020.

Edwards, Lillian. Lillian Ralston was born in 1906 in California. The former teacher married Kenneth Edwards and had three children. She was diagnosed as a manic depressive after the birth of her third child. She spent time in a San Francisco private hospital and a mental institution in Stockton, California, in 1940, before being allowed to go home to Fresno. On December 11, 1940, with her husband away overnight on a business trip and the housekeeper gone for the evening, Edwards strangled to death her children, using torn strips from the bed sheets. She was taken into custody the following morning, claiming she didn't remember what happened. Lillian Edwards was found mentally incompetent to stand trial and put back in an insane asylum where she spent the rest of her life.

Etheridge, Ellen. Jealousy, resentment, and hatred led Ellen Etheridge to commit murder in the family. She married wealthy Texas rancher, J. D. Etheridge, a widower with eight children. Ellen found herself unable or unwilling to compete with her husband's children and late wife for his affections. Feeling neglected and little more than a housekeeper, she used poison to kill two of her stepchildren in June 1913, and then killed two more by the same method in October 1913. Postmortem results revealed the manner of death and Ellen Etheridge was taken into custody. She confessed to the murders and was sentenced to life in prison.

Eubanks, Susan. On October 26, 1997, thirty-five-year-old Susan Eubanks took out her frustrations on her four young sons by shooting them to death in their San Marcos, California, home. The shootings of the four boys, ages four to fourteen, followed an argument with her boyfriend. Eubanks, an unemployed, divorced nursing assistant with a history of alcohol and drug problems and bad relationships with men, then tried to commit suicide by shooting herself in the stomach with the same .38-caliber revolver used on her children. She was arrested and charged with four counts of first-degree murder. Susan Eubanks was convicted on all counts in August, 1999 and sentenced to death. She is currently on death row at the Central California Women's Facility in Chowchilla.

Fiederer, Elizabeth. Married with three children, Elizabeth Fiederer lived in Passaic, New Jersey. The family lived in a small apartment above the tavern they owned. From October 1935 to January 1936, she was convinced she had terminal cancer. She repeatedly showed up at the hospital, but doctors could find no evidence of cancer or any other illnesses. Fiederer was terrified that she would spread her cancer to her family. On January 21, 1936, patrons who arrived at the tavern were angry that it was closed. They stormed upstairs and broke into the apartment. Greeted by gas fumes, they found Fiederer's husband and three children dead. Elizabeth was barely alive, but eventually recovered. She told authorities that she killed them so she wouldn't pass her cancer to them. She was charged with four counts of murder. At her trial in February 1936, Elizabeth Fiederer was found insane and committed to an insane asylum.

Foster, Lafonda Fay *see* PAIR AND GROUP KILLERS

Fuller, Edna. Born in California in 1890, Edna Fuller married Otto Fuller, a San Francisco night watchman. She had five children between 1915 and 1924 and murdered them all in 1926. The Fullers were destitute, barely making ends meet. They faced one eviction after another from their low income housing. In August 1926, Edna Fuller was declared an unfit mother by the Society for the Prevention of Cruelty to Children. A hearing was set for September, but not before the Fullers received yet another eviction notice on August 30, 1926. The following morning when Otto Fuller returned home from work, he found Edna and their five children dead. The gas jets were open, releasing deadly fumes. Officially, the deaths were listed as suicide by Edna Fuller and the mass murder of her children.

Garcia, Guinevere Falakassa. Born in Chicago, Illinois, in 1959, Guinevere Falakassa was raised by her grandparents. She had a troubled childhood, as her father left when she was born and her alcoholic mother died a year later. At age seventeen, after giving birth, she was convicted of prostitution and put on probation. On August 8, 1977, Garcia told police her infant daughter died when she accidentally crawled into a large plastic bag and suffocated. In 1981, she was arrested and charged with four counts of arson after setting four fires in the buildings where she lived, each occurring on the anniversary of her daughter's death. In custody, Garcia confessed to murdering her daughter and pleaded guilty. She received a sentence of twenty years and was paroled in March 1991. She quickly married sixty-year-old George Garcia, but they were separated by June that same year. On July 23, 1991, George was found dead in his pickup truck with a gunshot wound in his chest. Garcia denied killing him but later told police her twenty-eight-year-old boyfriend, John Gonzalez, killed him. They were both charged with murder. Gonzalez testified against her in exchange for a reduced sentence of seven years. Guinevere Garcia was convicted of murder on August 10, 1992, and sentenced to death on October 9, 1992. She was scheduled to die in January 1996 after she refused to appeal her sentence, claiming she wanted to die. However, on January 6, 1996, the Illinois governor commuted her sentence to life in prison without parole.

Grant, Rosalie. Born to a prostitute and murderess, Rosalie Grant already had violence in her blood by the time she took up residence in Youngstown, Ohio, in her teens. She had three children out of wedlock with two different men. Grant developed a reputation for a violent temper, often taking it out on her two young boys by physically abusing them. She took out life insurance policies on the boys, but not her daughter, two weeks before setting the boys on fire in their bedroom on April 1, 1983. They burned to death. Arson investigators concluded that the fire had been deliberately set. Grant produced various stories that did not add up. She was indicted for murder in the deaths of her two sons. Her daughter had spent the night with her grandparents when the fire occurred. Rosalie Grant was convicted on both counts of murder and sentenced to death on October 22, 1983. In 1991, the governor of Ohio commuted her sentence to life in prison, as he felt her sentence was not administered fairly.

Her, Khoua. On September 3, 1998, Khoua Her murdered her six children in her St. Paul, Minnesota, apartment. Police arrested her after getting a calling about a suicide in progress. They found Khoua Her with an extension cord around her neck after she had tried to kill herself. The six children had all been strangled with a strip of cloth during a game of hide and seek. Khoua was born in Laos and had been put in a Thailand refugee camp. She ended up in Minnesota with her family. Khoua claimed problems with her husband and his family, welfare, and public housing were the reasons she decided it would be better to die. Khoua Her, age twenty-five, was sentenced to fifty years in prison in January 1999 after she plea bargained for a second-degree intentional murder conviction.

Hilley, Audrey Marie. Audrey Marie Hilley was born in Alabama in 1933. She married Frank Hilley when she was eighteen and they had two children.

When her husband died in 1975 and then her mother in 1977, both allegedly from cancer, no one was suspicious. In early 1979, one of Hilley's daughters was close to death before doctors saved her. In November 1979, her mother-in-law died after being ill for a while. Police began suspecting Hilley when large amounts of arsenic were found in her sick daughter's blood. They then exhumed the bodies of dead family members and found arsenic. On October 25, 1979, she was indicted for the attempted murder of her daughter. Out on bond, she disappeared. On January 1, 1980, she was also indicted for murdering her husband. On the run, Hilley changed her name to "Robbi Hannon" and married a man in New Hampshire in May 1981. A month later, she asked for a divorce and fled to Texas. She tried to fake her death in 1982 while in Florida. She was finally arrested in Vermont in January 1983. Audrey Hilley was tried and convicted in Alabama on two counts of murder and sentenced to life. She was also convicted of the attempted murder of her daughter and sentenced to twenty years. Hilley was granted a three-day furlough on February 19, 1987, but never returned. Police found her on the porch of a home on February 26th suffering from hypothermia. She died of a heart attack on the way to the hospital.

Hogg, Megan. On March 23, 1998, Megan Hogg, suffering from depression, murdered her three daughters in their home in Redwood City, California. The twenty-seven-year-old Hogg suffocated the children—ages two, three, and seven—and then tried to commit suicide by drinking a mixture of cocoa, antidepressants, and painkillers. She was charged with three counts of murder on August 1, 1999, but pleaded no contest to avoid a trial. A judge sentenced Megan Hogg to a prison term of twenty-five years to life.

Hoyt, Waneta E. Born in 1946 in New York, Waneta Hoyt was nineteen when she began killing her children from 1965 to 1971. Likely to have suffered from Munchausen syndrome by proxy, Hoyt blamed the deaths, which had all previously been attributed to sudden infant death syndrome (SIDS), on their nonstop wailing. It took more than two decades for authorities to make a case against her. On March 23, 1994, forty-seven-year-old Waneta Hoyt, a housewife living in Oswego, New York, was arrested and charged with the murder of all five of her children. She confessed to the deaths in which each victim had been suffocated. Though she tried to recant her confession, the case went to trial. Waneta Hoyt was found guilty on all counts on April 21, 1995, and sentenced to seventy-five years to life in prison. In August 1998, Hoyt died of cancer in prison.

Hultberg, Violet. In 1928, at age nineteen, Violet Hultberg was living in Long Lake, Minnesota. She became intimately involved with Herbert Moreau, a man fourteen years older who was separated but had custody of his four young sons. After Hultberg moved to Minneapolis with Moreau in September, things apparently went sour between the couple. On November 5, 1928, Violet Hultberg did the unthinkable. While Moreau was at work, she turned up the gas jets on the stove, making sure all windows and doors were sealed, killing herself and all four boys in a murder-suicide. She left a suicide note, but no real explanation surfaced for her brutal actions.

Johnson, Martha Ann. This thrice married, vindictive female killer from Georgia murdered all four of her children between 1977 and 1982. Born in 1955, Martha Ann Johnson was twenty-two when she began killing. She was motivated by revenge against her fourth husband, Earl Bowen, with whom she had a stormy relationship. The 250-pound Johnson suffocated her children by rolling over them while they were asleep, following a confrontation with Bowen. The first two child deaths were initially diagnosed as due to SIDS and the third to a seizure. With the death of her fourth child under suspicious circumstances on February 21, 1982, her murder spree came to an end. An autopsy performed on the eleven-year-old victim indicated death by asphyxia. However, it was not until July 3, 1989, that Martha Ann Johnson was finally arrested and charged with murder. She confessed to killing two of her children, but retracted the confession by the time her trial began on April 30, 1990. A jury found her guilty of murder on May 5, 1990, and sentenced her to death.

Jones, Annie. The mother of five, Canadian born Annie Jones and her husband, Erwin, lived in Madison, Wisconsin. On June 21, 1936, Annie went on a murder-suicide shooting spree, killing three of her children. The thirty-two-year-old had been under a doctor's care for two years for physical and psychological problems. Her shocking crime occurred in a wooded area behind the family house where, after tying up her three young boys, she shot each in the head at point-blank range with a rifle. She then shot herself in the head. Her husband discovered the four bodies.

Jones, Roxanne. Born in California in 1958, Roxanne Jones had two rocky marriages producing three children, all of which she killed before taking her own life. Separated from her husband in 1989, Jones encountered difficulties in trying to make ends meet on part-time jobs in Reseda, California. Known to be suicidal, she took it one step further on March 19, 1990. She used a .22-caliber rifle to shoot to death her two teenage daughters and young son while they slept, then shot herself in the head. The police found several suicide notes in the house in which Roxanne Jones spoke of her troubles.

Kantarian, Nancy Lee. Mental illness drove Nancy Lee Kantarian to brutally take the lives of her two children in a shocking case of familicide and arson. Born to wealth in 1959, the former Nancy Heselden was the daughter of media mogul John Heselden. She married attorney Harry Kantarian at age twenty-five and bore him two children. The family lived in Great Falls, Virginia. Something snapped inside Nancy on the evening of May 23, 1984, when she murdered her two daughters, age five and six, including stabbing one thirty-two times, then set the house ablaze. She was arrested for murder and arson. Psychologists deemed her irrational. On October 2, 1984, Nancy Kantarian pleaded guilty to two counts of voluntary manslaughter. She was given a ten-year suspended sentence, provided she checked herself into a mental treatment facility.

Kimura, Fumiko. On January 29, 1985, swept up in a wave of depression, betrayal, and two cultures, Japanese immigrant Fumiko Kimura took her two young children out to sea and drowned them in a murder and attempted suicide. Married for the third time to an unfaithful man and blaming it on herself along with other insecurities—including the well being of her children and reconciling differences in Japanese and American cultures—Kimura planned to "make things right" by ending her suffering with murder and suicide. She survived and was charged with two counts of first-degree murder and special circumstances, meaning she could get the death penalty. Diagnosed as suffering from severe postpartum depression, Fumiko Kimura was allowed to plea bargain to two counts of involuntary manslaughter and given probation.

King, Kathleen. Plagued by a history of mental illness, Kathleen King bludgeoned to death her three young children on April 12, 1956, in the family's home in Xenia, Ohio. Born in California in 1922, King had undergone various treatments over the years to deal with depression, suicide attempts, and other mental problems including electroshock therapy. Even after marrying Charles King, moving to Ohio, and having three children, she was unable to escape her unstable behavior and depression. She used a hammer to kill her children—ages five, three, and two—then attempted to commit suicide by slashing her wrists and drinking oven cleaner. She survived the ordeal and was arrested. On April 16, 1956, Kathleen King was charged with three counts of murder. After prosecution psychiatrists found her competent, her trial began in December 1960. She was found not guilty of murder by reason of insanity and sent to Lima State Hospital. Kathleen King was given her unconditional release in December 1967, after she was found sane.

Knapp, Lorraine. Lorraine Knapp was born in Butte, Montana, in 1928. She moved to Dillon in 1949 to work as a secretary. After losing her job in November that same year, she returned to Butte acting moody and sullen. On New Year's Eve 1949, Knapp took a .22-caliber rifle and killed her mother, seven-year-old sister, three-year-old brother, and twelve-year-old brother. She then shot and killed herself. When her two older brothers returned home from a party, they discovered the carnage. Police never discovered a motive for Lorraine Knapp's rampage.

Lumbrera, Diana. From 1977 to 1990, this murderess killed six of her children to collect on insurance policies. Diana Lumbrera was born in Texas in 1957, married at seventeen, and divorced in her early twenties from the father of her first three children. Three more children followed from three different boyfriends. Lumbrera began murdering her children at age twenty and continued until she was thirty-three. The methods of death were strangulation and suffocation, occurring in Texas and Kansas. It was with the death of her third son and sixth child on May 1, 1990, that suspicious hospital staff and local law enforcement began to uncover the horrifying truth about Lumbrera and her progeny. In July 1990, she was indicted for first-degree murder in Palmer County, Texas, for the deaths of her first three children. A jury found her guilty on all counts in September 1990, sentencing her to life in prison. Two more indictments in other jurisdictions for the murder of her three other children resulted in confessions by Diana Lumbrera to the deaths and two more life sentences.

Lyles, Anjette Donovan. Born in 1925, Anjette Donovan Lyles operated a popular restaurant in Macon, Georgia, during the 1950s. The restaurant was originally owned by her father-in-law, but her husband took over the business in 1945 when his father died. He sold the place in 1951. When her husband died suddenly in January 1952, Anjette bought the restaurant back. She then married an airline pilot, but he died unexpectedly on December 2, 1955. After his death, she took back her first married name—Lyles—and invited her mother-in-law, Julia Lyles, to live with her. Julia died suddenly on September 29, 1957. Then Anjette's nine-year-old daughter died on April 4, 1958, after an undiagnosed illness. Shortly after that, a waitress at Anjette's restaurant became ill and her symptoms seemed to get worse every time she was given Anjette's coffee. Police were curious enough to exhume the four bodies of her relatives at the end of April. When they searched her home, they found bottles of arsenic and occult-type items. Police also discovered that Anjette had received life insurance payments totaling $50,000 from the four deaths. She was convicted of first-degree murder in October 1958 for the poisoning death of her daughter. After being sentenced to death, a sanity hearing in 1960 found her insane. Anjette Lyles was transferred to the State Hospital in Milledgeville, Georgia, where she died of natural causes in December 1977.

McDonald, Carol. Born as Carol Tiedeman in 1923 in New Jersey, Carol McDonald came from a wealthy family and was a college graduate in 1944 when she married former football star Kenneth McDonald. The couple had four children and lived in a New Jersey suburb. They separated in 1953 amidst accusations of infidelity on the part of the wife. On May 2, 1953, depressed about the upcoming divorce, visitation rights, and the end of what seemed like a storybook marriage, Carol McDonald murdered her four young children by carbon monoxide poisoning, leaving them in a car in the closed garage with the motor running. She was arrested the following day and told police she had planned it to be a murder-suicide, sparing her children the shame of a divorce.

McAninch, Alma May. On October 30, 1937, Alma May McAninch used a shotgun to murder five of her seven children before shooting herself to death in their small home in Norwalk, Iowa. In 1920, at age eighteen, Alma May married Gurness McAninch, a semi-skilled worker whose low income and troubles with the law left the ever growing family often unable to meet basic expenses. Concern over their financial woes and a history of threats to commit suicide may have pushed Alma May McAninch over the edge in perpetrating the mass murder and suicide, in which all the victims were shot in the head. A suicide-murder note was left in the family Bible.

Nollen, Elsie. In a family mass murder motivated by wife battering and alcohol abuse, Elsie Nollen killed her six children and herself by carbon monoxide poisoning on August 28, 1937. Born in Iowa as Elsie Jones in 1907, she married farmer Albert Nollen when she was sixteen. He turned out to be an alcoholic and batterer. Finding herself unable to cope with the burdens of a rural and abusive life, Elsie Nollen chose to take drastic measures. With her children all asleep in the family farmhouse, she connected a washing machine hose to the exhaust pipe of the car, placed it in a bedroom window, and started the engine. She went inside and, like her six offspring, died from the poisonous fumes. Elsie Nollen left behind a six-page suicide note.

Pasos, Marie. Born in 1894, Marie Pasos committed mass murder on February 14, 1929, when she turned the gas jets up on the stove in her New York City apartment, killing all six of her children and herself. Married to Joe Pasos, the family was impoverished in spite of Joe having two jobs. He discovered the seven bodies after a neighbor reported gas fumes coming from the apartment. Marie Pasos left no suicide note or advance warning of the tragedy that was to come.

Powell, Tina Marie *see* PAIR AND GROUP KILLERS, Foster, Lafonda Fay

Rowney, Margaret. On December 14, 1950, Margaret Rowney, a widow and mother suffering from mental illness, killed her four young children and herself in their station wagon in Van Nuys, California. The mass murder and suicide occurred through carbon monoxide poisoning when Rowney placed a hose from the exhaust pipe of the running car into the window. Authorities believed that the mentally unstable murderess went over the edge after the premature death of her husband.

Schreuder, Frances. On July 23, 1978, socialite Frances Schreuder orchestrated the murder of her father, Mormon millionaire Franklin J. Bradshaw. He was shot to death in a warehouse he owned in Salt Lake City, Utah. The seventy-six-year-old eccentric owner of a chain of auto parts stores was killed with a .357 magnum by his seventeen-year-old grandson, Marc Schreuder, on orders from his mother, Frances, who feared she was about to be disinherited by her wealthy father. Marc Schreuder was arrested in 1981 and convicted one year later of second-degree murder in his grandfather's death. In 1983, after unsuccessfully fighting extradition from New York—where she lived on the Upper East Side of Manhattan—Frances Schreuder was brought to trial in Salt Lake City on a first-degree murder charge. She was convicted of killing her father and sentenced to life imprisonment at Utah State Prison. Marc Schreuder was paroled in 1995 and Frances was paroled in 1996. She died on March 30,

2004. *See also* The 1970s – The Murder of Multimillionaire Mormon Franklin J. Bradshaw; Adult Victims, Bradshaw, Franklin J.

Shoaf, Mamie Shey. On May 24, 1929, in Lebanon, Kentucky, a depressed Mamie Shey Shoaf, mother of seven, killed her three youngest children and then took her own life. Having been married for almost twenty years to a lumber company employee, Shoaf apparently became increasingly frustrated over the family's struggle to make ends meet. The murder-suicide took place at the local cemetery where Mamie Shoaf cut the throats of her children, age two to eleven, before turning the knife on herself.

Sims, Paula Marie. In a tale of infanticide, lies, and missed opportunity to prevent future tragedy, between June 1986 and April 1989 Paula Marie Sims killed her two young daughters. Born as Paula Blew in 1959, her childhood included substance abuse, promiscuity, and the death of a brother in an automobile accident. She married Robert Sims in 1981 and the couple ultimately settled into a ranch house in a wooded area of Brighton, Illinois. On June 20, 1986, police discovered the skeletal remains of Loralei Sims—who had been born only fifteen days earlier—in the woods near the Sims home. Though both Paula and Robert Sims failed lie detector tests, a coroner's jury could not positively link the couple to their daughter's death. Unfortunately, another tragedy awaited their third child, Heather. Her remains were found in a garbage can along a St. Charles County, Missouri, highway on May 3, 1989, less than two months after she had been born. Paula was arrested in July 1989 and indicted for first-degree murder. After a change of venue for her trial, Paula Sims was convicted of Heather's murder on January 27, 1990, and sentenced to life in prison without the possibility of parole. Robert Sims was granted custody of their remaining child after authorities were unable to link him to the other children's deaths. Paula remains in prison at the Logan Correctional Center in Lincoln, Illinois.

Smith, Susan Vaughan. In a shocking murder case that gripped the nation and stirred racial tensions, Susan Vaughan Smith confessed to murdering her two young children on October 19, 1994, in Union, South Carolina. Smith, twenty-three, had initially told authorities that her fourteen-month-old and three-year-old boys were abducted by a black man during a carjacking. However, nine days later, under pressure, she admitted that she had killed her sons. They were found strapped in their car seats in the back of Smith's car at the bottom of a lake. She was arrested and charged with murder. Molested by her stepfather when she was young and now estranged from her husband, Smith had a history of mental problems and apparently wanted her children out of the way so she could be with her boyfriend. Although suicidal, Smith was ruled mentally fit to stand trial. She was found guilty of two counts of first-degree murder in the deaths of her sons. Six days later, Susan Smith was sentenced to life imprisonment. In September 2000, Smith was embroiled in a prison sex scandal. She admitted to having sex with two guards at the Women's Correctional Institution in South Carolina. The guards were disciplined and Smith was transferred to Leath Correctional Institution in Greenwood County. *See also* The 1990s – The Susan Smith Case of Filicide.

Sorenson, Della. A grudge family killer, Della Sorenson was born in Nebraska in 1897. She married in

1915 and had two children. She began to grow irritated by everything and little fights turned into huge feuds. Sorenson decided to get even with her sister-in-law, Mrs. Cooper, by killing her children. In July 1918, she killed Mrs. Cooper's thirteen-month-old daughter with poison candy. She poisoned her live-in mother-in-law in July 1920 because she was too burdensome. On September 7, 1920, Sorenson poisoned her own three-year-old daughter because she suffered from an intellectual disability. A few days later, on September 20, she poisoned her husband after they had a fight. She married her second husband in February 1991—two weeks after they met—and eventually had two more children. Sorenson killed her four-month-old niece in August 1992 to continue her revenge against her sister-in-law. She killed her own baby in February 1923 with poison because it was ill and always crying. That same month, she killed a friend's newborn baby with poison while they were visiting. Sorenson then tried to poison her husband and daughter, but was unsuccessful. In February 1925, she fed poison cookies to her neighbor's two young children because she was angry with their father. When they got sick, doctors discovered poison in their vomit. Sorenson was arrested on April 17, 1925. She confessed to numerous killings, telling police that it made her happy when someone died. Della Sorenson was diagnosed as schizophrenic and unable to stand trial. Criminal charges were dismissed and she was committed to the state asylum on April 20, 1925.

Tinning, Marybeth. This New York murderess is suspected of killing eight of her children by suffocation between 1972 and 1985, following the death of her first child by natural causes. Most of the deaths had initially been attributed to SIDS, including her last child, Tami Lynne, on December 20, 1985. An investigation led to Marybeth Tinning's arrest on February 4, 1986, for the murder of three-month-old Tami Lynne. She confessed to murdering three of her children by smothering them with a pillow and described herself as a bad mother. On July 17, 1987, Tinning was found guilty of second-degree murder in the death of Tami Lynne. She was given a prison sentence of twenty years to life. Though certain Marybeth Tinning had murdered eight of her children, authorities were unable to prove it or establish a clear-cut motive. She has been denied parole numerous times.

Urdanivia, Ruth. Born in 1918, Ruth Urdanivia married Jose Urdanivia, a Peruvian diplomat. The couple produced five children in the 1940s and 1950s while living in San Francisco and Washington, D.C. After her husband died of a heart attack in November 1957, Ruth moved back to her hometown of Allentown, Pennsylvania, where she struggled to care for her children and stay above the poverty line. On October 14, 1959, she committed mass murder when she gave her five children a fatal overdose of barbiturates. She attempted suicide, but survived to be charged with murder. Found sane enough to stand trial in April 1960, Ruth Urdanivia pleaded guilty to second-degree murder in the deaths of her five children. On April 7, 1960, she received a sentence of five concurrent terms in prison. She was paroled in January 1967.

Walkup, Marie. On July 23, 1937, Marie Walkup stabbed and strangled her four children to death in their home in Flagstaff, Arizona, before driving to a local golf course and committing suicide. Born in 1905 as

Marie Green, she married Army veteran and businessman James Walkup. The couple had four children between 1927 and 1936. Depressed and afflicted with a chronic intestinal condition, and fearing that it might be hereditary apparently triggered Marie to commit the murders. It concluded with her using a rifle to take her own life. She left a suicide note, insisting that her children were happier being dead.

Williamson, Stella. In a mysterious case of infanticide, Stella Williamson murdered her five infants between 1923 and 1933, but the deaths were not discovered for another forty-three years. Born in 1900, Williamson lived in New York and Pennsylvania. She died in 1976 while living in the town of Gallitzin, Pennsylvania. She left behind a sealed envelope to be opened upon her death. It contained instructions about a trunk long hidden in the recluse spinster's attic. Inside the trunk were the remains of five infants—four were newborns and the other approximately eight months old when they died. There was no explanation for the murders, but speculation was that Stella Williamson had given birth to the children out of wedlock while in her early twenties to early thirties.

Wise, Martha Hasel. Martha Hasel was born in 1883 in Ohio. She married Albert Wise in 1906 and had five children, one who died shortly after birth. Money was hard to come by and when her husband died in 1923, Wise was able to get by on the small insurance payment. Having heard voices all her life as well as inventing imaginary friends, she began hearing the voices tell her to murder. She went to her mother's house in late 1924 and put arsenic in her water bucket. Her mother died shortly thereafter. Wise then visited her aunt and uncle's farm and began poisoning them and their six children. Her aunt and uncle died in early 1925 and the children were sent to live with neighbors. In February 1925, police began investigating the deaths and discovered it was arsenic poisoning. When Wise was brought in for questioning, she confessed to the poisoning murders. She claimed that Satan had told her to do it. Martha Wise was tried for first-degree murder and convicted on May 13, 1925. She was sentenced to life in prison where she died on June 28, 1971.

Woods, Martha. Afflicted with the psychological disorder called Munchausen syndrome by proxy, Martha Woods murdered seven children between 1946 and 1969. Woods, married to a military officer, committed her crimes throughout the United States. Her victims died by suffocation and smothering and included three of her own children, an adopted child, a nephew, niece, and neighbor's child. Two other children survived her onslaught. Woods was arrested in Baltimore, Maryland, following the death of her adopted son, who was seven months old. She was found to be competent to stand trial and was found guilty of first-degree murder. Martha Woods received a sentence of life in prison and an additional seventy-five years for other crimes, including attempted murder and child mistreatment. The U.S. Supreme Court rejected an appeal brought by Wood.

Wright, Jeanne Anne. On November 10, 1983, Jeanne Anne Wright tossed her four sleeping children into the Cooper River in New Jersey, killing them. Born in 1958, she was living with her parents on welfare, had a personality disorder, and suffered from chronic depression and abuse at the hands of her boyfriend. On February 21, 1984, she was indicted on four counts of murder and pled guilty to killing her children. Jeanne

Anne Wright received a sentence of four concurrent life terms on April 19, 1984.

Yesconis, Jennifer Nicole *see* PAIR AND GROUP KILLERS

INTIMATE KILLERS - WOMEN

Adams, Millicent. A scorned wealthy Philadelphia socialite, Millicent Adams shot and killed her lover Axel Schmidt in October 1962. Adams became suicidal and jealous after Schmidt, who apparently used women to climb the social ladder, met another woman that was even more socially prominent. She purchased a Smith and Wesson .22-caliber pistol and shot her dog to test the gun's reliability. Then she lured Schmidt to bed and shot him to death. After pleading guilty to manslaughter, she was sentenced to ten years' probation and committed to a mental health facility. A few months after the murder, she gave birth to Axel Schmidt's baby. After spending three years institutionalized, Millicent Adams was released and moved to California.

Harris, Jean. On March 10, 1980, in a shocking crime that made national headlines, Jean Harris murdered her lover, Doctor Herman Tarnower, in his home in Purchase, New York. At the time, the fifty-six-year-old Harris was in charge of one of the country's most prestigious schools, the Madeira School for Girls in McLean, Virginia. She had been in a fourteen-year abusive relationship with Tarnower, who gained national recognition for his book, *The Scarsdale Diet*, when he became involved with another woman. Harris, addicted to prescription drugs, claimed she had planned to commit suicide when she shot and killed Tarnower during a struggle. She was convicted of murder in 1981 and sentenced to fifteen years to life. In January 1993, Jean Harris was released from prison when the governor commuted her sentence. She died on December 23, 2012, at the age of eighty-nine.

Hartman, Brynn *see* Celebrity Killers – Women

Haun, Diana J. *see* PAIR AND GROUP KILLERS, Dally, Michael

Lambert, Lisa Michelle *see* PAIR AND GROUP KILLERS

Price, Patricia Mildred *see* PAIR AND GROUP KILLERS

Smart, Pamela *see* PAIR AND GROUP KILLERS

Stangel, Linda Jean. On November 12, 1995, David Ronald Wahl plunged 320 feet to his death off a cliff in Ecola State Park on Oregon's coast. He had been shoved over by his girlfriend, Linda Jean Stangel. The incident followed a stormy one-year relationship between the twenty-three-year-old Stangel and the twenty-seven-year-old Wahl. The couple lived in the suburbs of Portland, Oregon, and both often abused alcohol in their relationship. After having initially told authorities that Wahl had simply vanished, Stangel, a cosmetologist, confessed to pushing her lover off the cliff in a fit of rage. She was indicted in August 1996 and charged with first-degree manslaughter in a case that attracted nationwide attention. Unsuccessful in her attempt to withdraw her confession, Linda Jean Stangel was convicted of second-degree manslaughter on January 16, 1997. She was sentenced to six and a half years in prison. She was released in February 2003. *See also* Adult Victims, Wahl, David Ronald.

MASS MURDERERS - WOMEN

Bacher, Johanna *see* Familial Killers – Women
Basore, Eleanor *see* Familial Killers – Women
Bearce, Mrs. Leon *see* Familial Killers – Women
Bolin, Patricia *see* Familial Killers – Women
Calbeck, Lorene *see* Familial Killers – Women
Campbell, Inez Ethel *see* Familial Killers – Women
Collins, Opal Juanita *see* Familial Killers – Women
Cooper, Glenda *see* Familial Killers – Women
David, Rachal *see* Familial Killers – Women
Dcyzheski, Nellie *see* Familial Killers – Women
Edwards, Lillian *see* Familial Killers – Women
Eubanks, Susan *see* Familial Killers – Women
Fiederer, Elizabeth *see* Familial Killers – Women
Ford, Priscilla Joyce. Born in 1929 as Priscilla Joyce Lawrence in Berrien Springs, Michigan, she was one of the first African American women mass murderers. Married four times, she had three children. Her first marriage resulted in her arrest for shooting her husband and herself. She eventually left Michigan with

her daughter and began drifting from state to state taking menial jobs. During this time, she became obsessed with religion and started proclaiming that she was Jesus. Ford was arrested on minor charges a number of times from 1972 to 1974. In 1979, she moved to Buffalo and was arrested numerous times for drug possession, theft, and writing bad checks. While undergoing psychiatric evaluation, Ford told her counselor that she had a fantasy of driving her car through a crowd of people and killing a bunch of them. In late 1980, she drove to Reno and got a job at Macy's department store. During that time she began drinking heavily and blaming the world for her problems. On Thanksgiving Day, fulfilling her fantasy, Priscilla Ford drove her black Lincoln down a crowded sidewalk in front of the casinos. Authorities said she was legally drunk at the time. In all, she killed six people and wounded twenty-three. Ford was arrested and charged with six counts of first-degree murder and twenty-three counts of attempted murder. After months of psychiatric evaluation, she was ruled competent to stand trial in July 1981. Priscilla Ford was convicted on all counts and sentenced to death by lethal injection on April 29, 1982. While on death row, she died of emphysema in January 2005.

Foster, Lafonda Fay *see* PAIR AND GROUP KILLERS

Fuller, Edna *see* Familial Killers – Women
Hogg, Megan *see* Familial Killers – Women
Hultberg, Violet *see* Familial Killers – Women
Jones, Annie *see* Familial Killers – Women
Jones, Roxanne *see* Familial Killers – Women
King, Kathleen *see* Familial Killers – Women
Knapp, Lorraine *see* Familial Killers – Women

McAninch, Alma May *see* Familial Killers – Women

McDonald, Carol *see* Familial Killers – Women

Nollen, Elsie *see* Familial Killers – Women

Pasos, Marie *see* Familial Killers – Women

Powell, Tina Marie *see* PAIR AND GROUP KILLERS, Foster, Lafonda Fay

Rowney, Margaret *see* Familial Killers – Women

Seegrist, Sylvia. On October 30, 1985, Sylvia Seegrist entered the Springfield Mall in Delaware County, Pennsylvania, and opened fire with a semiautomatic rifle, killing three people and wounding seven. The twenty-five-year-old woman, who wore camouflage pants and combat boots during the attack, was arrested shortly after the incident. Seegrist, described as out of touch with reality, was found guilty of first-degree murder, but mentally ill, on June 27, 1986. She was sent to a mental institution. In 1988, after she was found competent, Seegrist was transferred to Muncy State Prison in Lycoming County, to serve three life sentences for her crimes.

Shoaf, Mamie Shey *see* Familial Killers – Women

Urdanivia, Ruth *see* Familial Killers – Women

Walkup, Marie *see* Familial Killers – Women

Wright, Jeanne Anne *see* Familial Killers – Women

SERIAL KILLERS - WOMEN

Beck, Martha *see* PAIR AND GROUP KILLERS, Fernandez, Raymond Martinez

Brown, Debra Denise *see* PAIR AND GROUP KILLERS, Coleman, Alton

Bundy, Carol Mary Bundy *see* PAIR AND GROUP KILLERS, Clark, Douglas D.

Coffman, Cynthia *see* PAIR AND GROUP KILLERS

Copeland, Faye *see* PAIR AND GROUP KILLERS, Copeland, Ray

Favato, Carino *see* PAIR AND GROUP KILLERS, Bolber, Morris

Gallego, Charlene Williams *see* PAIR AND GROUP KILLERS, Gallego, Gerald Armond

Graham, Gwendolyn *see* PAIR AND GROUP KILLERS

Hahn, Anna Marie. A German immigrant to Cincinnati, Ohio, Anna Maria Hahn murdered for profit elderly sick men who were in her care. Between

1932 and 1937, she was the nurse to eleven of these men whom she poisoned in order to gain their money or possessions. In 1937, she was in Colorado with an elderly man who suddenly died. Police were suspicious when they learned he had left all of his money to Hahn. The police in Ohio were alerted and also grew suspicious and began exhuming the bodies of the victims who had been under her care. Hahn was indicted for two murders in Cincinnati. At her trial in 1937, she was found guilty of first-degree murder. Ohio had a policy at that time of not executing women. However, the judge and jury made an exception and she became the first woman in Ohio to go to the electric chair. Anna Marie Hahn was executed on June 20, 1938.

Neelley, Judith Ann *see* PAIR AND GROUP KILLERS, Neelley, Alvin

Puente, Dorothea Montalvo. Born in 1929, Dorothea Montalvo Puente was raised in an orphanage. Married at least four times, she was diagnosed as schizophrenic and delusional. Puente opened a boarding house in Sacramento, California, in 1978. In 1982, she was convicted for robbing and drugging strangers she met in bars and spent two and a half years in prison. In 1986, she began boarding elderly people on Social Security. In May 1988, neighbors began complaining about flies and a terrible odor in Puente's yard. She told them it was the fish emulsion she used in her garden. On November 7, 1988, police went to her house to check on a tenant missing since August. Noticing the horrible smell, they came back with shovels five days later after another tenant was reported missing. On November 11, police began digging up bodies but Puente disappeared before they could arrest her. They had dug up seven bodies by November 14. Puente was now suspected of killing as many as twenty-five tenants who were missing. Police believed she murdered them for their Social Security checks. Puente was arrested in Los Angeles on November 17 and charged with seven murders. Two more murders were added two weeks later. Dorothea Puente was tried and convicted of three murders in December 1993 and sentenced to life in prison without parole. She died on March 27, 2011, of natural causes.

Wood, Catherine May *see* PAIR AND GROUP KILLERS, Graham, Gwendolyn

Wright, Blanche *see* PAIR AND GROUP KILLERS, Young, Robert

Wuornos, Aileen "Lee" Carol. As a sexual serial murderess who also killed for profit, Aileen Wuornos differs from most female killers. Born in Michigan in 1956 as Aileen Carol Pittman, Wuornos endured a childhood of sexual and physical abuse, rejection, and alcoholism before becoming a bisexual drifter, prostitute, and murderer. She was thirty-three when she began a two-year stint in Florida from 1989 to 1990 as a serial killer of men who paid her for prostitution. Wuornos killed at least seven of her clients with a .22-caliber pistol, before robbing them of whatever possessions she could. Her killing spree ended when authorities arrested her in Ormond Beach, Florida, on January 9, 1991. Seven days later, prompted by her lesbian lover, she confessed to the murder of six johns, though insisting each murder had been in self-defense. Wuornos went to trial on January 13, 1992, for the murder of her first victim, Richard Mallory, a fifty-one-year-old convicted rapist with a history of alcohol abuse and addiction to pornography. She was found guilty of first-degree murder and sentenced to death on January 29, 1992. A second death sentence came on May 7, 1992, following her confession to three other murders. Aileen Wuornos was executed by the State of Florida by lethal injection on October 9, 2002.

OTHER KILLERS - WOMEN

Arrington, Marie Dean. Involved in crime most of her life, Marie Dean Arrington had been convicted of assault and battery, robbery, grand larceny, forgery, and escape from custody. She shot and killed her husband in July 1964, and was convicted of manslaughter and sentenced to twenty years. While out on appeal, Arrington murdered again in April 1968. She kidnapped the Lake County, Florida, public defender's secretary, Vivian Ritter, hoping to bargain for a release of her two children from prison. Arrington's son was serving a life sentence for armed robbery and her daughter was in for two years for forgery. She threatened to kill Ritter if her children weren't released immediately. When police refused to cooperate, Arrington shot and killed Ritter and dumped her body in an orange grove, running over her body with a car several times to make sure she was dead. She was convicted of first-degree murder and sentenced to death. Arrington escaped from prison on March 1, 1969, and was then charged with unlawful flight. Still on the run, Arrington sent the judge a voodoo doll with pins stuck in it, along with a threatening letter. By May 1969, she was added to the FBI's Ten Most Wanted Fugitives list. Marie Arrington was finally arrested by the FBI in New Orleans on December 22, 1971, and returned to Florida to wait for her execution. When the U.S. Supreme Court abolished the death penalty in 1972, her sentence was commuted to life in prison without parole. She died on May 10, 2014.

Jackson, Patricia Ann. Born in 1949 to a poor African American family in Alabama, Patricia Ann Thomas had a troubled life. She dropped out of school in the eighth grade and got her education on the streets, carrying a blade for protection. In 1966, she had a fight with her boyfriend and killed him with a straight razor. Patricia was charged with first-degree murder but plea bargained to second-degree. She was sentenced to twelve years and paroled after four. In 1972, she married a man named Jackson. They split up shortly after when she caught him with another woman. When her mother died soon after that, Patricia became an alcoholic. She was soon arrested for hit and run, malicious destruction of property, resisting arrest, assaulting an officer, and disorderly conduct. She got in a fight with the owner of a bar on February 28, 1981, when the woman refused to serve her more alcohol. Patricia stuck a knife in her chest and killed her in front of several witnesses. Patricia Jackson was convicted of first-degree murder on December 28, 1981. Because it was her second murder conviction in twenty years, Alabama law mandates the death penalty and that was her sentence. In 1990, her sentence was commuted to life in prison.

Washington, Annette. Working as a nurse employed by a home health care service on Long Island, New York, Annette Washington was fired in July 1986. At twenty-eight, she was single and had a nine-year-old son. Washington was also supporting her boyfriend's drug habit on the side. Angry and bitter over losing her job, she decided to kill and rob her former patients. In August 1986, Washington murdered eighty-five-year-old Loretta O'Flaherty by cutting her throat with two kitchen knives. Two weeks later, she murdered sixty-eight-year-old Edna Fumasoli by stabbing her ninety times. Both homes had been ransacked and valuables stolen. Detectives soon discovered Washington had a common link to both victims. She was arrested in September 1986 and pleaded guilty to two counts of murder as well as assault and weapons charges. In July 1987, Annette Washington was sentenced to fifty years to life in prison.

SECTION 3 – JUVENILE KILLERS

FAMILY KILLERS - JUVENILE

Bailey, Susan, and **Roger Bailey**. On June 8, 1969, fifteen-year-old Susan Bailey and her thirteen-year-old brother, Roger, committed mass murder and familicide when they set fire to the family house in Parkersburg, West Virginia, leaving twelve family members dead. Included among the victims were the killers' parents and ten siblings. Susan Bailey's incestuous relationship with a first cousin that her parents disapproved of, along with overall behavioral problems, set the stage for the shocking crime. Under police interrogation, Susan confessed to getting her brother to assist in her murderous plan—which included taking gasoline from the pickup truck owned by the family and pouring it on the floor in the rooms where the family members were sleeping. Susan and Roger Bailey were charged with the mass murder and given a mental evaluation. Both were found guilty of their crimes and placed in juvenile detention.

Brom, David. In February 1988, sixteen-year-old David Brom killed his parents, his brother, and sister with an axe at their home in Minnesota. He was arrested and charged with four counts of murder. Brom pleaded not guilty by reason of insanity. A psychiatrist found him to be depressed, psychotic, and developing multiple personalities. The jury felt he was sane at the time of the murders and convicted him on all counts. In 1988, David Brom was sentenced to three consecutive life terms. He is currently incarcerated at the St. Cloud Correctional Facility in Minnesota. He will be eligible for parole in 2041.

DeGelleke, Patrick. In Rochester, New York, on September 8, 1984, fifteen-year-old Patrick DeGelleke set the house of his adoptive parents on fire while they slept. His mother died in the fire and his father died eleven days later. Frequently suffering from outbursts of violence and an uncontrollable temper, DeGelleke was angry with his parents for taking him to court because he was a truant and thief and they could no longer control him. He was found sane and convicted of murder. After serving nine years, he was released.

Dutton, Herman, and **James Dutton**. On July 12, 1993, fifteen-year-old Herman Dutton and twelve-year-old James Dutton used a deer rifle to shoot their abusive father, Lonnie Dutton, to death while he slept in their home in Rush Springs, Oklahoma. The two young boys were arrested and charged with first-degree murder and conspiracy. They blamed their actions on years of physical and sexual abuse by Lonnie Dutton—a big man who often abused alcohol and terrorized his family, including his wife and ten-year-old daughter. Herman and James Dutton were allowed to plead no contest to manslaughter and placed in foster homes.

Freeman, Bryan, and **David Freeman**. On February 27, 1995, skinheads Bryan Freeman, seventeen, and David Freeman, fifteen, stabbed and bludgeoned to death their parents and eleven-year-old brother, Erik, in the family's Pennsylvania home. The violent brothers, with neo-Nazi connections, had often threatened their parents, culminating in the vicious attack with a baseball bat, pickaxe handle, and metal bar from a weight lifting machine. Bryan and David Freeman were arrested three days later in Michigan and charged with murdering their parents and brother. Both pleaded guilty to murder and received life sentences with no possibility of parole.

Gasparovich, Matthew Jr., and **Heidi Gasparovich**. On February 17, 1986, juvenile siblings Matthew Gasparovich Jr. and Heidi Gasparovich committed patricide in murdering their father, Matthew Gasparovich Sr., in his home in Iowa. The fifteen-year-old Matthew Jr., and his twelve-year-old sister, Heidi, had only recently been sent to live with their father by their mother, who lived in California and felt they needed more discipline in their lives. Matthew Gasparovich Sr. was shot five times while he slept. After the murder, the killers stole his car and headed back to California. Tried as juveniles, Matthew and Heidi Gasparovich were both found guilty of killing their father and placed in juvenile custody until they turned eighteen. The Iowa Supreme Court rejected an appeal by Heidi Gasparovich.

Hernandez, Jose. On March 14, 1988, seventeen-year-old Jose Hernandez killed his family in Philadelphia, Pennsylvania. He shot his father and pregnant stepmother, strangled his six-year-old half-brother, and beat to death his eight-month-old half-brother. Police found all four bodies piled in the bathtub. Jose Hernandez was convicted of all four murders and sentenced to four life terms on June 7, 1989.

Jahnke, Richard Jr. On November 16, 1982, Richard Jahnke Jr., age sixteen, shot and killed his father in the driveway of their home in Wyoming. Richard was charged with first-degree murder. His seventeen-year-old sister, Deborah, was charged with conspiracy for helping to plot the murder. At the trial, Richard claimed he did it in self-defense after years of abuse by his father towards him, his sister, and his mother. Evidence proved that over a fourteen-year period, Mr. Jahnke had often psychologically and physically abused his family. He had also sexually abused his daughter. The jury convicted Richard Jahnke Jr. of manslaughter and sentenced him to five to fifteen years. Deborah Jahnke was convicted of aiding and abetting and sentenced to three to eight years. They were both released a few years later when the governor commuted their sentences.

Jenkins, Joshua. Fifteen-year-old Joshua Jenkins was angry with his adoptive parents for sending him to a boarding school for troubled kids in West Los Angeles, California. His parents and sister, who lived in Las Vegas, picked Jenkins up at the school on February 2, 1996, so he could spend the weekend with his grandparents at their condo in San Diego. At the condo, he had an argument with his mother. Shortly after that, Jenkins got a hammer and bludgeoned to death his parents and grandparents. He was somehow able to hide the murders from his ten-year-old sister, Megan. The next morning, he took Megan with him to the store to buy an axe and then killed her with it when they got back to the condo. That afternoon, he set the condo on fire and left in his family's Mercedes. He was arrested the next day when a convenience store clerk recognized him and called police. Jenkins initially pleaded not guilty due to insanity, but changed his plea to guilty the day before his trial. He was found mentally ill but sane and convicted of five murders. In June 1997, Joshua Jenkins was sentenced to 112 years in prison with no chance of parole.

Justice, John. In Buffalo, New York, seventeen-year-old John Justice stabbed to death his mother, brother, and father on September 16, 1985. He then rammed his father's car into another car, killing a neighbor who was driving. Justice hated his mother and was upset that his parents were not going to pay for his upcoming college expenses. He confessed to police and was charged with four counts of second-degree murder. Psychiatrists could not agree on a diagnosis, but it was determined that he suffered from some type of psychosis. The jury found John Justice not guilty by reason of insanity for killing his father and brother and guilty of murder for killing his mother and neighbor.

Kellum, Britt. Near Flint, Michigan, nine-year-old Britt Kellum fought with his eleven-year-old brother and then killed him with a 16-gauge shotgun in April 1985. Because he was too young to be held accountable, he underwent counseling. On October 30, 1989, after four years of psychotherapy, Kellum shot and killed his six-year-old brother with his father's .38-caliber handgun while playing Russian roulette.

Kinkel, Kip *see* SCHOOL KILLINGS

Kszepka, Jennifer, Dominic Hendrix, and **Michael Gaumar**. On June 7, 1992, Jennifer Kszepka, her boyfriend Dominic Hendrix, and a friend, Michael

Gaumar, conspired to murder Jennifer's father and sister in their home in Gloucester, Virginia. Linda Kszepka discovered the bodies of her husband, Army Sergeant Jerome Kszepka, and her twenty-one-year-old daughter, Ranae. She also saw their fleeing killers— including her seventeen-year-old daughter, Jennifer, who had a history of trouble. The murderous trio was arrested while driving a stolen car in Nevada and extradited back to Virginia. Jennifer Kszepka was fingered as the mastermind behind the familicide. On February 1, 1993, Kszepka pleaded guilty to murdering her father and sister. She was sentenced to life in prison plus ninety years. Dominic Hendrix was sentenced to life in prison plus ninety years and Michael Gaumar was sentenced to sixty years in prison. All three have been denied parole at their parole hearings.

Oberst, Owen. On April 21, 1928, seventeen-year-old Owen Oberst murdered his entire family of seven in Kansas. Reportedly angry over being denied use of the family car, the mass murderer shot his parents and five siblings and then set the house on fire to try and cover up the murders. After first denying involvement, Oberst confessed to the shocking crime, was convicted, and sentenced to life in prison.

Sellers, Sean. A multiple murderer at age sixteen, Sean Sellers was also a Satan worshipper. He shot and killed a convenience store clerk in September 1985 during a robbery. Then, in March 1986, he shot and killed his mother and stepfather in their Oklahoma City home because they were interfering in his life. Sellers was arrested and charged with the murders. Tried as an adult, he was convicted and sentenced to death by lethal injection. Diagnosed as suffering from multiple personality disorder, Sellers drew support from death penalty opponents around the world to no avail. On February 4, 1999, twenty-nine-year-old Sean Sellers became the first murderer executed in the United States in forty years for offenses committed at the age of sixteen.

Stevenson, Sean. At age sixteen, Sean Stevenson shot and killed his parents and then raped and killed his eighteen-year-old sister on January 1, 1987, at their home in Washington state. He murdered them after an argument with his father over attending a New Year's party. After the murders, Stevenson called his fifteen-year-old girlfriend and told her what he had done. He then went to the police station and confessed. Sean Stevenson was found guilty of first-degree murder for killing his parents and one count of aggravated murder for the rape and murder of his sister. He was sentenced to life in prison without parole.

Turnmire, Ginger. On April 26, 1986, in Tennessee, Ginger Turnmire, age fifteen, shot and killed her parents after they returned from a church picnic. After the murders, she went to a local arcade and calmly told her friends what she had done. In court, Turnmire tried to blame the murders on a motorcycle gang leader that she said had broken into the home looking for drugs, had killed her parents, and threatened to kill her if she did not confess to the murders. Psychiatrists determined that she had severe identity problems, behavior problems, had previously tried to commit suicide, was suspended from school, and addicted to Valium. She was tried as an adult and convicted of first-degree murder. Ginger Turnmire received a sentence of life in prison.

Underwood, Wesley. In 1986 at age fifteen, Wesley Underwood shot and killed his mother in their Texas home after they argued about the disappearance of one of her knitting needles. Underwood shot her three times in the back while she sat watching TV. He had been drinking and sniffing gasoline fumes shortly before the murder. Wesley Underwood pleaded guilty to murder and was sentenced to eighteen years in prison on December 19, 1986.

Whipple, Dale. In 1985, seventeen-year-old Dale Whipple murdered his parents at their home in Indiana. After years of physical, sexual, and psychological abuse by both of his parents, he decided to put an end to it. He met his mother in the garage and hacked her to death with an axe. Whipple then went in the house and murdered his sleeping father with the axe. At his trial, he claimed self-defense and said he killed them to protect himself from his father's beatings and his mother's recent sexual advances. The jury found him guilty but mentally ill. On June 18, 1985, Dale Whipple was sentenced to two concurrent forty year sentences. He was released on parole in 1999.

Williams, Alonzo. On October 6, 1987, at seventeen, Alonzo Williams shot and killed his mother with a .22-caliber semiautomatic rifle at their New York home. After the murder, he left to go to work. When he came back at lunchtime, he opened all the gas jets on the stove and left, thinking the house would burn down. It didn't, and he was arrested that night when the body was discovered. Williams claimed he killed his mother because she had been physically, verbally, and sexually abusing him for years. He was charged with and convicted of murder. In March 1989, Alonzo Williams was sentenced to twenty years to life in prison.

MASS MURDERERS - JUVENILE

Bailey, Roger *see* Familial Killers – Juvenile, Bailey, Susan

Bailey, Susan *see* Familial Killers – Juvenile

Brom, David *see* Familial Killers – Juvenile

Carneal, Michael Adam *see* SCHOOL KILLINGS

DeFord, Ray Martin. On June 29, 1996, Ray Martin DeFord set fire to an apartment complex near Portland, Oregon, killing eight people. The eleven-year-old DeFord, a tenant, had initially been hailed as a hero in helping other tenants escape the burning building until he confessed to the slayings three days later. The victims, all Mexican, included a family of six and a three-month-old child. Ray DeFord, who has the mental age of seven, was charged with eight counts of murder. On August 22, 1997, a state judge found him guilty of eight counts of felony murder and criminally negligent homicide, and one count of arson. He was sentenced to thirteen years of state custody in September 1997.

Freeman, Bryan *see* PAIR AND GROUP KILLERS

Freeman, David *see* PAIR AND GROUP KILLERS, Freeman, Bryan

Golden, Andrew *see* SCHOOL KILLINGS, Johnson, Mitchell

Hernandez, Jose *see* Familial Killers - Juvenile

Jenkins, Josh *see* Familial Killers – Juvenile

Johnson, Mitchell *see* SCHOOL KILLINGS

Justice, John *see* Familial Killers – Juvenile

Klebold, Dylan *see* The 1990s – The Mass Murder at Columbine High School; SCHOOL KILLINGS, Harris, Eric

Oberst, Owen *see* Familial Killers - Juvenile

LaPlante, Daniel. In the small city of Townsend, Massachusetts, Daniel LaPlante, age seventeen, murdered a pregnant mother and her two children on December 1, 1987. Mrs. Gustafson, three months pregnant, was found tied to the bed. She had been raped and sodomized before being shot twice through a pillow on her head. Her five-year-old son and seven-year-old daughter had been strangled. Police tracking dogs led them to LaPlante, who was currently out on bail for chasing his girlfriend's family around with a hatchet in 1986. He was arrested and charged with three counts of murder. LaPlante was found competent to stand trial and convicted. Daniel LaPlante was sentenced to three consecutive life terms with no parole, no commutation, and no furloughs.

Loukaitis, Barry *see* SCHOOL KILLINGS

Porrell, Steven. On June 16, 1989, in New Hampshire, Steven Porrell, age seventeen, went on a murder spree. The day before his high school graduation, he argued with his father and stabbed him, though not fatally. He then went to an ice cream parlor and shot and killed the owner and a seventeen-year-old girl who had recently broken up with him. When the police arrived and surrounded the ice cream parlor, Steven Porrell shot and killed himself.

Stevenson, Sean *see* Familial Killers - Juvenile

Ward, Ronald. On April 11, 1985, Ronald Ward, age fifteen, murdered three people at a house in West Memphis, Arkansas. The victims were two women, age seventy-two and seventy-five, and their twelve-year-old grandnephew. Each had been stabbed repeatedly with a butcher knife. Ward, an African American, was arrested when a neighbor identified him from a yearbook photo as the person he had seen in the neighborhood around the time of the murders. Police found Ward's fingerprints throughout the victims' house. He was tried as an adult and convicted of murder. Ronald Ward was sentenced to death in September 1985, making him the youngest person on death row in the United States. He was re-tried in 1988 and again found guilty, but this time he was sentenced to life in prison without parole.

SEXUAL KILLERS - JUVENILE

Bey, Marko. This sexual murderer raped and killed two women New Jersey in 1983. Marko Bey was seventeen when he sexually attacked and beat to death a nineteen-year-old female on April 2, 1983. On April 26, now eighteen years old, Bey sexually assaulted and strangled a forty-six-year-old woman, then stole her car. He was arrested, tried, and convicted of the two murders and sexual assaults, receiving the death penalty in both cases. The New Jersey Supreme Court overturned the death sentence in the first murder, as Bey was a minor at the time of the crime. Marko Bey was also granted a new trial for the second rape-murder because his rights had been violated by law enforcement during questioning. He was resentenced to life in prison with no parole.

Cooper, Curtis. In Southern California on March 23, 1989, Curtis Cooper strangled and sexually assaulted a seven-year-old girl. Cooper, age fifteen, had recently moved to California from Florida where he had been arrested for burglaries and petty thefts. On March 26, 1989, Cooper's landlady searched his house looking for the source of a terrible odor. She found the dead girl's decaying body stuffed behind Cooper's waterbed headboard. He had put a fan in the window to help blow out the odor so he could still sleep in the room. After his arrest, it was determined he had mild brain damage but was not insane. Curtis Cooper pleaded guilty to first-degree murder and was sentenced to twenty-five years to life in prison. However, under juvenile sentencing guidelines, he was released from custody when he turned twenty-five.

Hughes, Kevin. Nicknamed "Peanut," Kevin Hughes, an African American boy, lived in Philadelphia, Pennsylvania. He was convicted of raping an eleven-year-old girl at knifepoint in 1976 at age fourteen and given three years' probation. On March 1, 1979, police found the body of a nine-year-old African American girl in an abandoned building. She had been strangled, sexually assaulted, and her body badly burned. Above her body, police found the word "Peanut" burned into the ceiling. On January 5, 1980, police were talking to a twelve-year-old girl who said a teenager had sexually assaulted her. She picked out Kevin Hughes from police photos. When searching his house, they found the word "Peanut" burned into the ceiling above his bed. Hughes confessed to killing the nine-year-old girl in 1979. Even though he was diagnosed as schizophrenic and having a very low IQ, Kevin Hughes was convicted of first-degree murder, rape, deviate sexual intercourse, and arson. He was sentenced to death. However, in 2005 the U.S. Supreme Court abolished the death penalty for offenders who were under the age of eighteen at the time they committed a crime. Kevin Hughes is currently serving a life sentence.

Milne, Shawn. Claiming his thirteen-year-old neighbor was always harassing and threatening him, fifteen-year-old Shawn Milne killed her. On November 12, 1985, Milne attacked her and dragged her through a wooded area in New Jersey. He told police that he dropped her on her head a few times and then threw her into the creek. An autopsy revealed that she had been brutally sodomized and beaten with a blunt object. She was also still alive when he threw her in the creek. Shawn Milne was tried as an adult in June 1987 and convicted of aggravated sexual assault and murder. He was sentenced to fifty years in prison. In November 2015, after serving thirty years, Shawn Milne was released from prison.

Pinkerton, Jay Kelly. In Amarillo, Texas, on October 26, 1979, seventeen-year-old Jay Kelly Pinkerton brutally murdered Sarah Lawrence in her home while her three young children slept. Pinkerton had entered the house planning to rob it. Autopsy reports stated she had been stabbed over thirty times, her abdomen had been cut open and ejaculated in, and her throat had been slit. Pinkerton also had sex with her after he killed her. Footprints led to Pinkerton's house, where he was arrested. He was charged with capital murder, found guilty, and sentenced to death. He was also convicted and sentenced to death for another sexual murder that occurred after Mrs. Lawrence's murder but before he was arrested. On May 15, 1986, Jay Kelly Pinkerton was executed by lethal injection at age twenty-four.

Rosenberg, Matthew. When he turned fourteen in 1983, Matthew Rosenberg had already sexually molested twenty young boys in Massachusetts. In October 1983, he sexually molested a five-year-old boy. After beating and drowning him, he put the boy's naked body in a trash bag and hid it in his closet. He was convicted of murder and sent to a state juvenile facility. While incarcerated, he was accused of assaulting younger inmates. In 1989, at age twenty, he was transferred to an adult prison for sexual offenders. Matthew Rosenberg was released in 1992 after completing his sentence.

Shedrick, Donald. At age sixteen, Donald Shedrick committed murder on September 15, 1988. While living at a motel in Ohio, he raped, stabbed, and murdered the thirteen-year-old girl who lived in the next room with her parents. She was stabbed seven times and had a broken neck. Shedrick was charged with rape and murder. His first trial ended in a mistrial because the jury didn't feel they had enough evidence. At his second trial, a girl that he had allegedly tried to rape and murder testified against him. This time the jury found Donald Shedrick guilty of aggravated murder, rape, and burglary. He was sentenced to life plus seventy-five years.

OTHER KILLERS - JUVENILE

Abraham, Nathaniel. On October 29, 1997, Nathaniel Abraham, age eleven, shot to death an eighteen-year-old male outside a Pontiac, Michigan, convenience store. In a murder case that drew national attention and controversy because of the age of the accused, Abraham was arrested two days later and charged with first-degree murder. He became the first juvenile to face first-degree murder charges under a 1997 Michigan law that permits children of any age to be tried as an adult for serious felonies. In spite of criticism from organizations such as Amnesty International, Nathaniel Abraham was convicted of second-degree murder on November 16, 1999. Had the jury opted for guilty of first-degree murder, Abraham could have been sentenced to life in prison as one of the nation's youngest convicted murderers. Instead, the thirteen-year-old African American boy was sentenced to juvenile detention and was released when he turned twenty-one.

Bankston, Clinton, Jr. Living in Georgia, Clinton Bankston Jr. was a high school dropout. In April 1987, at age fifteen, he robbed and killed two retired college professors in their home. He killed them when he discovered they had no money or valuables in their home. In August 1987, now sixteen years old, Bankston went to the house of three women, planning to rob them. After he robbed and stabbed them, he mutilated their bodies with a hatchet so they were barely recognizable. He was arrested that day while driving one of the victims' cars. He pleaded guilty but mentally ill to five counts of murder. He was sentenced to five consecutive life terms.

Cannon, Joseph John. In September 1977, seventeen-year-old Joseph John Cannon was high on drugs and alcohol when he murdered attorney Anne Walsh, age forty-five and mother of eight, in her San Antonio, Texas, home. Cannon, who was living with Walsh at the time, was on probation for burglary. He was arrested, convicted of murder, and sentenced to death by lethal injection. On April 22, 1998, Joseph Cannon was executed. He was the fifth inmate to die in Texas since the state reinstated capital punishment in 1982.

Cooper, Paula. In May 1985, Paula Cooper, age fifteen, and three teenage accomplices entered the Indiana home of a seventy-eight-year-old Bible teacher named Ruth Pelke. The intoxicated group of teenagers was intent on robbery and auto theft. Cooper used a butcher knife to fatally stab the victim thirty-three times before the group stole ten dollars and Pelke's automobile. All were arrested shortly after. Paula Cooper, an African American, was charged with murder and tried as an adult. She pleaded guilty and was sentenced to death—becoming only one of two female murderers under the age of eighteen on death row. In 1989, the Indiana Supreme Court reversed Cooper's death sentence to sixty years in prison. She was released from prison in 2013 and committed suicide in May 2015.

Crane, Cheryl. The daughter of actress Lana Turner and Stephen Crane, Cheryl Crane committed murder at age fourteen. On April 4, 1958, Cheryl murdered her mother's lover, gangster John Stompanato. The murder occurred while Stompanato was attacking Lana Turner with a wooden coat hanger. Cheryl grabbed a butcher knife with a nine-inch blade and stabbed him once, killing him. She was charged with murder, but it was eventually reduced to manslaughter. Cheryl and her mother testified to the abuse Stompanato had subjected them to. The jury rendered a verdict of justifiable homicide. Cheryl Crane was made a ward of the state and placed in the custody of her grandmother. After running away several times, she was placed in a state home for girls until she reached adulthood.

McClure, James. Twelve-year-old James McClure was looking for something to steal in his California neighborhood. On May 7, 1985, he went into his elderly neighbor's house looking for money. Surprised that the eighty-year-old man was home, McClure panicked and stabbed him in the chest with a kitchen knife. After he plea bargained to a reduced charge of guilty of voluntary manslaughter, James McClure was sentenced to a juvenile facility until the age of twenty-one.

McDonald, Roland. In 1924, at age fifteen, Roland McDonald shot and killed his schoolmistress, Louise Gerrish, in Amhurst, Maine. He was found guilty of murder and sent to prison. A request for parole was rejected, even though a lie detector test suggested he was not guilty.

Novak, Shawn Paul. On March 4, 1991, Shawn Paul Novak murdered two young boys in Virginia Beach, Virginia. The two boys, age nine and seven, had ridden their bikes to the woods near their home when they ran into sixteen-year-old Novak who was target practicing on a tree with his hunting knife. After talking about the knife with them, he stabbed them and covered their bodies with branches. When a witness reported seeing Novak with the two boys, police questioned him. He eventually confessed to the murders, giving no motive. Charged with two counts of first-degree murder, the jury found him guilty on both counts in March 1992. On May 4, 1992, Shawn Novak was sentenced to life in prison. He has been denied parole several times.

Rumbaugh, Charles "Chuckie". Growing up in Texas, Charles Rumbaugh had been in trouble most of his young life. At age six, he committed his first burglary. He committed his first robbery when he was twelve. Rumbaugh spent most of his childhood in reform schools and mental hospitals. At age seventeen, he shot and killed a jeweler in Texas. Tried as an adult, he was convicted of capital murder and sentenced to death. After spending ten years on death row, Charles Rumbaugh was executed on September 11, 1985. It was the first time in over twenty years that a person was executed in the United States for a crime they committed as a juvenile.

Smalley, Michael. At age fourteen, Michael Smalley kidnapped a five-year-old girl in Ohio and slit her throat, killing her. Her body was found hidden in the attic of the home his parents were renting. He was convicted of kidnapping and aggravated attempted murder in a juvenile court. Because he was a juvenile, he was sentenced to one year at the State Department of Youth Services. In West Virginia on September 20, 1987, Smalley, seventeen, shot and killed his fifteen-year-old sister. He then hitchhiked to Arizona, where he was arrested. Michael Smalley pleaded guilty to first-degree murder and was sentenced to life in prison.

SECTION 4 – PAIR AND GROUP KILLERS

Bailey, Susan, and **Roger Bailey** *see* Familial Killers - Juvenile

Barker, Frederick. Born in 1902 in Missouri, Frederick Barker was the co-leader of the notorious Barker-Karpis gang that specialized in bank and train robbery, kidnapping, and murder. Other members of the outlaw gang included Barker's brother, Arthur Barker, and Alvin Karpis. Also believed to be part of the gang during her later years was the mother of the Barkers, Arizona Donnie Barker, who became infamous in her own right as Kate "Ma" Barker. Born around 1872, she was portrayed as the sinister criminal mind behind the gang, but her actual role was believed to be minimal. At least ten murders were attributed to the Barker-Karpis gang. Fred Barker was identified as the likely killer in two of the murders. The Barker-Karpis gang was responsible for the kidnappings for ransom of wealthy businessmen William A. Hamm Jr. and Edward G. Bremer. On January 16, 1935, FBI agents killed Fred Barker and Ma Barker in Ocklawaha, Florida, during a four-hour gunfight. *See also* Bandits, Outlaws, and Organized Crime Killers – Men, Karpis, Alvin.

Barrow, Clyde, and **Bonnie Parker**. This infamous pair of murderous lovers terrorized the Midwest and South in the 1930s. Clyde Barrow, a career criminal, was twenty-one when he met the nineteen-year-old Bonnie Parker in January 1930. At the time, she was married to an incarcerated murderer. Together, Barrow and Parker were involved in a series of headline murders, robberies, burglaries, and shootouts with law enforcement—some in conjunction with family and friends that came to be known as the Barrow gang. The pair alone was believed to have murdered at least thirteen people, including several lawmen. In November 1933, an effort by authorities to capture the elusive and violent lovers near Grand Prairie, Texas, failed. On January 16, 1934, Barrow and Parker orchestrated a prison break from the Eastham State Prison Farm in Waldo, Texas. Five inmates escaped while Barrow covered them with rapid-fire machine gun blasts. The end for Clyde Barrow and Bonnie Parker came on May 23, 1934, when a posse of law enforcement officers acting on a tip ambushed the killers on a highway near Sailes, Louisiana. Opening fire with a hail of bullets on their automobile, the unsuspecting Parker and Barrow were killed instantly. Their legend continues to live long after their deaths. *See also* The 1930s – The Deadly Saga of Bonnie and Clyde.

Berry, Shawn Allen, John William King, and **Lawrence Russell Brewer** *see* HATE CRIME KILLERS

Bianchi, Kenneth, and **Angelo Buono**. Between October 1977 and January 1979, sexual serial killer cousins Kenneth Bianchi and Angelo Buono terrorized Los Angeles, California, and later Bellingham, Washington, brutally murdering at least twelve women between them. The murders of prostitutes, students, and other young women were initially believed to have been the work of one man, dubbed by the press as the "Hillside Strangler." Instead, Bianchi, a security guard, and Buono, an ex-thief and owner of an upholstery shop, joined forces to operate a prostitution ring and violently rape and murder females. Many of the victims were found on hillsides with their legs spread-eagle, having been raped and strangled by both killers. The last two murders occurred in Bellingham, where Kenneth Bianchi had moved with his common-law wife and child. Bianchi had found work there with a security company. In January 1979, two young women, Karen Mandic and Diane Wilder, were found raped and strangled after being hired by Bianchi to housesit overnight while an alarm system was being installed. Law enforcement authorities were able to link Bianchi to the Bellingham and Hillside Strangler murders. After being found sane enough to stand trial, Bianchi avoided the death penalty by pleading guilty to seven murders between the two states and agreeing to testify against his killer cousin, Angelo Buono. Kenneth Bianchi was sentenced to life in prison in California and Washington. In November 1983, following a long and expensive trial, Angelo Buono was found guilty of one Hillside Strangler murder and sentenced to life in prison. He died of a heart attack in his cell on September 21, 2002. Bianchi is currently serving his life sentence at the Washington State Penitentiary in Walla Walla, Washington. He was denied parole in 2010 and will be eligible for parole again in 2025.

Bittaker, Lawrence, and **Roy Norris**. For four months in 1979, sexual psychopaths and serial murderers Lawrence Bittaker and Roy Norris killed five women in Southern California. The two men met while incarcerated and formed a friendship and homicidal relationship. They used a van they called "Murder Mac" to hunt down, abduct, sexually assault, torture, and murder their victims. Their last murder occurred on October 31, 1979, with the victim's tortured remains left on the front lawn of a home. One would-be murder victim of the pair was raped, but spared death. She was able to identify her assailants as Bittaker and Norris. Both men were arrested and faced numerous charges, including five counts of murder, forcible rape, sexual perversion, kidnapping, and criminal conspiracy. Norris confessed to the killings and led investigators to the burial sites. In exchange for his testimony against Bittaker, Roy Norris pled guilty, avoiding the death penalty. Norris was sentenced to forty-five years to life. He was denied parole in 2009 and will be eligible again in ten years. On February 17, 1981, Lawrence Bittaker was convicted on twenty-six counts, including five murders. He was sentenced to death and is currently on death row.

Black Hand. The Black Hand was a criminal group of extortionists, kidnappers, and killers who operated in America during the early 1900s. Originating in Italy and Sicily in the 1750s, the Black Hand preyed mostly on wealthy Italian and Sicilian immigrants in New York,

New Orleans, San Francisco, Chicago, Detroit, Kansas City, and other large urban regions. Black Handers often demanded money from targeted individuals with threats to kidnap, injure, or murder family members, or promises to destroy a business. Black Hand extortion notes typically included a black ink hand print or picture denoting such, along with some frightening and intimidating cryptic images such as a bloody knife, smoking gun, or exploding bomb.

The Black Hand victimized tens of thousands of fearful people between 1890 and the early 1920s, often ending fatally. In New York alone, Black Hander Ignazio Saietta—known as Lupo the Wolf—was reported to have murdered at least thirty people who rejected his extortion demands, often shooting, stabbing, strangling, dismembering, burning, and burying his victims. Saietta worked for other Black Hand extortionists as well, using his deadly skills to achieve their ends. He was eventually arrested and convicted on counterfeiting charges, and sentenced to thirty years in prison. Other infamous Black Hand killers include Kansas City Black Hander brothers Joseph and Peter DiGiovanni, and Chicago-based Black Hand extortionist-murderers James Belcastro, Sam Cardinelli, and Frank Campione. Many of the Black Hand criminals were themselves killed by racketeers or through legal executions.

Bolber, Morris, Paul Petrillo, Herman Petrillo, and **Carino Favato**. During the 1930s, this group of serial killers accounted for as many as fifty murders, thirty of which were documented by authorities between 1932 and 1937. Morris Bolber, a Philadelphia doctor, was the mastermind behind a murderous scheme that involved killing the husbands of dissatisfied women to collect on insurance. Bolber recruited his friend, Paul Petrillo, and his cousin, Herman Petrillo, for the deadly insurance scams. Later, Black Widow Carino Favato joined the team, having already rid herself of several husbands and already in the business of helping other women to be relieved of their husbands for a price. When an ex-con and would-be new partner to the scheme instead went to the police, the serial murderers were arrested, along with a number of their co-conspirators. Paul and Herman Petrillo were convicted of murder and sentenced to death. They were executed in the electric chair. Morris Bolber and Carino Favato were also found guilty of their deadly crimes and received sentences of life in prison.

Boyle, William Anthony (Tony), Paul E. Gilly, Claude E. Vealey, and Aubran W. Martin. On December 30, 1969, fifty-nine-year-old Joseph A. Yablonsky, his fifty-seven-year-old wife Margaret, and their twenty-five-year-old daughter Charlotte, were shot to death in the family's farmhouse in Clarksville, Pennsylvania. Charged with ordering the murders was William Anthony (Tony) Boyle, the president of the United Mine Workers Union (UMW). Boyle and Yablonsky had been in heated competition for the UMW presidency weeks earlier. UMW money was allegedly used to pay off the hit men: Paul E. Gilly, Claude E. Vealey, and Aubran W. Martin. In 1971, Vealey pleaded guilty to the triple murders. In 1971 and 1972, respectively, Martin and Gilly were convicted of the murders. In April 1974, Boyle, who was then serving time for embezzling and illegal campaign contributions, was tried and convicted of first-degree murder for ordering the executions of the Yablonskys.

He was sentenced to three consecutive life terms. After successfully appealing the verdict, Boyle was granted a new trial in 1977 and was again found guilty by a jury. On May 31, 1985, at the age of eighty-three, Tony Boyle died of a heart attack in the penitentiary.

Bryant, Ritch, Randall Lee Rojas, and **Jessica Colwell** *see* HATE CRIME KILLERS

Carson, Susan, and **James Clifford Carson**. Mixing drug abuse and a hippie lifestyle with murder, Susan Carson and James Clifford Carson killed three people between 1981 and 1983 in California. Born as Susan Barnes in 1941 to a prosperous family, Susan was divorced, the mother of two, heavily into the drug scene, practicing the occult, and an exhibitionist when she met James Carson in November 1977. Nine years younger, Carson was also abusing drugs and into the counter-culture movement. The two self-described Muslims were married on June 21, 1978. They moved around the Western U.S. working odd and illegal jobs, eventually resorting to vengeful and drug-crazed murder. On January 12, 1983, the pair was apprehended following the murder of a motorist who was stabbed and shot to death. The killers confessed to three murders. In June 1984, after being found competent to stand trial, Susan Carson and James Carson were convicted of one murder. On July 2, 1984, the pair was sentenced to twenty-five years to life in prison. They were eventually convicted for the other two murders and received the same sentences of twenty-five years to life behind bars.

Caston, James, Charles E. Caston, and **Hal Crimm** *see* HATE CRIME KILLERS

Clark, Douglas D., and **Carol Mary Bundy**. During 1980, sexual serial killers Douglas Clark and

Carol Mary Bundy terrorized Hollywood, California, by brutally murdering at least six females and possibly as many as fifty. The murders of mostly young prostitutes included stabbing, strangulation, shooting, and mutilation motivated by the couple's perverse sexual desires, including necrophilia. Bundy, a nurse, was thirty-eight when she met the dominating Clark. The two lovers turned sexual fantasies into sexual obsession, slavery, and murder, often luring their victims to their deaths. Clark—who became known as the "Sunset Slayer" and "Hollywood Slasher"—and Bundy's victims included her ex-boyfriend. The killing spree came to an end when Carol Bundy confessed the couple's serial homicides to police. They were arrested, tried, and convicted of multiple murders. In 1983, Douglas Clark was found guilty of six murders and sentenced to death. Carol Bundy was given two consecutive prison sentences, the worst being twenty-seven years to life. While Clark remains on death row in California, in 2003, Bundy died of heart failure during her incarceration.

Coffman, Cynthia, and **James Gregory Marlow**. For five weeks in 1986, serial killers Cynthia Coffman and James Gregory Marlow murdered at least four women in California and Oregon, motivated by robbery and sexual molestation. Coffman, born in 1962 in Missouri, had a history of drug and alcohol abuse and violent relationships. She met Marlow, an inmate, while visiting her boyfriend in jail. Coffman was quickly attracted to Marlow, a white supremacist and career criminal who was five years her senior. Upon his release, the two embarked on a life of robbery, sexual assault, and murder. The couple was arrested on November 14, 1986, in Big Bear City, California.

Cynthia Coffman confessed to the crimes and led police to one of their victims. The couple was charged with one count of murder and went to trial on July 18, 1989, in San Bernardino, California. Both were convicted and sentenced to death on August 30, 1989. Cynthia Coffman faced a second California murder trial on May 14, 1992. She was also found guilty in that trial and given a sentence of life in prison with no chance for parole. They are both currently on death row in California.

Coleman, Alton, and **Debra Denise Brown**. In the summer of 1984, Alton Coleman and Debra Denise Brown, both African American, went on a two-month robbery, rape, and murder spree in four states in the Midwest. The murders, which totaled at least eight, were primarily sexually motivated and included bludgeoning, torturing, and shooting their victims. Coleman was already a violent chronic offender and sexual sadist at age twenty-eight when he met the twenty-one-year-old Debra Brown. Immediately the two clicked in pursuing a path of violence and terror in Indiana, Illinois, Ohio, and Michigan. Coleman made the FBI's Most Wanted list. The killer couple was arrested in Evanston, Illinois, with bail set at $25 million for Coleman and $20 million for Brown. Each was tried and convicted of murder in different jurisdictions and twice sentenced to death. In 1991, the governor commuted one of Debra Brown's death sentences to life in prison. She is currently serving a life sentence in Ohio, though her death sentence in Indiana still stands. Alton Coleman was executed in Ohio on April 26, 2002, by lethal injection.

Collier, Cindy Lee, and **Shirley Wolf**. On June 14, 1983, teenage thrill killers Cindy Lee Collier and Shirley

Wolf viciously murdered eighty-five-year-old Anna Brackett in her home in Auburn, California. Collier, fifteen, and Wolf, fourteen, stabbed to death Brackett in the midst of a burglary. The girls, who described the killing as "lots of fun," stabbed the elderly woman more than twenty-eight times with a knife. Collier and Wolf were arrested and charged with Brackett's murder. On July 29, 1983, a juvenile court judge found the pair guilty of committing first-degree murder and burglary. Cindy Collier was committed to the custody of the California Youth Authority until she reached the age of twenty-seven. After an attempt to plead not guilty by reason of insanity failed, Shirley Wolf received the same maximum sentence allowed by state law as Cindy Collier.

Copeland, Ray, and **Faye Copeland**. This elderly couple may represent the oldest husband-wife American serial killer team in the 20th century. Ray Copeland, seventy-five, and Faye Copeland, sixty-nine, at the time of their arrest in 1989, murdered at least five drifters who worked on their farm near Chillicothe, Missouri. The Copelands were already being investigated for livestock fraud when a co-conspirator called a "Crime Stoppers" program to report finding a human skull and bones on the Copeland farm. Authorities uncovered the remains of five men, each of whom had been shot in the back of the head by a rifle belonging to the Copelands. Both were arrested and charged with five counts of first-degree murder. Faye Copeland, who had made a patchwork quilt using strips of clothing from their victims, went to trial on November 1, 1990. She was convicted on all counts and sentenced to die by lethal injection. Ray Copeland, whose insanity defense failed as well as a plea bargain to avoid the death penalty, went on trial on March 4, 1991. Like his wife, he too was found guilty on five counts of murder and sentenced to death. Ray and Faye Copeland became the oldest murdering pair to ever be condemned to die in Missouri. Ray Copeland died in 1993 at the age of seventy-eight while awaiting execution. In August 1999, Faye Copeland's death sentence was commuted to life in prison without parole. After suffering a stroke in 2002, she was granted medical parole. Faye died in a nursing home on December 28, 2003, at age eighty-two.

Corll, Dean, and **Elmer Wayne Henley Jr.** In the early 1970s, serial killer Dean Corll and his accomplice, Elmer Wayne Henley Jr., combined to rape, torture, and murder thirty-two boys in Corll's Pasadena, Texas, home. Dean Corll, a thirty-three-year-old electrician, and the seventeen-year-old Henley lured boys to the house to sniff glue or get high on drugs. The victims were then sexually assaulted, sodomized, and handcuffed to a "torture board" for further indignities before being strangled and shot. The dead boys were buried under a boat shed and in several other burial sites. Corll's serial murder came to an end on August 8, 1973, when Henley shot and killed him. Henley was arrested after he called the police to report the murder. In July 1974, he went to trial for murder and was convicted. Elmer Wayne Henley Jr. was sentenced to six consecutive 99-year terms of imprisonment. His killing of Dean Corll was found to be justifiable homicide. Henley implicated another young accomplice who was recruited by Corll named David Owen Brooks. He was also convicted of murder and sentenced to life in prison.

Creighton, Mary Frances, and **Earl Applegate**. Black Widow Mary Frances Creighton was involved in three murders for profit between 1923 and 1935 in New Jersey and New York. The first murder occurred when she and her husband, John Creighton, poisoned her brother, Raymond Avery, with arsenic to collect his life insurance. The Creighton's were tried and acquitted of murder, though there was significant forensic evidence against the pair. Mary Creighton was later acquitted of the arsenic poisoning death of her husband's mother. On September 25, 1935, Mary conspired with her lover, Earl Applegate, and poisoned his wife. The two couples were sharing a Long Island home with the Creighton's three children. Applegate, who was also sexually abusing the Creighton's fourteen-year-old daughter, was the mastermind behind the murder of his wife, Ada Applegate. The two killers were arrested and Mary Creighton confessed to Ada's murder after Applegate was charged with child rape. Creighton and Applegate went to trial and were found guilty of first-degree murder on January 30, 1936. They were both sentenced to death. On July 19, 1936, they were executed in the electric chair at Sing Sing prison.

Dally, Michael, and **Diana Haun**. In a lover's triangle killing, Michael Dally conspired with his lover and co-worker, Diana Haun, to murder his thirty-five-year-old wife, Sherri Dally. On May 6, 1996, Dally, mother of two sons and owner of a childcare center, was kidnapped from the parking lot of a Target store in Ventura, California. On June 1, her skeletal remains were discovered in a ravine. She had been stabbed and beaten to death. Investigators honed in on Michael Dally, thirty-six, a night supervisor at a Von's supermarket, and Haun, thirty-five, a Von's deli worker.

The two had been involved in an ongoing two-year affair. In November 1996, Haun and Dally were indicted for Sherri Dally's death and charged with kidnapping, murder, conspiracy, and special circumstances in killing for financial gain and lying in wait. On September 28, 1997, Diana Haun was found guilty of kidnapping, conspiracy, and murder in the first-degree and sentenced to life imprisonment without the possibility of parole. Michael Dally was convicted of the charges on June 9, 1998, and also received life with no chance of parole. Further, he was ordered to pay $15,000 in restitution to Sherri Dally's family.

Dutton, Herman, and **James Dutton** *see* Familial Killers – Juvenile

Fernandez, Raymond Martinez, and **Martha Beck.** From 1947 to 1949, serial killers Raymond Martinez Fernandez and Martha Beck preyed upon lonely, vulnerable women for their assets. They murdered at least twelve and as many as twenty victims in the Southeastern United States. Fernandez, a Hawaii native and con artist, met Beck through a lonely hearts advertisement in Pensacola, Florida. Weighing almost 300 pounds, Martha Beck, a registered nurse, dwarfed her soon-to-be-lover who was five years her senior. She was twenty-seven when the unlikely couple teamed up to defraud women that they met through lonely hearts clubs magazines and newspaper advertisements. Their scheme quickly escalated into jealousy and murder. It was after the murder of their last victims in January 1949—a twenty-eight-year-old single mother and her two-year-old daughter—that Fernandez and Beck were arrested following the discovery of the victims' buried remains. Both killers confessed to their heinous crime spree that included bludgeoning, poisoning, drowning, and strangling their victims. In July 1949, the couple, dubbed by the press as the "Lonely Hearts Killers," went to trial on multiple murder counts. In spite of an insanity defense strategy, a jury found Fernandez and Beck guilty on every count and sentenced them to death. Raymond Fernandez and Martha Beck were executed in the electric chair at Sing Sing prison on January 2, 1951. *See also* The 1940s – The Lonely Hearts Murders.

Foster, Lafonda Fay, and **Tina Marie Powell.** On April 23, 1986, bisexual mass murderers Lafonda Fay Foster and Tina Marie Powell went on a brutal murder spree in Lexington, Kentucky, leaving five people dead. When the two women met while both in their twenties, they each had a long criminal history and were abusing drugs and alcohol. This escalated into vengeful murder when they went berserk against five direct or indirect acquaintances with whom they had real or imagined conflicts. All five victims were stabbed repeatedly and shot in the head. Several had been run over by a car and three were left inside a car that was set on fire. Foster and Powell were soon arrested and charged in what was said to be Lexington's worst mass murder. In February 1987, a jury found both women guilty on five counts of first-degree murder. Lafonda Foster was sentenced to death and Tina Powell received a life sentence. In 1991, Foster's death sentence was reversed to life in prison.

Freeman, Bryan, and **David Freeman** *see* Familial Killers – Juvenile

Gallego, Gerald Armond, and **Charlene Williams Gallego.** During a twenty-six month stretch from 1978 to 1980 covering three Western states, this unlikely pair of husband and wife "sex slave" serial killers claimed ten lives, including college sweethearts Craig Miller and

Mary Beth Sowers. The killings, which included kidnapping and rape, were the result of Gerald Gallego's sex slave fantasies. Charlene acted as the lure in drawing unsuspecting victims to the man she had married twice. Gallego, born in 1946, came from a long line of deviants, including his father, Gerald Albert Gallego, a double murderer who was executed in Mississippi in 1955. Charlene, born in 1956, came from a privileged family but felt more at home with the domineering and charming Gallego. A career criminal, Gerald Gallego found the perfect mate in Charlene Williams, his fifth wife. Together they abused alcohol, drugs, and each other and perpetrated their sex slave murders in California, Oregon, and Nevada. Their reign of sexual homicide ended with the murders of Miller and Sowers, whose plans to marry on New Year's Eve 1981 ended with violence. Fugitives Gerald and Charlene Gallego were captured by FBI agents on November 17, 1980, in Omaha, Nebraska. The two were charged with murder and extradited back to California, where their final victims were murdered. A pregnant Charlene confessed to ten murders as part of a plea bargain to testify against Gallego in two trials. Gerald Gallego was convicted of four murders and implicated in several others in two states. He received the death penalty in California and Nevada, the last coming on June 25, 1984. After avoiding execution through years of appeals, on July 18, 2002, Gerald Gallego died of rectal cancer while on death row in Nevada. As part of her plea bargain, Charlene Gallego received a sentence of sixteen years and eight months behind bars in Nevada. She was released in July 1997. *See also* The 1970s − The Sex Slave Killings; Adult Victims, Sowers, Mary Elizabeth.

Garrett, Daniel, and **Karla Faye Tucker**. On June 13, 1983, Daniel Garrett and Karla Faye Tucker brutally bludgeoned to death two people during a robbery in Houston, Texas. The victims, Jerry Lynn Dean, twenty-seven, and Deborah Thornton, thirty-two, were killed in Dean's apartment where the killers had broken in looking for motorcycle parts. Tucker, a self-confessed drug-addicted prostitute, was dubbed the "pickaxe killer" after she used a fifteen-pound pickaxe to silence Dean as he was being beaten by Garrett with a hammer. She then turned the pickaxe on Thornton, who was hiding under the covers. Tucker later admitted to a friend that she received a sexual thrill with each swing of the axe. Garrett and Tucker were arrested shortly after the double murder. They were tried, convicted, and sentenced to death. Before he could be executed, Daniel Garrett died of liver disease in prison in 1993. Karla Faye Tucker became a born again Christian and gained worldwide support from death penalty opponents, including Pope John Paul II. However, the thirty-eight-year-old murderer could not prevent her fate. On February 4, 1998, Karla Faye Tucker was put to death by lethal injection. She was the first woman executed in Texas since the Civil War and the first woman executed in the United States since 1984.

Gasparovich, Matthew, Jr., and **Heidi Gasparovich** *see* Familial Killers – Juvenile

Graham, David, and **Diane Zamora**. On December 4, 1995—in a case that gained national attention—jealousy and alleged unfaithfulness led high school honor students and lovers, David Graham and Diane Zamora, to murder Adrianne Jones near Fort Worth, Texas. The pair lured sixteen-year-old Jones to a remote lake south of Fort Worth, where they bludgeoned her with a dumbbell and shot her twice in the head in retaliation for Graham's claim to have had sexual relations with her. The crime went unsolved for nine months while the killers entered military academies. Zamora entered the Naval Academy and Graham went into the Air Force Academy. They were arrested in September 1996, after midshipman Diane Zamora confessed to classmates about the slaying. Tried separately, Diane Zamora, twenty, was convicted of capital murder on February 17, 1998, and sentenced to life imprisonment without parole for at least forty years. On July 25, 1998, David Graham, the former cadet, age twenty, was also found guilty of capital murder and given a life sentence. They are both eligible for parole in 2036. The case inspired a made-for-television movie. *See also* Child Victims, Jones, Adrianne.

Graham, Gwendolyn, and **Catherine May Wood**. In 1987, lesbian lover serial killers Gwendolyn Graham and Catherine May Wood suffocated five elderly patients and attempted to kill five others in a nursing home where the two employees met in Walker, Michigan. The 450-pound Graham was the more dominating of the two lovers. Their murder spree was motivated by perverse sexual thrills in killing. Over a four-month stretch at the beginning of 1987, Graham and Wood carried out the cold, calculating murders of the aging victims. Their relationship had already ended when they were arrested in December 1988. The arrest came following an investigation after a jealous, lonely, and guilt-ridden Catherine Wood confessed to her ex-husband about the murders. Graham and Wood faced five counts of first-degree murder. On September 8, 1989, just before the start of her trial, Catherine Wood pled guilty to second-degree murder and became the prosecution's star witness against Gwendolyn Graham. On September 20, 1989, Graham was convicted of five counts of homicide and one count of conspiracy to commit murder. She was sentenced to six terms of life imprisonment with no parole. In October 1989, Wood was given twenty to forty years behind bars.

Hamlin, Louis, and **Jamie Savage**. In May 1991, in a planned crime of rape, torture, and murder, Louis Hamlin and Jamie Savage abducted two twelve-year-old girls in a wooded area in Vermont. They killed one and seriously injured the other. Sixteen-year-old Hamlin and fifteen-year-old Savage stabbed and shot both victims after they had gone out looking for some girls to rape. Louis Hamlin was tried as an adult, convicted, and sentenced to forty-five years to life behind bars. Jamie Savage was found guilty of murder and two counts of rape in juvenile court and placed in a juvenile institution until the age of eighteen.

Hardy, Jim, Pete Roland, and **Ron Clements**. On December 9, 1987, Steve Newton, nineteen, was beaten to death by three Missouri teenagers practicing Satanism and abusing drugs. Seventeen-year-olds Jim Hardy, Pete Roland, and Ron Clements were looking for a human sacrifice. They used baseball bats to murder Newton before tying a boulder to him and dumping his body into a well. The young killers were arrested one day later. The jury rejected insanity pleas by Roland and Clements and they were convicted of murder. Hardy pleaded guilty to the murder of Steve Newton. Each killer received a sentence of life in prison with no chance for parole.

Hayer, Talmadge, Norman Butler, and **Thomas Johnson**. On February 21, 1965, Talmadge Hayer,

Norman Butler, and Thomas Johnson assassinated former Nation of Islam Minister Malcolm X as he was giving a speech at the Audubon Ballroom in Harlem, New York. The three Black Muslims were suspected of being part of a faction within the Black Muslim movement dissatisfied with his defection from the organization, his outspokenness, or his stature as an independent black leader. In March 1966, Hayer, Butler, and Johnson were convicted of murder in the first degree for Malcolm X's death and imprisoned. In 1985, Norman Butler—who had changed his name to Muhammad Abdul Aziz—was paroled after spending nineteen years behind bars. In 1998, Nation of Islam leader Louis Farrakhan appointed Aziz to head a Harlem mosque where Malcolm X had preached in the 1950s. Johnson, who became Khalil Islam, was paroled in 1987, and Hayer, who changed his name to Mujahid Halim, was released in 2010. *See also* The 1960s – The Assassination of Malcolm X; Adult Victims, X, Malcolm.

"Hillside Strangler" *see* Bianchi, Kenneth, and Angelo Buono

"Hollywood Slasher" *see* Clark, Douglas D., and Carol Mary Bundy

Jones, Milton, and **Theodore Simmons**. In two shockingly brutal crimes involving the Catholic Church, Milton Jones and Theodore Simmons robbed, stabbed, and bludgeoned to death two priests in Buffalo, New York, on February 24 and March 27, 1987. Their bodies were found in their church rectories. The seventeen-year-old Jones and eighteen-year-old Simmons were apprehended shortly after committing the second robbery-murder. Both killers were tried, convicted, and sentenced to fifty years to life in prison.

Kovzelove, Kenneth, and **Dennis Bencivenga** *see* HATE CRIME KILLERS

Kszepka, Jennifer, Dominic Hendrix, and **Michael Gaumar** *see* Familial Killers – Juvenile

Lambert, Lisa Michelle, Tabitha Buck, and **Lawrence Yunkin.** On December 20, 1991, a romantic triangle turned into jealousy and murder in the death of sixteen-year-old Laurie Show in Lancaster County, Pennsylvania. Lisa Michelle Lambert, nineteen, was the mastermind behind the murder of the romantic rival for her boyfriend, twenty-year-old Lawrence Yunkin. At the time of the murder, Lambert was six months pregnant with Yunkin's child. Lambert and her accomplice, seventeen-year-old Tabitha Buck, brutally murdered Show and fled the scene of the crime with Yunkin. In 1992, Lambert and Buck were convicted of first-degree murder and sentenced to life imprisonment without parole, while Yunkin pleaded guilty to third-degree murder and received a ten to twenty year sentence. On April 22, 1997, a federal judge overturned Lisa Lambert's conviction, citing gross misconduct on the part of the prosecution, and ordered her to be released from prison, which she was. However, in December 1997, the Third U.S. Circuit Court of Appeals reinstated the conviction and Lambert was returned to prison to serve out her term. Lawrence Yunkin served twelve years and was released in 2004.

Lester, John, Scott Kern, and **Jason Ladone** *see* HATE CRIME KILLERS

Leopold, Nathan, and **Richard Loeb.** On May 21, 1924, in a crime that shocked the nation, Nathan Leopold and Richard Loeb brutally murdered fourteen-year-old Bobby Franks while he walked home from school in Chicago, Illinois. Loeb, eighteen and a graduate of the University of Michigan, and Leopold, a nineteen-year-old University of Chicago law student, both came from prominent families, as did Franks. The kidnapping and murder of Bobby Franks, who was randomly chosen by his killers, was well thought out. He was killed with a chisel, doused with hydrochloric acid, and dumped into a concrete drainage culvert. Leopold and Loeb confessed to the murder after evidence pointed towards them. The "trial of the century" took just over a month to complete and included competing psychiatric testimony, over one hundred prosecution witnesses, and highly regarded defense attorney Clarence Darrow, who conceded guilt on the part of his clients but was intent on keeping them from being put to death. In September 1924, due to the age of the defendants and the potential for criminological study, the judge sentenced Nathan Leopold and Richard Loeb to life in prison. In 1936, Loeb was killed in prison by inmate James Day, who slashed him to death with a razor. On March 15, 1958, Leopold was released after thirty-four years in prison. He died on August 30, 1971. *See also* The 1920s – The Kidnap and Murder of Bobby Franks; Child Victims, Franks, Bobby.

"Lonely Hearts Killers," *see* Fernandez, Raymond Martinez, and Martha Beck

Manson, Charles, Charles "Tex" Watson, Susan Atkins, Patricia Krenwinkel, Leslie van Houten, and the **Manson Family**. In 1969, a California cult led by Charles Manson committed a series of high-profile brutal murders that left their mark on American society. Born in 1934, the charismatic Manson, a career criminal, used drugs, sex, and his power of manipulation to attract and control a group of loyal and deadly followers known as the Manson Family. In all, it is believed that Manson and his followers killed at least twenty people from October 1968 to November 1970. It was the vicious murder spree in August 1969 that shocked the nation and proved to be the undoing of the Manson Family. On orders from Charles Manson, Tex Watson, Patricia Krenwinkel, Susan Atkins, Leslie van Houten, and other family members began a "helter skelter," or the start of a race war in which Manson would emerge as a new post-war leader. The killings started at the home of director Roman Polanski and his wife, pregnant actress Sharon Tate. Five people, including Tate and Abigail Folger, were viciously bludgeoned, stabbed, and shot to death. Two days later, the drug-crazed Manson Family stabbed to death businessman Leno LaBianca and his wife Rosemary LaBianca in their home. On December 1, 1969, Manson and his followers were arrested for what became known as the Tate-LaBianca murders. The killers went to trial in 1970 and 1971. On April 19, 1971, Manson, Krenwinkel, van Houten, and Atkins were convicted of the murders and sentenced to death. In a separate trial, Charles Watson was also found guilty of seven murders and conspiracy, and given a death sentence. When the Supreme Court overturned the death penalty in 1972, all the Manson Family member sentences were commuted to life in prison. Other Manson Family members were later convicted of other murders and crimes. Susan Atkins died on September 24, 2009, while battling brain cancer, and Charles Manson died of natural causes on November 19, 2017. The other participants remain behind bars and their applications for parole have been repeatedly denied. *See also* The 1960s – The Tate-Folger-LaBianca Cult Murders; Adult Victims, Tate, Sharon.

Matix, William, and **Michael Platt**. On April 11, 1986, in a shootout with FBI agents, bank robbery suspects William Matix and Michael Platt shot and killed two agents and wounded five others before being killed themselves in Miami, Florida. Matix, thirty-four, and Platt, thirty-two, were believed to have been responsible for a number of bank and armored car robberies before the confrontation on the street. The shootout that took the lives of FBI Special Agents Jerry Dove and Benjamin P. Grogan was one of the worst criminal fatalities in FBI history.

McCrary, Sherman, Carolyn McCrary, Raymond Carl Taylor, Daniel McCrary, and **Ginger Taylor**. Between late 1971 and mid-1972, the McCrary family— led by Sherman McCrary, his wife Carolyn McCrary, and their son-in-law Raymond Carl Taylor— orchestrated a series of robberies, rapes, kidnappings, and homicides across the country. Authorities believe that the McCrary family—including their daughter, Ginger Taylor, and son, Daniel McCrary—committed at least twenty-two abductions and murders. These violent offenses were motivated primarily by robbery and extortion of their victims. In June 1972, the crime wave ended in a shootout near Santa Barbara, California, after an unsuccessful supermarket robbery. The entire five-member McCrary family was arrested a short time later and faced a variety of charges, including armed robbery and harboring of fugitives. All were convicted and sent to prison for terms of anywhere from five years to life in prison. The FBI managed to connect Sherman McCrary, Raymond Taylor, and

Daniel McCrary, in particular, to at least ten female homicides in a number of states.

McKinney, Aaron, and **Russell Henderson** *see* HATE CRIME KILLERS

McVeigh, Timothy J., and **Terry Nichols** *see* The 1990s – The Oklahoma City Bombing of The Alfred P. Murrah Federal Building; Terrorist Killers – Men

Menendez, Lyle, and **Erik Menendez** *see* Familial Killers – Men

Murder, Incorporated. Beginning in the 1920s, a killer enforcement branch of the newly formed national crime syndicate was established that came to be known as Murder, Incorporated. Its purpose was to protect the syndicate's interests as well as enforce its edict among members. Meyer Lansky and Bugsy Siegel, who ran the Bugs and Meyer Mob in New York, started Murder, Inc. and lent out killers to other gangs. These professional killers were highly compensated to work exclusively for Murder, Inc. and included such murderers as Louis Buchalter, Albert Anastasia, Harry Strauss, and Abe Reles. These organized crime killers were believed to have been responsible for hundreds, if not thousands, of murders from the 1920s to the 1940s, using every means of killing—guns, ice picks, knives, and strangulation. When Murder, Inc. member Abe Reles turned informant in 1940, it led to the arrest, imprisonment, and execution of many of its killers—including Buchalter and Strauss—and the beginning of the end of this gang of ruthless mob killers. *See also* Bandits, Outlaws, and Organized Crime Killers – Men, Anastasia, Albert; Buchalter, Louis; Lansky, Meyer; Luciano, Charles; Reles, Abraham; Siegel, Benjamin; Strauss, Harry.

Neelley, Alvin, and **Judith Ann Neelley**. From 1980 to 1982, husband and wife serial killers Alvin Neelley and Judith Ann Neelley murdered at least fifteen women in Alabama, Tennessee, and Georgia. The killings were sexual in nature and included torture and robbery of the victims. Both of the Neelley's had extensive and violent criminal histories by the time they met and joined forces in committing murders and other crimes of violence. It was after the rape and murder of twenty-three-year-old Janice Chatman and the attempted murder of her boyfriend John Hancock in Rome, Georgia, that the Neelley's were identified and arrested. The murderous pair confessed to killing twelve women, giving details of the murders. In order to avoid the death penalty, Alvin Neelley pled guilty to two counts of murder in Georgia and was given two life sentences. Judith Neelley, who claimed to be a battered wife, was fingered by Hancock as the one that shot him. She was tried in Alabama for murder, convicted, and sentenced to death on April 18, 1983. In 1999, the governor of Alabama commuted her sentence to life in prison with no parole. Alvin Neelley died in prison on October 21, 2005. Judith Neelley remains behind bars.

Nelson, George, and **John Paul Chase**. In the 1930s, two of the most notorious and violent gangsters were George "Baby Face" Nelson and John Paul Chase. Born in 1908 in Chicago as Lester M. Gillis, "Baby Face" Nelson was already a career criminal by the time he turned twenty. He met John Chase in 1932 in California shortly after escaping from authorities while on trial for bank robbery. Chase, a railway worker born in 1901, had become involved with an underworld liquor smuggling operation in 1930. The two men became criminal associates and pair murderers, joining the John Dillinger gang in 1934. Nelson and Chase, either alone or together, were believed to have killed at least seven people. The last two—FBI Inspector Samuel Crowley and Special Agent Herman Hollis—were shot and killed in a shootout while pursuing the pair in Illinois in late November 1934. A critically wounded "Baby Face" Nelson died later that evening. Chase was apprehended in California in December 1934 for Inspector Crowley's murder. He went to trial on March 18, 1935, and was convicted. John Paul Chase was sent to Alcatraz Penitentiary and was later transferred to Leavenworth in 1954. He was paroled on October 31, 1966, and died of cancer in 1973.

Ng, Charles Chitat, and **Leonard Lake**. In 1984 and 1985, survivalists and serial killers Charles Chitat Ng and Leonard Lake abducted, sexually enslaved, tortured, and murdered at least eleven people and as many as nineteen in California. Some of the victims were lured to a cabin owned by Lake in Wilseyville in Calaveras County, some 150 miles east of San Francisco. In the cabin, he had constructed a bunker with a cell that was used to imprison, rape, sadistically torture, and murder female victims. Ng, born in Hong Kong in 1961, was an ex-Marine with a criminal record when he met Leonard Lake in the early 1980s. Lake, also a former Marine, was born in San Francisco in 1945 and had a history of mental problems. The two began living together at the Wilseyville cabin in 1984 and soon after began their sexual slavery and serial murder. In 1985, after being arrested for shoplifting, Lake committed suicide. Charles Ng fled to Canada, where he was arrested on July 6, 1985, on charges including attempted murder. It was not until September 1991 that the serial killer was extradited to California to face multiple murder charges in what proved to be one of the longest, most expensive criminal prosecutions in U.S. history. On February 24, 1999, Charles Ng was convicted of the sexual-torture murders of eleven people—including three women and two baby boys. Ng was sentenced to death on June 30, 1999, and is currently on death row at San Quentin prison.

Oklahoma City Federal Building Bombing *see* The 1990s – The Oklahoma City Bombing of The Alfred P. Murrah Federal Building; Terrorist Killers – Men, McVeigh, Timothy J.

Pica, Sean, and **Cheryl Pierson**. On February 6, 1986, teenagers Sean Pica and Cheryl Pierson conspired to murder Cheryl's father, James Pierson, in front of his Long Island, New York home. After being paid as a hit man, the seventeen-year-old Pica, a petty criminal and drug addict, shot to death the forty-two-year-old widower. Both Pica and Pierson were arrested and charged with murder. Cheryl Pierson, a sixteen-year-old cheerleader, claimed the killing was motivated by years of sexual and physical abuse by her father. In 1988, Sean Pica pleaded guilty to manslaughter and was sentenced to eight to twenty-four years in prison. Pierson also pleaded guilty to first-degree manslaughter but, in taking into account her victimization, a judge sentenced her to six months in jail. Cheryl Pierson was released after spending less than four months behind bars. After serving sixteen years in prison, Sean Pica was released in 2003.

Price, Patricia Mildred, and **Rayford Hagood**. In Alabama in 1994, Jesse "Buddy" Price was murdered by his wife, Patricia Mildred Price, and her lover, Rayford Hagood. Contending that he was abusive to her youngest son, whom Hagood claimed to have fathered, the pair beat Price with a pipe, and then used duct tape to wrap him like a mummy, before dumping him in the river, where he drowned. On November 19, 1999, Patricia Price pleaded guilty to murdering her husband, thereby avoiding the death penalty. She was given two life sentences behind bars. Rayford Hagood was convicted of first-degree murder and sentenced to death.

Ryan, Michael, and **Dennis Ryan**. In a brutal murder involving torture, sodomy, mutilation, and a sadistic survivalist cult, Michael Wayne Ryan, his son Dennis Ryan, and other followers murdered James Thimm on the cult's farm in Nebraska in April 1985. Thimm, a cult member, had been chained to a post prior to his death. Under the authority of Michael Ryan, who was the cult leader or "King," fifteen-year-old Dennis shot Thimm in the face. Over the next several days, the Ryans and other cult members inflicted unspeakable horrors on Thimm until he finally died. The Ryans were arrested and charged with murder. Michael Ryan was convicted of first-degree murder and given a death sentence in September 1985. He died of natural causes on May 24, 2015, while on death row. Dennis Ryan was found guilty of second-degree murder and sentenced to ten years to life in prison. He was released from prison in 1997.

Smart, Pamela, William "Billy" Flynn, Patrick Randall, Vance Lattime, and **Raymond Fowler**. On May 1, 1990, profit and infidelity led Pamela Smart, her teenage lover, William "Billy" Flynn, and three other teen accomplices—Patrick Randall, Vance Lattime, and Raymond Fowler—to murder her insurance salesman husband, Gregory Smart. He was shot to death in the couple's condominium in Derry, New Hampshire.

Pamela, twenty-two, was a media services coordinator at the local high school. She was having an affair with the fifteen-year-old Flynn, a student at the school, when she persuaded him and his friends to kill her husband. Following the murder, Pamela used some of the $140,000 she received from Greg's life insurance to buy a new car and move to a different condo in nearby Hampton. Law enforcement authorities pieced together the plot and charged Flynn with murder and Randall, Lattime, and Fowler as accomplices. Pamela Smart was arrested and charged with conspiracy to commit murder in the death of her husband. On March 22, 1991, she was convicted and sentenced to life in prison with no chance of parole. Three of her young accomplices also received life sentences, which were later reduced to twenty-eight years to life for their cooperation in the case. Raymond Fowler received a sentence of fifteen to thirty years in prison. The story was made into a movie.

Smart's appeal for a new trial was rejected in June 1997. In December 1997, two fellow inmates were found guilty of second-degree assault for beating up Pamela Smart in the Bedford Hills Correctional Facility in New York and sent to other prisons. Raymond Fowler was paroled in April 2003 and Vance Lattime was paroled in August 2005. In June 2015, William Flynn and Patrick Randall were both released on parole and will remain on lifetime parole. *See also* The 1990s — The Murder of Gregory Smart; Adult Victims, Smart, Gregory.

Smith, Perry Edward, and **Richard Eugene Hickock.** On November 15, 1959, ex-convicts Perry Edward Smith and Richard Eugene Hickock broke into the home of Herbert Clutter in Holcomb, Kansas, and murdered the wealthy farmer, his wife Bonnie, and their youngest children, sixteen-year-old Nancy and fifteen-year-old Kenyon. The victims of the mass murder died from shotgun blasts to the head at point-blank range. The forty-eight-year-old Herbert Clutter had once served on President Dwight Eisenhower's Agriculture Board and founded the Kansas Wheat Growers Association. Smith, thirty-one, and Hickock, twenty-eight, had targeted the Clutters believing they kept huge sums of money in a house safe. They ended up with less than fifty dollars for their trouble before fleeing. The two murderers were arrested in Las Vegas, Nevada, in early January 1960. They soon confessed to the mass slaying and went to trial on March 22, 1960. Both were found guilty on March 29, 1960, and sentenced to death by hanging. On April 14, 1965, Perry Smith and Richard Hickock were executed at the Kansas State Penitentiary. *See also* The 1950s – The Clutter Family Massacre; Adult Victims, Clutter, Herbert.

Starkweather, Charles, and **Caril Ann Fugate**. In 1958, juvenile serial killers Charles Starkweather and Caril Ann Fugate went on a murder spree in Nebraska and nearby states, leaving eleven victims in their wake, including three members of Fugate's family. The seventeen-year-old Starkweather, who had a history of trouble in his life, was quickly able to win the fourteen-year-old Caril Fugate over. Though the facts of their serial murders, insofar as Fugate's active participation, remain a mystery, the end result is that together they were judged to be responsible for a string of heinous murders by shooting, stabbing, and mutilating their victims over a one-month period. Starkweather raped at least one of their victims. On February 1, 1958, in Douglas, Wyoming, the killing pair was apprehended following the murder of a salesman and a high-speed car chase. Starkweather confessed to killing eleven and implicated Fugate as equally culpable in the murders. Fugate portrayed herself as a victim of her unstable, violent lover. They were both convicted of murder. Starkweather received the death penalty and Fugate was given a life sentence in prison. On June 24, 1959, Charles Starkweather was executed by electrocution in Nebraska. Caril Ann Fugate was paroled in 1976.

"Sunset Slayer" *see* Clark, Douglas D.

Tri-State Gang *see* Bandits, Outlaws, and Organized Crime Killers – Men, Mais, Robert Howard

World Trade Center Bombing *see* The 1990s – The Bombing of the World Trade Center; Terrorist Killers – Men, Yousef, Ramzi

Yesconis, Jennifer Nicole, Jeremiah Lee Wetmore, and **Michael Heath**. In a murder motivated by profit and greed, Jennifer Nicole Yesconis conspired with Jeremiah Wetmore and Michael Heath to murder her parents, Robert and Aletha Yesconis, in their Texas home on January 29, 1994. The twenty-year-old Yesconis, Robert's daughter by a previous marriage, enticed her eighteen-year-old live-in lover, Wetmore, and his seventeen-year-old friend, Heath, to kill her parents in order to collect on her father's insurance policy. Jeremiah Lee Wetmore and Michael Heath pleaded guilty to the murders and were sentenced to prison. After implicating Yesconis in the crime for pay, she was charged with solicitation to commit murder. A jury found Jennifer Yesconis guilty, convicting her of capital murder in the deaths of Robert and Aletha Yesconis. In October 1995, she was sentenced to life in prison with no chance for parole for forty years.

Young, Robert, and **Blanche Wright**. Between 1979 and 1980, contract killers Robert Young and

Blanche Wright murdered four people and attempted to murder two others in New York City. Young and Wright, both African American, had troubled backgrounds when they met in May 1977. Robert Young, a chronic violent offender who was mentally ill, was an escapee from a mental institution. Blanche Wright had been sexually abused as a child. Together they turned to murdering and robbing drug dealers and killing anyone else who stood in their way. In February 1980, a gun battle between the murderous couple, a drug dealer, and his body guard left the dealer and Robert Young dead. Blanche Wright was still on the loose, armed and dangerous. When she was finally apprehended, she confessed to participating in the murders, but claimed she had been forced to do it by Young. A jury felt otherwise, convicting her on several counts of murder. Blanche Wright was sentenced to eighteen years to life for one murder and given fifteen more years to life for two other slayings.

Yousef, Ramzi, and **Eyad Ismoil** *see* Terrorist Killers – Men, Yousef, Ramzi

SECTION 5 – HATE CRIME KILLERS

Beckwith, Byron De La. On February 5, 1994—more than three decades after NAACP activist Medgar Evers was slain in Jackson, Mississippi—white supremacist Byron De La Beckwith was convicted of his murder. Evers was shot to death in front of his home on June 12, 1963. The seventy-three-year-old Beckwith had twice before been tried for Evers' murder, but had escaped conviction after two all-white male juries deadlocked. Evers was a NAACP field secretary when he was gunned down, immediately becoming a martyr for racial violence in the South and helping to further the cause for civil rights. Byron De La Beckwith was sentenced to life in prison with a minimum of ten years behind bars before becoming eligible for parole. Beckwith's conviction was upheld by the Mississippi Supreme Court in 1997. He died in January 2001 at the age of eighty after suffering from numerous ailments. *See also* Adult Victims, Evers, Medgar.

Berry, Shawn Allen, John William King, and **Lawrence Russell Brewer**. In June 1998, a vicious hate crime occurred that sickened the nation due to its brutality when James Byrd Jr., a forty-nine-year-old African American, was beaten and dragged to his death by three white men in Jasper, Texas. White supremacists, Shawn Allen Berry, twenty-four, John William King, twenty-five, and Lawrence Russell Brewer, thirty-two, lured Byrd to their pickup truck. They beat him and then chained him to the truck and dragged him by his ankles for more than three miles. The trio was arrested, charged with murder, and convicted. In early 1999, John King and Lawrence Brewer were sentenced to death. In November 1999, Shawn Berry received a sentence of at least forty years behind bars before being eligible for parole. Lawrence Brewer was executed by lethal injection on September 21, 2011. John King remains on death row awaiting execution and Shawn Berry will be eligible for parole in 2038.

Bowers, Samuel H. On August 21, 1998, former Ku Klux Klan leader Samuel Bowers was convicted of the Mississippi firebombing that killed civil rights activist Vernon Dahmer more than three decades earlier. On January 10, 1966, two cars filled with Klansmen drove up to Dahmer's house and threw gasoline bombs into a window. Dahmer, a farmer who helped other African Americans register to vote, held off the racists with a shotgun as his family escaped the burning house, sustaining injuries that killed him a few hours later. In August 1998, the seventy-three-year-old Bowers—who had spent six years in prison for his role in another high-profile murder case involving the 1964 deaths of three civil rights workers near Philadelphia, Mississippi—was found guilty of murder and arson in Vernon Dahmer's death. He was sentenced to life imprisonment. It was Bowers' fifth trial for the murder. The previous trials took place in the 1960s and ended with the juries deadlocked—two of which consisted of all white jurors. Four other Klansmen involved in Dahmer's murder were convicted in the 1960s. Samuel Bowers died in prison in November 2006 at the age of eighty-two. *See also* The 1960s – The Mississippi Freedom Summer Murders of 1964; Adult Victims, Dahmer, Vernon.

Bryant, Ritch, Randall Lee Rojas, and **Jessica Colwell**. On November 25, 1995, in a vicious racially motivated hate crime attack, white supremacists Ritch Bryant, Randall Rojas, and Jessica Colwell beat a homeless man to death in Lancaster, California. The victim, Milton Walker Jr., was African American. He was murdered behind a McDonald's restaurant. Twenty-year-old skinhead Ritch Bryant led the trio. He hoped the killing would earn him a lightning bolt tattoo from a Mojave Desert white supremacist group. Bryant and Rojas, twenty-four, were convicted of first-degree murder in November 1999 and sentenced to life in prison without parole. Jessica Colwell, who was sixteen when the attack occurred, was convicted of involuntary manslaughter. On November 24, 1999, she was sentenced to nine years in prison for her role in Walker's death.

Caston, James, Charles E. Caston, and **Hal Crimm**. After nearly thirty years, white racists James Caston, sixty-six, his brother Charles E. Caston, sixty-four, and a half-brother, Hal Crimm, fifty, were brought to justice for the April 22, 1970, murder of Rainey Pool. Pool, an African American sharecropper with one arm, was attacked by a mob outside a nightclub and beaten to death near the small town of Louise, Mississippi. His body was thrown off a bridge into the Sunflower River. Charged with the murder after pressure from Pool's family, James and Charles Caston and Hal Crimm were found guilty of manslaughter on November 13, 1999. Each man was sentenced to twenty years in prison.

Cowan, Frederick. On February 28, 1977, a vengeful-minded suspended employee, Frederick Cowan, entered the offices of the Neptune Moving Company in New Rochelle, New York, with a small arsenal, killing four employees. The racist killer, who singled out black workers, also shot and killed a police officer as he arrived on the scene. In spite of pleas by his mother to surrender, Cowan put a gun to his head and killed himself.

Essex, Mark Robert James. On January 7, 1973, a sniper atop a New Orleans Howard Johnson Motor Lodge shot and killed six people and wounded fifteen others before being shot to death by Marine sharpshooters. The gunman, identified as twenty-three-year-old Mark Robert James Essex, was an African American who reportedly developed a hatred of whites while in the Navy. The rifle Essex used in the hotel assault was said to be the same one that killed two police officers in New Orleans on New Year's Eve, leading some law enforcement authorities to believe the mass murder was part of a national conspiracy to kill police. This was never proven.

Kovzelove, Kenneth, and **Dennis Bencivenga.** In a hate crime on November 8, 1998, two teenagers planning to join the Army went on a shooting spree, killing two Mexican laborers. The eighteen-year-old Bencivenga drove a pickup truck while the seventeen-year-old Kovzelove unloaded a semiautomatic rifle in back at their victims. In January 1989, Dennis Bencivenga confessed to participating in the double murder to an Army recruiter. Kenneth Kovzelove was arrested and charged with murder after enlisting in the Army, where he hoped to become a paratrooper. He admitted having a hatred for Mexicans, which prompted the murders. On October 13, 1989, Kenneth Kovzelove pleaded guilty to two counts of first-degree murder. He was sentenced to fifty years to life in prison. Dennis Bencivenga was sentenced to fourteen years in prison.

Lester, John, Scott Kern, and **Jason Ladone**. On December 19, 1986, in a racially motivated hate crime that stunned the nation, white teenagers John Lester, Scott Kern, and Jason Ladone, along with a number of other youths used bats and fists to severely beat three African American men in a predominantly white neighborhood in New York known as Howard Beach. One of the victims, in his bid to escape the attackers, ran onto a highway and was struck and killed by a car. Lester and Kern, both eighteen, and Ladone, seventeen, were arrested, tried, and convicted of manslaughter. They received sentences ranging from ten to thirty years in prison to five to fifteen years behind bars. Some of the other participants in the hate crime were convicted on riot charges. Jason Ladone was released in 2000, John Lester was released and deported back to Britain in 2001, and Scott Kern was released in 2002.

McKinney, Aaron, and **Russell Henderson**. On October 12, 1998, gay college student Matthew Shepard died as a result of being brutally beaten by Aaron

McKinney and Russell Henderson in Laramie, Wyoming. The hate crime murder took place when McKinney and Henderson, both twenty-one, lured Shepard from a bar near the University of Wyoming campus the night of October 6, 1998. After hitting him in the head eighteen times with a .357-caliber pistol, the men stole Shepard's wallet and tied him to a fence, leaving him for dead in frigid temperatures. McKinney and Henderson were arrested and charged with kidnap and murder. On April 5, 1999, Russell Henderson pleaded guilty to felony murder and kidnapping, avoiding a possible death sentence. He received two consecutive life sentences with no chance for parole. On November 2, 1999, a jury convicted Aaron McKinney of felony murder. He was sentenced to two consecutive life terms behind bars with no parole. The vicious nature of the attack galvanized and increased efforts towards anti-hate crime legislation. *See also* Adult Victims, Shepard, Matthew.

Purdy, Patrick Edward *see* SCHOOL KILLINGS

Ray, James Earl. On April 4, 1968, black civil rights campaigner, the Reverend Martin Luther King Jr., was shot to death on the balcony of the Lorraine Hotel in Memphis, Tennessee. On June 8, 1968, James Earl Ray was arrested in Britain for King's assassination. He had escaped from prison a year earlier and his 30.06 Remington hunting rifle was believed to be the murder weapon. At his murder trial, Ray pled guilty on March 10, 1969. He was sentenced to ninety-nine years in prison. Three days later, Ray recanted his guilty plea. He claimed he was innocent and had been set up by a mysterious man named "Raoul" as part of a broader conspiracy to assassinate King. Ray insisted on being granted a new trial to prove it. In spite of some fuel to the conspiracy theory debate over the years—including support of Ray by Martin Luther King Jr.'s family—he was never granted a new trial. James Ray died of liver disease due to cirrhosis at the age of seventy on April 23, 1998, still professing his innocence in King's death. *See also* The 1960s – The Assassination of Dr. Martin Luther King Jr.; Adult Victims, King, Martin Luther, Jr.

Smith, Roland. On December 8, 1995, vengeful African American activist Roland Smith entered a Harlem clothing store armed with a .38-caliber revolver and opened fire before setting the business ablaze, killing eight people, including himself. Smith, fifty-one and a career criminal, barricaded himself and the other victims inside the store and exchanged gunfire with the police prior to setting several fires that erupted in flames. The racially motivated mass murder at a white owned Freddie's Fashion Mart across the street from the famed Apollo Theater was in response to the store's plan to expand at the expense of a black owned record shop next door.

White, Dan *see* Politically Motivated Killers – Men

SECTION 6 - SCHOOL KILLINGS

Allaway, Edward Charles. On July 12, 1976, Edward Charles Allaway went on a shooting rampage on the college campus of California State University at Fullerton, killing seven and wounding two others. The shootings occurred in the basement of the school library where the thirty-seven-year-old Allaway worked as a janitor. He was arrested shortly thereafter at a nearby Hilton Inn Hotel where his estranged wife worked. In court, Allaway was found not guilty by reason of insanity, and confined to the Napa State Hospital. He was released back into the community as sane in 1992.

Carneal, Michael Adam. On December 1, 1997, Michael Adam Carneal went on a shooting rampage at Heath High School in West Paducah, Kentucky, killing three students and wounding five. The fourteen-year-old murderer had recently watched a movie, "The Basketball Diaries," in which in a dream the main character enters a classroom and shoots five classmates.

Carneal was arrested and charged as an adult with the multiple murders and attempted murders, which left one victim paralyzed. On October 6, 1998, Michael Carneal pleaded guilty but mentally ill to the charges. He was sentenced to life imprisonment with no chance for parole for twenty-five years.

Dann, Laurie Wasserman. On May 20, 1988, Laurie Wasserman Dann went on a shooting rampage at Hubbard Woods Elementary School in Winnetka, Illinois. She killed one eight-year-old second grader and wounded six others before eventually taking her own life. The thirty-year-old divorced babysitter had a history of mental illness and was licensed to own three guns when she went on her deadly rampage in the North Shore suburb. Prior to the shooting, Dann had given milk laced with arsenic to preschoolers she had been babysitting, sent poisoned food to nearly two dozen homes and two fraternity houses, and tried to burn down a daycare center and school. After hiding out in a house, Laurie Dann shot herself to death. An autopsy on the killer revealed that she was being treated for a psychiatric disorder with the experimental drug clomipramine.

Elliott, Nicholas. Nicholas Elliott was a shy boy with learning problems. In 1987, his mother put him in a private Christian school in Virginia, hoping he would improve. One of only a few African American students in the mostly white school, Elliott was teased and often the victim of racial slurs. On December 16, 1988, at age sixteen, he arrived at the school with a semiautomatic pistol and 200 rounds of ammunition. He entered a classroom and began shooting. When the gun jammed, he was disarmed and arrested. He had killed a teacher and seriously injured another. Charged as an adult,

Nicholas Elliott pleaded guilty to murder and attempted murder. He was sentenced to life in prison plus 114 years on December 13, 1989.

Ferris, Nathan. Living in Missouri, Nathan Ferris was an overweight honor student described as a loner. On March 2, 1987, at age twelve, he took his father's .45-caliber pistol to school in his gym bag. He pulled the gun out and threatened his classmates. When one of them teased him about it being a toy, Nathan Ferris shot and killed the boy and then himself. One week earlier, Ferris had told a friend he was going to shoot everyone at school.

Harris, Eric, and **Dylan Klebold**. On April 20, 1999, students Eric Harris and Dylan Klebold entered Columbine High School in Littleton, Colorado, armed with semiautomatic weapons. They opened fire on students and teachers in the cafeteria, library, and other rooms, killing thirteen and injuring twenty-five before committing suicide. Harris, eighteen, and Klebold, seventeen, wore long black trench coats during the murder spree as part of a so-called "Trench Coat Mafia" they belonged to at the school. In addition to firearms, the teenage killers planted homemade bombs and explosive devices throughout the school and in cars on school grounds. The attack was motivated by revenge against those Harris and Klebold felt had wronged and ridiculed them. A journal found in Harris's bedroom indicated that the murderers had hoped to kill as many as 500 people in their deadly rampage. At least one other person was convicted of illegally selling one of the firearms used by the killers. *See also* The 1990s – The Mass Murder at Columbine High School.

Johnson, Mitchell, and **Andrew Golden**. On March 24, 1998, Mitchell Johnson and Andrew Golden, dressed in camouflage, opened fire on fellow students and teachers outside a middle school in Jonesboro, Arkansas, killing five and wounding ten others. Johnson, fourteen, and Golden, twelve, pulled a fire alarm to lure classmates and teachers out of the school. The two boys, hiding in the nearby woods, began shooting. The killers then headed to a van packed with ammunition, food, and camping gear, before being arrested by police. In court, Johnson pled guilty to five counts of murder and ten counts of battery. Golden tried to plead temporary insanity. On August 12, 1998, both Mitchell Johnson and Andrew Golden were adjudicated delinquent by a juvenile court judge, the equivalent to a guilty verdict in the criminal court. As juvenile murderers in Arkansas, the state was only able to hold the two until they reached the age of twenty-one.

Kehoe, Andrew. A farmer and school board member, Andrew Kehoe lived in Bath, Michigan. On May 18, 1927, he blew up a school there, killing forty-five people, thirty-seven of them children. He had planted explosives under the school. After the school bombing, he blew up his pickup truck, killing the Bath school superintendent and himself. No explanation was ever given as to why he did it.

Kinkel, Kip. On May 21, 1998, fifteen-year-old Kip Kinkel entered Thurston High School in Springfield, Oregon. Heavily armed, he went on a shooting rampage killing two students and wounding twenty-five others. The day before, after being expelled from school when a stolen gun was found in his locker, Kinkel shot to death his mother and father. He was arrested and charged as an adult with four counts of aggravated murder and twenty-six counts of attempted murder. He claimed voices in his head had commanded him to kill. Psychiatrists testified in court that Kinkel was psychotic, schizophrenic, and severely depressed. In September 1998, Kip Kinkel pleaded guilty to murdering his parents and two students, agreeing to serve at least twenty-five years behind bars. However, following a six-day hearing, the judge sentenced the multiple murderer to 112 years in prison with no chance for parole.

Loukaitis, Barry. In Moses Lake, Washington, on February 2, 1996, Barry Loukaitis killed two students and a teacher at Frontier Junior High School. An honor student, fourteen-year-old Loukaitis wore a black outfit, cowboy boots, cowboy hat, ammunition belt, and long coat when he entered an algebra class. He was carrying two handguns, a high-powered rifle, and seventy-eight rounds of ammunition. Loukaitis shot and killed the forty-nine-year-old algebra teacher, Leona Caires, while she wrote on the blackboard. He then shot and killed two fourteen-year-old students, Manuel Vela and Arnold Fritz. Loukaitis then gathered the students at the back of the room, planning to take a hostage. He tried to force the gym teacher, Jon Lane—who had entered the room when he heard shots—to be his hostage. Lane was able to grab the rifle and pin Loukaitis to the wall until police arrived and arrested him. He confessed to the killings and claimed he had only meant to kill Manuel Vela for making offensive remarks. Tried as an adult, Loukaitis was convicted of two counts of aggravated murder and one count of second-degree murder. In October 1997, Barry

Loukaitis was sentenced to two consecutive life terms plus 205 years.

Purdy, Patrick Edward. On January 17, 1989, Patrick Edward Purdy entered the school yard of Cleveland Elementary School in Stockton, California. Armed with a semiautomatic AK-47, he opened fire and killed five children, wounded twenty-nine other children, and one teacher, before killing himself. The twenty-six-year-old drifter wore combat fatigues and fired at least 106 rounds in gunning down five Southeast Asian refugees. Purdy had an extensive criminal history and was described by authorities as antisocial. There was no clear-cut motive for the shootings, though the chosen victims would suggest it was a hate crime.

Ramsey, Evan. On February 19, 1997, sixteen-year-old Evan Ramsey arrived at Bethel Regional High School in Bethel, Alaska, armed with a shotgun and ammunition. He entered the main lounge area where students had gathered before school started. Ramsey began firing, wounding several students. He then went to the principal's office and shot him, and then continued down the hall still firing. When it was over, Ramsey had killed Joshua Palacious, sixteen, and the principal, Ron Edwards, age fifty. Two others were wounded, though not seriously. After Ramsey's arrest, police learned he had told friends he was going to kill the principal and Palacious and make them suffer. In 1998, he was tried as an adult and charged with two counts of first-degree murder. He was found guilty of the murder, one count of attempted murder, and fifteen counts of assault. On December 2, 1998, Evan Ramsey was sentenced to 210 years in prison.

Spencer, Brenda. Born in 1963, Brenda Spencer was a drug user, truant, and thief who loved guns and violence. She lived with her father in San Diego, California, after her parents divorced. For Christmas in 1978, Spencer's father gave her a .22-caliber semiautomatic rifle and 500 rounds of ammunition. In early January 1979, she told her friends she was planning something that would get her on TV. On January 29, 1979, Spencer watched and waited in her house—which was directly across the street from the Cleveland Elementary School—while the principal opened the gates for the waiting children. She suddenly began firing, killing the principal and a custodian. Spencer fired the rifle for twenty minutes, wounding nine young children and a police officer. She surrendered six hours later after talking to the media and police on the phone while they surrounded the house. She told them she did it for fun and because she didn't like Mondays. Spencer was charged with two counts of murder and multiple counts of aggravated assault. She was convicted of the two murders and one count of assault. Brenda Spencer was sentenced to two concurrent terms of twenty-five years to life and forty-eight years for assault with a deadly weapon.

Whitman, Charles Joseph. On July 31, 1966, former Marine and ex University of Texas student Charles Whitman stood atop the thirty story watchtower building on the campus in Austin, Texas. The twenty-five-year-old, armed with an arsenal of weapons and ammunition, opened fire on everything that moved, killing fourteen on campus and wounding more than thirty. In total, Whitman took sixteen lives—including stabbing to death his mother and wife the previous night—before police broke through a barricade he had set up and shot him to death. Whitman had complained of having violent impulses and severe headaches. An autopsy revealed that he had a brain tumor, but it was concluded that it was not directly related to his shooting rampage. *See also* The 1960s – Massacre at the University of Texas.

Wurst, Andrew. On April 24, 1998, fourteen-year-old Andrew Wurst entered the banquet hall at James W. Parker Middle School in Edinboro, Pennsylvania, armed with a .25-caliber handgun and shot to death science teacher John Gillette. The shooting was apparently random by the mentally disturbed student. Wurst was arrested and charged as an adult with criminal homicide, aggravated assault, possession of marijuana, and other offenses. In September 1998, Andrew Wurst pled guilty to third-degree murder and was sentenced to thirty to sixty years in prison.

PART III

A CENTURY OF VICTIMS

ADULT VICTIMS

"The Black Dahlia" *see* Short, Elizabeth

Bradshaw, Franklin J. On July 23, 1978, multimillionaire Mormon businessman Franklin J. Bradshaw was shot to death by his seventeen-year-old grandson, Mark Schreuder, at his warehouse in Salt Lake City, Utah. The murder was ordered by Bradshaw's daughter, Frances Schreuder. The socialite, who lived in Manhattan with her three children from two failed marriages, had wanted her father dead because she feared he would disinherit her. Bradshaw had amassed his fortune through ownership of a chain of auto parts stores. In 1981, Marc Schreuder was arrested and charged with murder. The following year, he was convicted of second-degree homicide in the death of Franklin Bradshaw. After fighting extradition to Salt Lake City in 1983, Frances Schreuder was found guilty of first-degree murder by a jury in the death of her father. The forty-five-year-old Schreuder was sentenced to life imprisonment. Marc Schreuder was paroled in 1995 and Frances was paroled in 1996. She died on March 30, 2004. *See also* The 1970s – The Murder of Multimillionaire Mormon Franklin J. Bradshaw; Familial Killers – Women, Schreuder, Frances.

Cermak, Anton Joseph. On February 15, 1933, the mayor of Chicago, Anton Joseph Cermak, was gunned down at a parade in Miami, Florida. The bullet was intended to strike the President-elect of the United States, Franklin D. Roosevelt. Born in 1873 in what is now the Czech Republic, Cermak moved to Chicago in 1890 and rose up the ranks of the local Democratic Party before becoming mayor in 1931. He was highly influential in Illinois, siding with Roosevelt during the 1932 Democratic National Convention. The fifty-nine-year-old Cermak was mortally wounded while riding in Roosevelt's open convertible and died on March 6, 1933. His assassin was Guiseppe Zangara, a bricklayer and naturalized Italian. The thirty-two-year-old killer pleaded guilty to murder on March 10, 1933, and was given a death sentence. On March 20, 1933, Guiseppe Zangara was put to death in the electric chair in the fastest legal execution of the 20th century. *See also* Politically Motivated Killers – Men, Zangara, Guiseppe.

Chaney, James, Andrew Goodman, and **Michael Schwerner** *see* The 1960s – The Mississippi Freedom Summer Murders of 1964

Clutter, Herbert. On November 15, 1959, wealthy farmer Herbert Clutter was shot to death along with his wife, Bonnie, and the youngest two of their four children—Nancy, sixteen, and Kenyon, fifteen—in their home in Holcomb, Kansas. The Clutter family was slain during a robbery by ex-convicts Richard Eugene Hickock and Perry Edward Smith, who believed Clutter kept a large stash of money in a safe in the house. In fact, the forty-eight-year-old Clutter, who was once a member of President Dwight Eisenhower's Farm Credit Board and the founder of the Kansas Wheat Growers Association, had less than fifty dollars in the house and no safe. Smith, thirty-one, and Hickock, twenty-eight, were arrested in Las Vegas, Nevada, in early January 1960. Both confessed to the horrific crime and were put on trial on March 22, 1960. Seven days later on March 29, 1960, the two men were found guilty of the mass slaying of the Clutter family and sentenced to die in the gallows. On April 14, 1965, Perry Smith and Richard Hickock were executed at the Kansas State Penitentiary. *See also* The 1950s – The Clutter Family Massacre; PAIR AND GROUP KILLERS, Smith, Perry Edward.

Crane, Bob. On June 29, 1978, actor Bob Crane was bludgeoned to death in his apartment in Scottsdale, Arizona. Born in 1928 in Waterbury, Connecticut, the forty-nine-year-old star of the 1960s television series "Hogan's Heroes" was a family man who also had a secret lifestyle: he was addicted to sex. Crane liked to take nude pictures of himself and women and also filmed himself having sex with women. At the time of his death, he was starring in the romantic comedy "Beginner's Luck," performing in dinner theaters across the country. Cast member, Victoria Berry, discovered Crane's body the following day. Suspected in Crane's death was his friend, videotape equipment salesman John Henry Carpenter, who had been with the actor in the hours leading up to his death. In 1994, Carpenter went to trial for Bob Crane's murder and was acquitted by the jury. The homicide case remains unsolved.

Crum-Wills, Julie Anne. On April 14, 1996, model-actress Julie Anne Crum-Wills was found stabbed to death in her Boca Raton, Florida, apartment. The thirty-three-year-old divorced former research chemist won the Mrs. Texas title in 1992 and appeared as an extra in several movies, including "Striptease." Suspected in her death was her boyfriend Steven Flaco, the beneficiary of her life insurance policy. The case has been shown twice on the crime series "America's Most Wanted" and remains unsolved.

Dahmer, Vernon. On January 10, 1966, civil rights activist Vernon Dahmer was murdered when members of the Ku Klux Klan went to his house in Hattiesburg, Mississippi, and fired shots into it while tossing gasoline bombs inside a window. The killing was in response to Dahmer's role in getting other African Americans to vote. While four Klansmen were convicted during the 1960s for their participation in Dahmer's murder, it was only in August 1998 that the man who masterminded the killing was brought to justice. Samuel H. Bowers, a seventy-three-year-old former leader of the Ku Klux Klan, was convicted of ordering the firebombing attack that killed Vernon Dahmer. He was sentenced to life in prison and died in November 2006 at the age of eighty-two. *See also* HATE CRIME KILLERS, Bowers, Samuel H.

Evers, Medgar. On June 12, 1963, NAACP activist and field secretary Medgar Evers was shot and killed getting out of a car in front of his home in Jackson, Mississippi. Three decades later, white supremacist Byron De La Beckwith was convicted of killing Evers and sentenced to life in prison. Beckwith's conviction was upheld by the Mississippi Supreme Court in 1997. He died in January 2001 at the age of eighty. Evers' murder helped draw national attention to the civil rights movement and racial injustice and bigotry in the South. *See also* HATE CRIME KILLERS, Beckwith, Byron De La.

El-Shabazz, El-Hajj Malik *see* X, Malcolm

Falater, Yarmila. On January 16, 1997, Yarmila Falater was brutally stabbed and drowned in the family swimming pool outside her home in Phoenix, Arizona. The killer was her husband of twenty years—and the father of their two children—Scott Falater. A Mormon electrical engineer for Motorola, the forty-two-year-old Falater claimed that he had been sleepwalking when he killed his wife. Yarmila Falater, a preschool aid, was stabbed forty-four times with a hunting knife and then her head was held under water in the swimming pool. Falater was arrested and charged with murder. In spite of a history of sleepwalking and work-related stress that, according to his attorneys, could have triggered the attack, Scott Falater was convicted by a jury of first-degree murder on June 24, 1999. On January 10, 2000, a judge sentenced him to life in prison with no chance of parole. *See also* The 1990s – The Case of the Sleepwalker Killer; Intimate Killers – Men, Falater, Scott.

Folger, Abigail *see* The 1960s – The Tate-Folger-LaBianca Cult Murders; Adult Victims, Tate, Sharon Marie; PAIR AND GROUP KILLERS, Manson, Charles

Gaye, Marvin. On April 1, 1984, singer Marvin Gaye was shot to death by his father, Marvin P. Gay Sr., at the family's home in Los Angeles, California. Born in 1939 in Washington, D.C., as Marvin Pentz Gay Jr., Gaye later added the "e" to his last name. He gained fame as a rhythm and blues singer in the 1960s with Motown Records—recording such classics as "You're All I Need To Get By" and "What's Going On"—and winning two Grammy awards in his career. Marvin Gaye moved in with his parents after reportedly suffering from depression, paranoia, and drug dependency. Following a physical confrontation with his father, who was an ordained minister, Gaye was killed with a gun he had given to the elder Gay. The singer was forty-four years old at the time of his death. Marvin Gay Sr. pled no contest to voluntary manslaughter and was given a sentence of five years' probation. He died in 1998 at the age of eighty-four. *See also* Celebrity Killers – Men, Gay, Marvin P., Sr.

Goldman, Ronald *see* The 1990s – The Murders of Nicole Brown Simpson and Ronald Goldman; Adult Victims, Simpson, Nicole Brown

Hall, Reverend Edward Wheeler *see* The 1920s – The Murders of Reverend Edward Wheeler Hall and Choir Singer Eleanor Mills

Hartman, Phil. On May 28, 1998, comic actor Phil Hartman, forty-nine, was found dead in his Encino, California, home. His wife, forty-year-old Brynn Hartman, shot him to death and then killed herself. Phil Hartman was best known as a cast member of the TV show "Saturday Night Live" from 1986 to 1994. In 1989, he shared an Emmy with the writing staff of the show. He also did frequent voice-over work and appeared in several commercials and movies. The couple married in 1987 and had two children. Brynn Hartman, a former model, was known to be temperamental and jealous. At the time of the murder-suicide, she was legally drunk and traces of cocaine and a prescription anti-depressant drug were found in her system. *See also* Celebrity Killers – Women, Hartman, Brynn.

Hoffa, James "Jimmy" Riddle. Born on February 14, 1913, in Indiana, James Riddle Hoffa disappeared on July 30, 1975, and was never seen again. Working in Detroit, Michigan, Hoffa organized his first union in 1931 and went on to organize several other unions, including the International Brotherhood of Teamsters. In 1957, Hoffa became the president of the Teamsters union, becoming one of the most powerful men in the country. Federal investigators pursued him throughout the 1950s and 1960s and labeled him a "ruthless" union official on the take. In 1964, he was found guilty of jury tampering and sentenced to eight years in prison. Shortly after that, he was sentenced to an additional five years when he was convicted in Chicago of fraud and conspiracy in handling a union benefits fund. President Richard Nixon commuted his sentence on December 23, 1971. That same day, he returned home and plotted his strategy to once again become the president of the Teamsters union. When he disappeared in 1975, his family and the police felt he had been murdered. Federal investigators believe mob bosses had him killed to prevent him from regaining the union presidency. Hoffa's disappearance remains a mystery. In 1982, James Riddle Hoffa was declared legally dead.

Kennedy, John Fitzgerald. On November 22, 1963, John Fitzgerald Kennedy, the thirty-fifth President of the United States, was assassinated in Dealey Plaza in downtown Dallas, Texas, as he rode in an automobile procession. Born in Massachusetts in 1917, Kennedy, the first Roman Catholic president, was shot to death at the age of forty-six by Lee Harvey Oswald. The former Marine and Marxist who spent a few years living in the Soviet Union, took a job at the Texas School Book Depository five weeks before assassinating Kennedy through an upper floor window of the depository. After killing a policeman later, Oswald was apprehended at a theater and charged with two murders. On November 24, 1963, Dallas nightclub owner Jack Ruby gunned down Lee Harvey Oswald while he was in police custody. Ruby died from a blood clot on January 3, 1967. In spite of conspiracy theorists, with the deaths of the principals, the world would forever be left wondering if a conspiracy ever existed to assassinate President Kennedy. *See also* The 1960s – The Assassination of President John F. Kennedy; Politically Motivated Killers – Men, Oswald, Lee Harvey; Ruby, Jack.

Kennedy, Robert Francis. On June 5, 1968, Robert Francis Kennedy, U.S. senator from New York, was gunned down in the pantry of the Ambassador Hotel in Los Angeles, California. The former U.S. Attorney General and brother of the late President John F. Kennedy, was leaving a victory celebration after winning the California presidential primary when he was fatally wounded by a gun held by Sirhan Bashara Sirhan, a twenty-five-year-old Palestinian Arab. Kennedy died the next day at the age of forty-two. The assassin was quickly apprehended and charged with first-degree murder. His trial began on January 7, 1969. Sirhan was convicted of the murder of Robert Kennedy and five additional counts on April 17, 1969, and given a death sentence. This was later commuted to life in prison when California outlawed the death penalty in 1972. Sirhan remains incarcerated at Richard J. Donovan Correctional Facility in San Diego County, having been turned down for parole numerous times.

See also The 1960s – The Assassination of Robert F. Kennedy; Politically Motivated Killers – Men, Sirhan, Bashara Sirhan.

King, Martin Luther, Jr. On April 4, 1968, civil rights leader Dr. Martin Luther King Jr. was assassinated at the Lorraine Hotel in Memphis, Tennessee. On June 8, 1968, James Earl Ray, an escaped convict, was arrested for the murder. Born in 1929 in Atlanta, Georgia, the thirty-nine-year-old King was a Baptist minister who devoted his life to racial equality and integration through nonviolence. In 1964, at the age of thirty-five, he won the Nobel Peace Prize. On March 10, 1969, James Earl Ray pleaded guilty to King's murder and was sentenced to ninety-nine years behind bars. Three days later, Ray withdrew his plea, claiming he was innocent and had been manipulated into confessing guilt as part of a broader conspiracy. He stuck to his position for nearly three decades until his death on April 23, 1998, from liver diseases. Though James Earl Ray continues to be regarded as King's assassin, conspiracy theories still abound. *See also* The 1960s – The Assassination of Dr. Martin Luther King Jr.; HATE CRIME KILLERS, Ray, James Earl.

LaBianca, Leno, and **Rosemary LaBianca** *see* The 1960s – The Tate-Folger-LaBianca Cult Murders; PAIR AND GROUP KILLERS, Manson, Charles

Lennon, John. On December 8, 1980, John Lennon—of Beatles fame—was shot to death in front of his apartment building, the Dakota, where he lived with his wife, Yoko Ono, in Manhattan, New York. His killer was an obsessed, delusional fan named Mark David Chapman, whom he had given an autograph to earlier in the day. Born in Liverpool, England, in 1940, Lennon was part of the successful British rock group,

The Beatles, who produced a string of hit songs mostly during the 1960s before the group broke up in 1970. Lennon and his second wife, Yoko, were returning from a recording session when the shooting occurred. Chapman was arrested after the crime without incident. In 1981, he pleaded guilty to murdering Lennon and was sentenced to twenty years to life at Attica Prison in upstate New York. He has been denied parole nine times. *See also* The 1980s – The Killing of John Lennon; Celebrity Killers – Men, Chapman, Mark David.

McKinley, William. On September 6, 1901, William McKinley—the 25th President of the United States—was assassinated. He was shot to death at a reception while attending the Pan-American Exposition in Buffalo, New York. His assassin was twenty-eight-year-old Leon Czolgosz, a blacksmith from Cleveland, Ohio. Czolgosz was found guilty of first-degree murder in late September 1901, and sentenced to death. On October 29, 1901, he was executed in the electric chair at Auburn Prison. *See also* The 1900s – The Assassination of President William McKinley; Politically Motivated Killers – Men, Czolgosz, Leon.

Menendez, Jose and Mary *see* The 1980s – The Murders of Jose and Mary Menendez

Milk, Harvey. On November 27, 1978, gay activist and San Francisco City Supervisor Harvey Milk was gunned down in City Hall along with San Francisco Mayor George Moscone. Their killer was embittered ex-City Supervisor Dan White. Born in 1931, the forty-seven-year-old Milk—often referred to as the "Mayor of Castro Street"—was the first openly gay person elected to the San Francisco Board of Supervisors. He became a close political associate of Mayor Moscone and played a key role in the enactment of the city's first gay civil rights ordinance. White, a thirty-two-year-old former policeman, had opposed the bill and resigned from the board in protest. Upon murdering Milk and Moscone, White turned himself in to the authorities. During his trial, he used a "Twinkie Defense," blaming the killings on eating too much junk food, causing him to have a "diminished capacity." On May 21, 1979, a jury convicted White of manslaughter in the deaths of Moscone and Milk, sentencing him to seven years in prison. After being released on parole in January 1984, Dan White committed suicide on October 21, 1985. *See also* Adult Victims, Moscone, George; Politically Motivated Killers – Men, White, Dan.

Miller, Craig *see* Sowers, Mary Elizabeth

Mills, Eleanor *see* The 1920s – The Murders of Reverend Edward Wheeler Hall and Choir Singer Eleanor Mills

Moore, Harry T., and **Harriet Moore**. On December 25, 1951, pioneer civil rights workers Harry T. Moore and his wife, Harriet, were murdered when their home in Mims, Florida, exploded from a bomb placed in their bedroom. It was the couple's twenty-fifth wedding anniversary and the first homicides of prominent human rights activists in the country. Harry Moore, forty-six, and Harriet Moore, forty-nine, organized the first chapter of the NAACP in Brevard County, Florida. Both were educators and Mr. Moore, as the executive secretary of the Progressive Voters League, played a key role in getting tens of thousands of African Americans in Florida registered to vote. The murderers of the Moores were never apprehended and the case remains officially classified as unsolved.

Moscone, George. On November 27, 1978, San Francisco Mayor George Moscone and gay activist and

City Supervisor Harvey Milk were shot to death by former City Supervisor Dan White in City Hall. Born in 1929, the forty-nine-year-old Moscone, a former County Supervisor and state senator, had aligned himself with Milk—the first openly gay person to be elected to the San Francisco Board of Supervisors—in the passage of the city's first gay civil rights statute. White, a thirty-two-year-old ex-policeman, had opposed the measure and resigned from the Board of Supervisors. After the double homicide, he turned himself in to authorities. Using a defense of "diminished capacity," due to eating too many Twinkies and other junk food, Dan White was convicted of manslaughter on May 21, 1979, and sentenced to a seven-year prison term. On January 6, 1984, he was paroled and then committed suicide by asphyxiation on October 21, 1985. *See also* Adult Victims, Milk, Harvey; Politically Motivated Killers – Men, White, Dan.

Nash, Frank *see* The 1930s – The Kansas City Massacre

Opsahl, Myrna Lee. On April 21, 1975, Myrna Lee Opsahl was shot to death in a robbery of the Crocker National Bank in Carmichael, California. The forty-two-year-old wife of a surgeon, mother, and devoted church member, had gone to the bank to deposit the weekend collection from the local Seventh Day Adventist Church. She was the victim of a double-barreled shotgun blast as part of a robbery committed by four members of the radical group, the Symbionese Liberation Army (SLA). Though Opsahl's killer was never brought to justice, according to kidnapped heiress and SLA participant Patricia Hearst, one of the armed robbers was Kathleen Soliah. The former SLA fugitive, now known as Sara Jane Olson, pled guilty in 2001 to two counts of possessing explosives with intent to murder stemming from her SLA activities in the 1970s and sentenced to fourteen years in prison. After serving seven years, she was released on March 17, 2009.

Quintanilla, Selena *see* Selena

Sabich, Vladimir "Spider". On March 21, 1976, Vladimir Sabich, a champion skier, was shot to death in his Aspen, Colorado, home. His killer was live-in lover, Claudine Longet. The thirty-four-year-old former showgirl and actress and the thirty-one-year-old Sabich lived with her three children from her marriage to Andy Williams in the Rocky Mountain resort area. Longet claimed that the shooting with Sabich's .22-caliber pistol was accidental. Authorities thought otherwise and on April 8, 1976, she was charged with reckless manslaughter and pleaded innocent. On January 14, 1977, Claudine Longet was found guilty of criminally negligent homicide. She was sentenced to thirty days in jail, given two years' probation, and ordered to pay a fine of $250. *See also* The 1970s – The Murder of Champion Skier Vladimir Sabich; Celebrity Killers – Women, Longet, Claudine.

Selena. Selena Quintanilla, the Grammy winning Latino recording artist, was shot and killed on March 31, 1995, at the age of twenty-three. Yolanda Saldivar, thirty-four, murdered Selena outside a motel room in Corpus Christie, Texas. Saldivar—the former president of Selena's fan club and current head of Selena Etc. Inc.—was suspected of embezzling funds from the company and was going to be fired when the shooting occurred. In 1987, Selena won the Tejano Music Award for best female vocalist and performer of the year. She married her band's guitarist, Chris Pérez, in 1992. A jury convicted Yolanda Saldivar of first-degree murder on October 23, 1995. She was sentenced to life in prison. *See also* Celebrity Killers – Women, Saldivar, Yolanda.

Shepard, Matthew. On October 7, 1998, Matthew Shepard, a gay college student, was severely beaten, tied to a fence, and left to die by his attackers outside of Laramie, Wyoming. His comatose body was discovered eighteen hours later. The twenty-one-year-old University of Wyoming student died on October 12, 1998. Charged with his kidnapping and murder were Aaron McKinney and Russell Henderson, both twenty-one. The brutal attack shocked the nation and put the spotlight on hate crimes. On April 5, 1999, Henderson pleaded guilty to felony murder and kidnapping. McKinney was convicted of felony murder on November 3, 1999. Both men were sentenced to two consecutive life terms in prison. *See also* HATE CRIME KILLERS, McKinney, Aaron.

Sheppard, Marilyn Reese. On July 4, 1954, thirty-one-year-old Marilyn Reese Sheppard was bludgeoned to death in the family's suburban Cleveland, Ohio, home. The housewife was four months pregnant at the time she was murdered. Dr. Samuel Sheppard, her thirty-year-old husband, was charged with the murder after authorities rejected his insistence that the real killer was a "bushy-haired intruder." Sheppard was indicted and put on trial for his wife's murder on October 28, 1954. A jury convicted him of second-degree murder on December 21, 1954, and Sheppard was sentenced to life in prison. In 1966, the conviction was overturned by the U.S. Supreme Court due to prejudicial publicity. A retrial resulted in Sheppard's acquittal on November 16, 1966. Suffering from depression and liver disease, Sam Sheppard died on

April 6, 1970, at the age of forty-six. Richard Eberling, a former window washer for the Sheppards, was suspected by some as being Marilyn Sheppard's killer. Eberling, who was convicted of another murder in 1989, died in prison in 1998. In April 2000, a Cleveland jury ruled against Samuel Sheppard's son, Samuel Reese Sheppard, in a wrongful imprisonment civil suit. *See also* The 1950s – The Murder of Marilyn Sheppard.

Short, Elizabeth. On January 15, 1947—while on her way to a shoe repair shop in the Leimert Park section of Los Angeles, California—a housewife discovered the horrific remains of a young woman. Her pale body had been completely separated at the waist, with the two parts morbidly posed about a foot apart. Multiple lacerations to the face made identification nearly impossible. Through fingerprints, the FBI identified the victim as Elizabeth Short, a twenty-two-year-old attractive, aspiring actress. She had been called "The Black Dahlia" because of her long black hair and her desire for wearing black dresses. The mutilation and murder of Short created frenzy in Hollywood and elsewhere. In spite of an exhaustive investigation, the police were never able to officially solve Elizabeth Short's homicide. *See also* The 1940s – The Case of The Black Dahlia.

Simpson, Nicole Brown. On June 12, 1994, thirty-five-year-old Nicole Brown Simpson and her waiter friend, twenty-five-year-old Ronald Goldman, were brutally stabbed to death outside of her swank townhouse in Brentwood, California. Simpson, an ex-waitress, was married to former Heisman Award winner and professional football star Orenthal James (O. J.) Simpson, before the couple divorced in 1992. The Simpsons' stormy relationship had been marked by physical and psychological abuse. On June 17, 1994, O. J. Simpson, forty-seven, was arrested for the murder of his ex-wife and Goldman. The arrest came after a low speed chase of Simpson's Bronco by police with a national television audience watching. Opening statements in his murder trial began on January 24, 1995. With the nation continuing to be riveted, the controversial trial ended on October 3, 1995, with Simpson being acquitted in the murders of Nicole Simpson and Ron Goldman. On February 4, 1997, a civil jury found the ex-football player liable in the double homicide, awarding a total of $33.5 million in damages. Simpson continues to declare his innocence of the murders. *See also* The 1990s – The Murders of Nicole Brown Simpson and Ronald Goldman.

Smart, Gregory. On May 1, 1990, Gregory Smart, a twenty-four-year-old insurance salesman, was shot and killed in the condo where he lived with his twenty-two-year-old bride, Pamela Smart, in Derry, New Hampshire. The two were married for less than a year when the murder occurred. Arrested and charged with the homicide were Pamela Smart, her fifteen-year-old student lover, Billy Flynn, and two of his friends, Patrick Randall and Vance Lattime. Smart, who worked for the Winnacunnet High School's media office, seduced and manipulated Flynn into carrying out her deadly plan—the motive being insurance money and getting out of a marriage in which both parties were unfaithful. Pamela Smart's trial was widely publicized as a young wife turned cold-blooded killer. On March 22, 1991, she was found guilty of conspiracy to commit murder in the death of Gregory Smart and sentenced to life in prison with no chance for parole. Her teenage co-conspirators also received life sentences, which were later reduced to twenty-eight years to life behind bars. Smart's appeal for a new trial was rejected in June 1997. In December 1997, two fellow inmates were found guilty of second-degree assault for beating up Pamela Smart in the Bedford Hills Correctional Facility in New York and sent to other prisons. In April 2003, Raymond Fowler was paroled and in August 2005, Vance Lattime was paroled. William Flynn and Patrick Randall were both released on parole in June 2015 and will remain on lifetime parole. *See also* The 1990s – The Murder of Gregory Smart; PAIR AND GROUP KILLERS, Smart, Pamela.

Sobek, Linda. On November 16, 1995, model Linda Sobek was sodomized and strangled to death by photographer Charles Rathbun in the Los Angeles National Forest, then buried in a shallow grave. The twenty-seven-year-old Sobek, a former Los Angeles Raiders cheerleader, was lured to her death on the promise of a modeling assignment for a magazine. An autopsy report revealed that Linda Sobek was legally intoxicated at the time of death. Charles Rathbun was convicted on November 1, 1996, of first-degree murder and sodomy. On December 16, 1996, Rathbun was sentenced to life imprisonment with no possibility of parole. *See also* Celebrity Killers – Men, Rathbun, Charles.

Sowers, Mary Elizabeth, and **Craig Miller**. On November 2, 1980, college sweethearts Mary Elizabeth Sowers and Craig Miller were abducted at gunpoint from a Sacramento, California, shopping center. Engaged to be married on New Year's Eve 1981, the twenty-two-year-old Miller and twenty-one-year-old Sowers had just left a Founder's Day dance when they were kidnapped by serial killer husband and wife team,

Gerald and Charlene Gallego. Unbeknownst to the coeds, the Gallegos had already murdered eight people as part of their "sex slave" fantasies. Sowers and Miller became the ninth and tenth victims when they were assaulted and shot to death.

Their vicious killers were arrested on November 17, 1980, by FBI agents in Omaha, Nebraska. Both were charged with the murders of Sowers and Miller. Charlene Gallego, twenty-four, turned state's evidence against her thirty-four-year-old husband, Gerald Gallego, and avoided the death penalty. Gallego's trial for the kidnap and murder of Sowers and Miller began in November 1982. On June 21, 1983, the serial murderer was convicted and sentenced to death. A year later, he was found guilty of two additional murders in Nevada and given the death penalty. Charlene Gallego served nearly seventeen years in prison after her plea bargain and was released in July 1997. Gerald Gallego died of cancer while on death row in Nevada on July 18, 2002. *See also* The 1970s – The Sex Slave Killings; PAIR AND GROUP KILLERS, Gallego, Gerald Armond.

Stratten, Dorothy. On August 14, 1980, model-actress Dorothy Stratten was murdered by her husband, Paul Snider. The twenty-year-old Stratten, a native of Vancouver, British Columbia, was the *Playboy* magazine Playmate of the Year in 1980. Snider, who was jealous and vindictive, shot her to death after he learned she was planning to divorce him. After the murder, he committed suicide by turning the gun on himself. *See also* The 1980s – The Murder of Playmate Dorothy Stratten; Celebrity Killers – Men, Snider, Paul.

Stuart, Carol. On October 23, 1989, Carol Stuart— a thirty-year-old tax lawyer who was seven months pregnant—was shot to death in her car after leaving a birthing class in the Mission Hill district of Boston, Massachusetts. Also shot was her husband, Charles Stuart, a thirty-year-old manager of a furrier. It was Charles Stuart—who was shot in the abdomen—who reported the crime to police on his car cell phone. He identified the perpetrator as an African American man, striking fear and condemnation into the hearts of white America. Christopher Stuart was delivered by Cesarean section and died seventeen days later due to complications from the fatal wounds Carol Stuart had sustained. Law enforcement authorities investigating the murder turned their suspicions toward Charles Stuart, who was having an affair and experiencing financial problems at the time of his wife's death. On January 3, 1990, Stuart's brother, Matthew Stuart, admitted to police that Charles had given him the .38-caliber pistol believed to be the murder weapon and other incriminating items. The following day, as police began to close in on Charles Stuart for his wife's murder, he killed himself by jumping off a bridge into the Mystic River. *See also* The 1980s – The Murder of Carol Stuart; Intimate Killers – Men, Stuart, Charles.

Tate, Sharon Marie. On August 9, 1969, actress Sharon Tate was the victim of a vicious murder—along with four other people, including coffee heiress Abigail Folger—at the home she shared with her director husband Roman Polanski in Beverly Hills, California. The victims were killed by members of the Charles Manson Family on orders from Manson, who saw it as the start of a race war that he called "helter skelter." Born in 1943, the twenty-six-year-old Tate, who starred in the film "Valley of the Dolls," was eight months pregnant when she was murdered. On August 11, 1969, the Manson followers added two more victims to their sadistic murderous spree—Leno and Rosemary LaBianca, who lived nearby. The killers, including Charles Manson, were arrested, tried, convicted of murder, and sentenced to death. When California outlawed capital punishment in 1972, the cult members' sentences were commuted to life in prison. Susan Atkins died on September 24, 2009, while battling brain cancer, and Charles Manson died of natural causes on November 19, 2017. The other participants remain behind bars and their applications for parole have been repeatedly denied *See also* The 1960s – The Tate-Folger-LaBianca Cult Murders; PAIR AND GROUP KILLERS, Manson, Charles.

Taylor, William Desmond *see* The 1920s – The Murder of William Desmond Taylor

Tippit, J. D. *see* Politically Motivated Killers – Men, Oswald, Lee Harvey

Tupper, Jack *see* The 1970s – The Murder of Restaurateur Jack Tupper

Versace, Gianni. Italian designer Gianni Versace was shot to death in front of his Miami Beach, Florida, mansion on July 15, 1997. Versace, fifty-one and openly gay, was best known for his flamboyant collections. Twenty-seven-year-old serial killer Andrew Cunanan shot the designer twice in the head at close range. Between April and May 1997, Cunanan murdered four other men. After the murder of Versace, the FBI initiated one of the largest unsuccessful manhunts in U.S. history—with alleged sightings of Cunanan in virtually every state. On July 23, 1997, Cunanan shot and killed himself while hiding out in a houseboat in Miami Beach. *See also* Serial Killers – Men, Cunanan, Andrew Phillip.

Wahl, David Ronald. On November 12, 1995, following a lover's quarrel, twenty-seven-year-old David Ronald Wahl of Tualatin, Oregon, was pushed to his death from a 320-foot cliff at a state park near Cannon Beach, Oregon. His badly decomposed, headless body washed ashore two weeks later on the Washington coast. Wahl's twenty-three-year-old girlfriend, Linda Jean Stangel, was charged with his murder, which came amid a tumultuous, violent relationship where both had problems with alcohol abuse. In January 1997, Stangel was found guilty of second-degree manslaughter and received a seventy-five month prison sentence. She was released in February 2003. *See also* Intimate Killers – Women, Stangel, Linda Jean.

Walcker, Marie *see* The 1900s – The Death of Marie Walcker

White, Stanford *see* The 1900s – The Murder Case of Harry Thaw

X, Malcolm. On February 21, 1965, former Black Muslim Malcolm X was assassinated while delivering a speech in the Audubon Ballroom in Harlem, New York. Born in 1925 in Omaha, Nebraska, as Malcolm Little, the thirty-year-old ex-con became a powerful voice in the Black Muslim movement as a Minister of the Nation of Islam. He had left the black organization and changed his name to El-Hajj Malik El-Shabazz when he was shot to death by Black Muslims Norman Butler, Talmadge Hayer, and Thomas Johnson. In March 1966, the three men were convicted of first-degree murder and sentenced to prison. Butler (now Muhammad Abdul Aziz) was released on parole in 1985. Johnson, who became Khalil Islam, was paroled in 1987, and Hayer, who changed his name to Mujahid Halim, was released in 2010. *See also* The 1960s – The

Assassination of Malcolm X; PAIR AND GROUP KILLERS, Hayer, Talmadge.

Youk, Thomas. On September 17, 1998, Thomas Youk was administered a lethal dose of drugs by Dr. Jack Kevorkian, a retired pathologist and proponent of doctor assisted suicide. The fifty-three-year-old Youk was suffering from Lou Gehrig's disease. Kevorkian, seventy-one, had gained a national reputation for assisted suicide, admitting to participating in at least 130 such deaths in various states around the country. On November 25, 1998, after sending a videotape of Youk's death by injection to CBS, Kevorkian was charged with murder, assisted suicide, and delivering a controlled substance. The man referred to as "Dr. Death" had previously been tried four times on assisted suicide charges. Three trials resulted in acquittals and the other a mistrial. In Oakland County, Michigan, on March 26, 1999, Dr. Jack Kevorkian was found guilty of murder in the second degree and delivery of a controlled substance. He was sentenced to serve ten to twenty-five years behind bars. On June 1, 2007, he was released on parole. He died on June 3, 2011, at age eighty-three. *See also* Other Killers – Men, Kevorkian, Jack.

CHILD VICTIMS

Clutter, Kenyon and Nancy *see* The 1950s – The Clutter Family Massacre; PAIR AND GROUP KILLERS, Smith, Perry Edward.

Franks, Bobby. On May 21, 1924, in one of the century's most sensationalized murder cases, fourteen-year-old Bobby Franks was abducted, bludgeoned to death, and then mutilated in Chicago by fellow teenagers, Richard Loeb and Nathan Leopold. Both Franks and his killers were from prominent Chicago families. The well planned kidnapping and murder, which may have been sexually motivated, shocked the nation. Franks was apparently a random but targeted victim as a child of wealth and a potentially large ransom. The eighteen-year-old Loeb and nineteen-year-old Leopold confessed to the homicide after their arrests. Both pleaded guilty to the crime. During their trial, attorney Clarence Darrow argued on their behalf against the death penalty. In September 1924, Nathan Leopold and Richard Loeb were sentenced to life imprisonment. Loeb was stabbed to death by a fellow inmate with a razor in 1936. Leopold was released from prison in 1958, having spent thirty-four years behind bars. He died in 1971. *See also* The 1920s – The Kidnap and Murder of Bobby Franks; PAIR AND GROUP KILLERS, Leopold, Nathan.

Jones, Adrianne. High school student Adrianne Jones was beaten and shot to death outside of Fort Worth, Texas, on December 4, 1995, because of a romantic rivalry. Convicted of the sixteen-year-old's murder were former lovers David Graham and Diane Zamora. Both were attending prestigious military academies when arrested in September 1996. In 1998, Zamora and Graham were found guilty of capital murder and sentenced to life in prison. They will both be eligible for parole in 2036. *See also* PAIR AND GROUP KILLERS, Graham, David.

Kanka, Megan. On July 29, 1994, seven-year-old Megan Kanka was brutally raped and murdered by a twice-convicted sex offender who lived across the street from her in Hamilton Township, New Jersey. Jesse K. Timmendequas, a thirty-six-year-old sexual predator, was arrested and tried for the kidnapping, aggravated sexual assault, and murder of Megan Kanka. On May 31, 1997, Timmendequas was convicted on all counts in connection with the crime and sentenced to death. Megan's parents, Richard and Maureen Kanka's determined efforts to change the laws led to New Jersey's passage of Megan's Law in October 1994, requiring public notification when a convicted sex offender is released into the community. A similar federal law was enacted on May 17, 1996. Timmendequas was on New Jersey's Death Row until December 17, 2007, when the New Jersey legislature abolished the state's death penalty. His sentence was commuted to life in prison without parole. *See also* Child Killers – Men, Timmendequas, Jesse K.

Klaas, Polly Hannah. On October 1, 1993, Polly Hannah Klaas was abducted from her home during a slumber party in Petaluma, California, by Richard Allen Davis and murdered. The disappearance of the twelve-year-old led to a nationwide manhunt involving thousands of volunteers and law enforcement personnel. In early December her body was found thirty miles from where she had been kidnapped. Davis, a twice-convicted kidnapper, was arrested and charged with murdering Polly Klaas. He was ordered to stand trial in May 1994 and was subsequently convicted of kidnapping and murder. On September 26, 1996, Richard Davis was sentenced to death. He is currently on death row at San Quentin prison. The tragedy of Polly Klaas's murder resulted in the formation of the Klaas Foundation for Children in 1997. Its objective is to prevent crimes against children. *See also* Child Killers – Men, Davis, Richard Allen.

Lamana, Walter *see* The 1900s – The Kidnapping and Murder of Walter Lamana

Likens, Sylvia. On October 26, 1965, Sylvia Likens was discovered dead by police in a second floor bedroom of a house owned by Gertrude Baniszewski in Indianapolis, Indiana. The sixteen-year-old girl had been the victim of horrifying crimes at the hands of Baniszewski, her children, and some neighborhood boys. Likens and her fifteen-year-old sister, Jenny, were staying with Baniszewski while their parents traveled around the Midwest with the circus. Gertrude Baniszewski was a thirty-six-year-old divorcée who struggled to make ends meet between low paying jobs and child support payments from her ex-husband. Taking her frustrations out on the Likens sisters, she led vicious attacks on them that included severe beatings and cigarette burns.

Sylvia Likens bore the brunt of the assaults and mistreatment, as she was burned more than 150 times, was forced to insert a Coke bottle into her vagina as part of a sadistic striptease, and starved into eating and drinking her own feces and urine. Baniszewski punctuated the torture by heating a needle and using it to carve the words "I am a prostitute and proud of it" on Sylvia's stomach. Sylvia Likens died after Baniszewski slammed her head onto a concrete floor to silence her from alerting neighbors of the atrocity. After being arrested for murder, Gertrude Baniszewski was convicted in 1966 and sentenced to life in prison. Despite public protests, she was released on parole in 1985. *See also* Child Killers – Female, Baniszewski, Gertrude.

Lindbergh, Charles Augustus, Jr. On March 1, 1932, twenty-month-old Charles Augustus Lindbergh Jr., son of Charles and Anne Lindbergh, was abducted from the family home near Hopewell, New Jersey. His remains were discovered on May 12, 1932, some four and a half miles away near Mount Rose, New Jersey. Arrested for the kidnapping-murder was Bruno Richard Hauptmann, a thirty-five-year-old German carpenter. Hauptmann was indicted for murder on October 8, 1934. After a five-week trial, he was found guilty on February 13, 1935, and sentenced to death. After several denied appeals, Bruno Hauptmann was electrocuted on April 3, 1936. *See also* The 1930s – The Lindbergh Baby Kidnapping and Murder; Child Killers – Men, Hauptmann, Bruno Richard.

Moxley, Martha. On October 30, 1976, fifteen-year-old Martha Moxley was bludgeoned and stabbed to death outside her family's home in the private Bell Haven community in Greenwich, Connecticut. Her corpse was found the following day under a pine tree on the three-acre estate belonging to the Moxleys. The night of her death, Moxley had attended a gathering of teenagers across the street at the Skakel residence. The murder weapon was a six-iron from a golf club set identified as belonging to the Skakel family. Among the suspects in the homicide were teenagers Thomas and Michael Skakel, nephews of the late Senator Robert Kennedy and Ethel Skakel Kennedy, his widow. On January 19, 2000, Michael Skakel was arrested for murder in Greenwich following the findings of a grand jury convened in 1998. The thirty-nine-year-old Skakel was charged as a juvenile because he was only fifteen at the time of the crime. On August 17, 2000, a juvenile court judge ruled that there was sufficient evidence for Michael Skakel to stand trial for the murder of Martha Moxley. In January 2001, Skakel's case was transferred to adult court. On June 7, 2002, Michael Skakel was found guilty in the murder of Martha Moxley and sentenced to twenty years to life behind bars. On May 4, 2018, the conviction was vacated by the Connecticut Supreme Court. *See also* The 1970s – The Murder of Martha Moxley.

Parker, Marion *see* The 1920s – The Kidnap and Murder of Marion Parker

Phagan, Mary. On April 27, 1913, thirteen-year-old Mary Phagan was found beaten and strangled in the basement of the National Pencil Factory in Atlanta, Georgia. She worked at the factory, putting erasers on pencils. The four-foot-eleven-inch girl had gone to the factory the previous day to pick up her paycheck. Arrested for her brutal murder was the factory superintendent, Leo Frank. The twenty-seven-year-old Jewish man from Brooklyn was convicted of the crime on August 25, 1913, and sentenced to die by hanging. Frank's sentence was commuted to life imprisonment in June 1915. With anti-Semitism sentiments running high, a mob calling itself the Knights of Mary Phagan removed Leo Frank from the Milledgeville prison by force and lynched him. His killers were never tried for the murder. *See also* The 1910s – The Murder of Mary Phagan; Child Killers – Men, Frank, Leo.

Ramsey, JonBenet. On December 26, 1996, six-year-old JonBenet Ramsey was found murdered in her parents' home in Boulder, Colorado. The child beauty queen was beaten, strangled, and possibly sexually assaulted. A three-page ransom note was found by Patsy Ramsey, JonBenet's mother, some eight hours before JonBenet's body was discovered in a basement room by her father, John Ramsey. The well-to-do Ramseys became the chief suspects in the brutal murder that was characterized by sloppy police work and tainted evidence as well as controversies about the district attorney's investigation into the murder. In September 1998, a grand jury was convened to hear evidence in the case. Just before the October 20, 1999, grand jury deadline, it was announced that no indictments would be issued due to insufficient evidence. The governor of Colorado declined to appoint a special prosecutor in the case. However, the targets of the investigation continued to be the parents of JonBenet Ramsey. Handwriting samples given by Patsy Ramsey could not rule her out as the person who wrote the ransom note. In May 2000, John and Patsy

Ramsey held a news conference to announce they had each passed a lie detector test in denying any involvement in their daughter's death. Boulder law enforcement officials dismissed the results, as the tests were not conducted by the FBI and thereby not considered credible. In August 2000, the Ramseys were interviewed by Boulder police investigators and neither cleared nor implicated in JonBenet's murder. On July 9, 2008, the Boulder district attorney officially cleared the Ramseys of involvement in the case, citing new DNA sampling and testing procedures. In June 2006, Patsy Ramsey died from ovarian cancer. The case remains unsolved. *See also* The 1990s – The Murder of JonBenet Ramsey.

Walsh, Adam. On July 27, 1981, six-year-old Adam Walsh was abducted from a department store in Hollywood, Florida. Two weeks later, his severed head was found in a canal along the Florida Turnpike. Suspected in the kidnapping-murder was convicted killer Ottis Elwood Toole—who confessed to the crime in October 1983 while incarcerated. He later retracted the confession and died in prison without ever being charged with the murder. Adam's parents, John and Reve Walsh, turned their tragedy into a crusade to help other missing and exploited children. They helped to gain passage of the 1982 Missing Children Act and the 1984 Missing Children's Assistance Act, resulting in the establishment of the National Center for Missing and Exploited Children. In 2006, President George W. Bush signed into law The Adam Walsh Child Protection and Safety Act, establishing the national child abuse registry and broadening the national sex offender registry. In December 2008, the police officially closed the case with the belief that Ottis Toole had murdered Adam

Walsh. The abduction and murder of Adam Walsh was the basis of two television movies, "Adam" and "Adam: The Song Continues."

Weinberger, Peter. On July 4, 1956, one-month-old Peter Weinberger was abducted from his carriage in the family home in Westbury, New York. A ransom note was left demanding $2,000 for the infant's safe return. An analysis of handwriting specimens and the ransom note resulted in the arrest of Angelo LaMarca on August 23, 1956. The taxi dispatcher confessed to the kidnapping. Shortly thereafter, authorities discovered the remains of Peter Weinberger in an area off the highway. LaMarca was charged with, tried, and convicted of kidnapping and murder. On December 14, 1956, he was sentenced to death. In spite of numerous appeals, Angelo LaMarca was executed in Sing Sing prison's electric chair on August 7, 1958. *See also* The 1950s – The Kidnapping and Murder of Peter Weinberger; Child Killers – Men, LaMarca, Angelo.

PART IV

A CENTURY OF MURDERERS AND MURDERS OUTSIDE OF THE U.S.

BLACK WIDOWS

Becker, Marie Alexander. Born in 1877 in Belgium, Marie Becker began her murder for profit killings at the age of fifty-five using digitalis, a heart stimulant. She murdered her first husband by poisoning him in 1932 and received a large insurance payment. Then she murdered her lover, rather than marry him. Becker used the money from that insurance settlement to open a dress shop for senior women. Over four years she became friends with ten of her customers, stole their assets, and poisoned them. She made the mistake of telling a friend about the ten women, who then told the police. Marie Becker was arrested in October 1936 and confessed to twelve murders. The bodies were exhumed and the digitalis discovered. She was tried and found guilty and received a life sentence. On June 11, 1942, Marie Becker died in prison.

de Melker, Daisy. Born in 1885 in South Africa, Daisy de Melker was a classic Black Widow who murdered for profit. She murdered two husbands by serving them arsenic in their meals to collect on their life insurance. Her son, Rhodes Cowle, helped her with the murders. However, he began telling friends about the murders and then tried to blackmail his mother. She murdered him with arsenic shortly after that. Authorities, suspicious over her son's sudden death, exhumed the bodies of her three victims and discovered arsenic poisoning. Daisy de Melker was arrested and confessed to the crimes. She was found guilty and hanged on December 30, 1932.

Renczi, Vera. Born in 1903 in Hungary, Vera Renczi used arsenic to murder thirty-five people because she could not deal with rejection. Renczi married her first husband while she was a teenager, and had a son. She became jealous and her husband soon disappeared. Renczi's second husband also disappeared after she became convinced he was unfaithful. She didn't marry again, but had at least thirty-two lovers who all eventually suddenly disappeared. Her son disappeared after he accidentally discovered the remains of her missing husbands and lovers and tried to blackmail his mother, so she poisoned him. When her last lover's wife complained to police about her missing husband after he had gone to Renczi's house, they went there to investigate. Renczi immediately confessed. In the basement, they found the remains of thirty-five men, each preserved in an expensive zinc coffin. Vera Renczi was found guilty of murder and sentenced to life in prison, where she eventually died.

MASS MURDERERS

Asahara, Shoko, Yasuo Hayashi, Masato Yokoyama, Yoshihiro Inoue, and other members of the Aum Shinrikyo cult. On March 20, 1995, thirteen people were killed and thousands of others injured when deadly sarin gas was released in the subway in Tokyo, Japan. Implicated in connection with the mass murder were followers of the Japanese Aum Shinrikyo doomsday cult, including its spiritual leader, Shoko Asahara. Asahara and a number of other Aum members were convicted of charges stemming from the gas attack—called Japan's worst act of terrorism in recent memory—and sentenced to death. Shoko Asahara and several other cult members were executed in early July 2018.

Borel, Eric. On September 24, 1995, a French teenager named Eric Borel went berserk in bludgeoning to death his family members with a hammer and baseball bat. The victims included his mother, stepfather, and brother. Borel then armed himself with a .22-caliber rifle and walked into the nearby village of Cuers, where he began to shoot anyone in sight before fatally wounding himself. In all, thirteen people died at the hands of Eric Borel, whose father had recently died from cancer. The mass murderer was a neo-Nazi and had posters of Adolf Hitler on the walls of his bedroom, possibly contributing to the massacre.

Bryant, Martin. On April 28, 1996, Martin Bryant became Australia's worst mass murderer. Armed with an arsenal of weapons, including an AR-15 and FN semiautomatic rifle, he went on a shooting spree in Tasmania's historical town of Port Arthur, leaving thirty-five dead and wounding many others. The twenty-eight-year-old Bryant, who had a history of mental problems, shot and killed twenty in the Broken Arrow Café before methodically executing others he came in contact with. He ended up at a seaside bed and breakfast, Seascape Cottage, where he took hostages and was soon surrounded by more than 200 police officers. Several hours later, Bryant set the cottage on fire and ran out with his clothes ablaze, leaving behind the dead bodies of two hostages. Police arrested the mass murderer and soon-to-be suspected serial killer, implicating him in the deaths of five people, including his father. Found to be legally sane, Mark Bryant went to trial for the mass killing on November 7, 1996. He was found guilty of his crimes and sentenced to life imprisonment without the possibility of parole. Bryant, who has since attempted suicide multiple times, is kept in protective custody in prison.

de Franca, Genildo Ferreira. On May 21 and 22, 1997, former soldier Genildo Ferreira de Franca—dressed in camouflage and carrying an automatic pistol and silencer-equipped .38-caliber revolver—mowed down fifteen people in the town of São Goncalo do Amarante, some 1,800 miles northeast of São Paulo, Brazil. His victims included his wife, mother-in-law, ex-wife, and her parents. Police killed the twenty-seven-year-old drug-crazed mass murderer on the second day of his killing spree, after he shot himself. A suicide note found on his body blamed the murders on his ex-father-in-law spreading rumors that he was gay, which he denied. A fellow army friend and drug addict, Francisco de Assis dos Santos, confessed to assisting de Franca in the first five murders.

Delgado, Campo Elias. On December 4, 1986, mentally unstable Campo Elias Delgado went on a shooting spree in his native Bogotá, Columbia. He killed twenty-eight people before he was shot and killed by police. The fifty-two-year-old electronics engineer had served in the United States Air Force and had returned home to live with his mother, whom he hated. She was his first victim, as he shot her to death and then set her on fire. Twenty-one of Delgado's victims were dining in a posh restaurant where he opened fire, shooting indiscriminately.

Flink, Mattias. In June 1994, Mattias Flink armed himself with an AK-5 and additional ammunition clips and opened fire in the town of Falun, Sweden. He killed seven people and wounded two others. The murder spree by Flink, who was in the Swedish army, came after some heavy drinking and anger over the breakup of a relationship. Mattias Flink was shot by police and arrested two hours after the rampage. He was tried, convicted, and given life imprisonment. His sentence was commuted to thirty-two years in prison in 2010. In June 2014, Flink was released from prison.

Goldstein, Baruch. In February 1994, Baruch Goldstein, a Jewish settler, went on a shooting rampage at a Hebron mosque in Israel, gunning down twenty-nine Arab worshippers. Goldstein was quickly overcome by a vengeful mob and beaten to death. The massacre by the physician, an immigrant from New York, occurred at a shrine known as the Cave of the Patriarchs and the traditional burial place of Abraham. Though the killer was Jewish, the road leading to the mosque—occupied by 500 Jewish settlers—was closed for five years to Palestinian traffic, for fear of retaliation.

Gray, David. On November 13, 1990, David Gray became New Zealand's worst mass slayer when he went on a shooting spree in the small seaside hamlet of Aramoana in the Otago province in the South Island. He killed thirteen people before he was shot and killed by police.

Hamilton, Thomas. On March 13, 1996, former scoutmaster and pedophile Thomas Hamilton went berserk at a primary school in Dunblane, Scotland. Carrying four guns, he shot to death seventeen people, including sixteen children, before committing suicide. The mass murder occurred forty miles from Edinburgh by the revenge-seeking Hamilton, who had been dismissed by the Boy Scouts in the early 1980s due to his unnatural attraction to young boys.

Hirasawa, Sadamichi. In January 1948 in a Tokyo suburb in Japan, Sadamichi Hirasawa murdered twelve bank employees. Hirasawa was a bank robber who arrived at the Teikoku Bank just before it closed. He informed the bank employees that he was a doctor who had orders to inoculate the staff for dysentery and they each drank a drink mixture he gave them. Ten of the sixteen died immediately and two more died later. They had all been poisoned with cyanide. After poisoning them, he stole all the money he could find, which totaled about $720 U.S. dollars. Hirasawa was arrested several days later when one of the surviving employees identified him. He was convicted in 1950 and sentenced to death. In 1987, he died in prison at the age of ninety-five.

Jones, Jim, and the Jonestown Massacre. On November 18, 1978, Guyana was the sight of the century's worst mass murder-suicide when 913 people were either executed or took their own lives as part of the Reverend Jim Jones People's Temple, located in Northwest Guyana. The communal village was commonly referred to as "Jonestown." Jones and his followers had moved to Guyana from the U.S. in hopes of establishing a self-sufficient community using the principles of socialism. But it all went horribly wrong when Jim Jones and more than 900 of his estimated 1,100 people in Jonestown swallowed poisonous drinks. Those who refused to commit suicide were shot to death. Jones himself was among the victims. Preceding the mass suicide-murder were the murders of U.S. Congressman Leo J. Ryan and four others, who had come to Guyana to investigate reports of people of Jonestown being held against their will, human rights violations, and other abuses. A drug-crazed, paranoid Jones and his supporters' horrific actions were apparently prompted by fears that political forces would destroy the People's Temple and kill its members.

Lepine, Marc. In December 1989, graduate student Marc Lepine went into the University of Montreal École Polytechnique and opened fire on females, killing fourteen students. He then shot himself to death. The twenty-five-year-old French-Canadian's love for guns and hatred of women—feminists in particular—led to the slaughter. A suicide note sent to a Canadian newspaper blamed his troubles and disadvantages in life on feminists, having developed a hit list to that effect.

Qashash, Saeed. In June of 1998, Jordanian student Saeed Qashash gunned down a fellow student and eleven of his family members in Jordan, hiding the corpses behind a brick wall in his family's basement. Among the victims were the nineteen-year-old killer's parents, four sisters, and two brothers. Qashash was arrested and confessed to the mass murder, blaming it on family pressures to pass his school final exams. In November 1998, Qashash was convicted of his crimes and sentenced to death. He was hanged on June 6, 1999.

Ryan, Michael. On August 19, 1987, Michael Ryan went on a killing spree in Hungerford, Berkshire, sixty miles west of London. He shot to death sixteen people and wounded fourteen. The twenty-seven-year-old shooter—described as a loner with a penchant for television violence and guns—wore combat fatigues as he embarked on his homicide mission. Among the victims was Ryan's elderly mother. After holing up at the John O'Gaunt High School for four hours, surrounded by police, Michael Ryan used a 9mm pistol to take his own life. Following the massacre, the British government took measures to outlaw the right to bear firearms and reduce violence on television.

Vaganov, Artur. On June 7, 1997, Russian soldier Artur Vaganov shot and killed ten fellow soldiers and wounded three more while stationed in a unit in Abkhazia in Georgia, the former republic of the Soviet Union. The mentally unbalanced sergeant then shot himself to death in a murder spree that was reminiscent of others in recent years by soldiers in a demoralized Russian military.

SERIAL KILLERS

"Acid Bath Murderer" *see* Haigh, John George

Barbosa, Daniel Camargo. In Columbia, Daniel Barbosa was convicted of brutally raping and killing a nine-year-old girl. He escaped from prison in 1986 and fled to Ecuador, where he began raping and killing children. In fourteen months, fifty-five young girls had disappeared, most of them never found. Those that were discovered had been raped and bludgeoned with a machete type instrument. Barbosa was arrested in 1988 based on a fingerprint and a photo of one of the missing girls in his pocket. He confessed to killing seventy-one children and led police to the bodies of six victims. In 1989, Daniel Barbosa was sentenced to sixteen years in prison—the maximum punishment allowed under Ecuador's laws. In November 1994, Barbosa was killed by a prisoner who was the cousin of one of Barbosa's victims.

"Berlin Butcher" *see* Grossmann, Georg Karl

Bernardo, Paul, and **Karla Homolka**. Canadian husband-wife sexual serial killers Paul Bernardo and Karla Homolka abducted, sexually tortured, and murdered at least three teenage girls between December 1990 and April 1992 in one of the most shocking and heinous crimes in Canada's history. Included among the victims was Karla Homolka's fourteen-year-old sister, who was raped and murdered on Christmas Eve in 1990. Paul Bernardo was an accountant and serial rapist in a suburb of Toronto in 1987 when he met Homolka who, at seventeen, was six years his junior. By the time the two married in June 1991, their perverted sex life—including making videotapes of each other while sexually assaulting their victims—had escalated to serial murder and domestic violence. In January 1993, a battered Homolka implicated the two in several sexual murders and Bernardo as the wanted "Scarborough Rapist." Bernardo was arrested in February 1993 and charged with forty-three counts of sexual assault. Later, he would face multiple charges in the kidnapping, rape, and murder of two of his victims. On July 15, 1993, in exchange for testifying against her husband, Karla Homolka pled guilty to manslaughter and was sentenced to twelve years in prison. On September 1, 1995, Paul Bernardo was convicted on all counts against him involving the two homicides, and sentenced to life in prison with no parole for at least twenty-five years. He was also designated as a dangerous offender, which means he will probably never be released. On July 4, 2005, after completing her twelve-year sentence, Karla Homolka was released from prison.

Brady, Ian, and **Myra Hindley**. Born in 1938 in England, Ian Brady was a sexual sadist who was fascinated with the leaders of Nazi Germany. He met

Myra Hindley, nineteen, in 1961 while they were both working at the same company. Hindley was intrigued with Brady's dark side and they soon became inseparable. Involved in pornography and fascinated with murder and sex, the couple soon acted out their fantasies. From 1963 to 1965, Brady and Hindley sexually molested, tortured, stabbed, and strangled at least five children age ten to seventeen and buried their bodies on Saddleworth Moor. For "entertainment," Brady decided to let his eighteen-year-old brother-in-law, David Smith, watch one of his sadistic murders. Hindley brought Smith to the house where Brady was hacking to death a seventeen-year-old victim with a hatchet. Hindley urged Smith to help kill the girl, but Smith was horrified. The next morning, October 7, 1965, the police arrived after Smith told them about the murder. They found the victim's body in Hindley's bedroom, along with other evidence. Brady and Hindley—known as the Moors Murderers—were arrested and charged with three murders. In May of 1966, they were both convicted and sentenced to life in prison. In 1986, Myra Hindley confessed that they had murdered two other children. Hindley died in prison on November 15, 2002. Ian Brady was serving his sentence in a hospital for the criminally insane after being diagnosed as a schizophrenic until his death on May 15, 2017, at the age of seventy-nine.

"Butcher of Hanover" *see* Haarmann, Fritz

Chikatilo, Andrei. Born in 1936, Andrei Chikatilo would eventually be known as the Rostov Ripper. From 1982 to 1990, he murdered children and young women and left their bodies in wooded areas throughout the USSR. Chikatilo was arrested in 1990 after being stopped for having blood on his face near a wooded area where a body was found. The fifty-four-year-old confessed to committing at least fifty-two murders—thirty-five children and eighteen young women. The victims had all been stabbed in their eyes and their genitals mutilated. In 1992, Chikatilo was found legally sane and charged with fifty-two murders. He was found guilty and sentenced to death. Andrei Chikatilo was executed in 1994.

Cummins, Gordon. Aircraftman Gordon Cummins of the Royal Air Force in London murdered four women over a four-day period in February 1942. The twenty-eight-year-old strangled his first victim. His next three victims were strangled and their genitals horribly mutilated. Cummins was discovered on February 13 after unsuccessfully attempting to strangle two women. When his last would-be victim screamed and struggled, he ran off, leaving behind his gas mask that contained his name, rank, and serial number. Gordon Cummins was tried and convicted of four murders. He was hanged on June 25, 1942.

"Devil of Turin" *see* Giudice, Giancarlo

"Doorbell Killer" *see* Szczepinski, Waldemar

Dzhumagaliev, Nikolai. In 1980, Nikolai Dzhumagaliev was murdering women in the Soviet Republic of Kazakhstan. Called "Metal Fang" because of his white metal false teeth, he had already served time for manslaughter when his reign of horror began. Dzhumagaliev enjoyed being with tall, attractive women and liked to take them for walks along the river. Once they were isolated, he would rape them and hack them to death with an axe and knife. He would then light a fire and cook them, asking his friends to join him for some roasted meat. Dzhumagaliev was finally captured when two men he had invited over found a woman's head and intestines in the kitchen. He was charged with seven murders but found insane. Nikolai Dzhumagaliev was committed to a mental institution and escaped in 1989 while being transferred to another mental hospital, though the public was never told as authorities didn't want to cause a panic. He was finally recaptured in Moscow in 1991 after he was reportedly trying to proposition women.

Enriqueta, Marti. In Spain in the early 1900s, Marti Enriqueta killed at least six children. Involved in Satanism, she would sexually molest, torture, boil, and eat her victims. She was convicted of murder in 1912 and received a death sentence.

Erskine, Kenneth. Kenneth Erskine was murdering elderly residents of London during 1986. Dubbed by the press as the "Stockwell Strangler," Erskine murdered seven elderly victims by sexually assaulting them and strangling them. Most of his victims were found tucked in their beds with no sign of a struggle. Erskine—twenty-four-years-old and a homeless drifter with the mental capacity of an eleven-year-old—was discovered when police identified him through a palm print. He was arrested and charged with seven murders and one count of attempted murder. Kenneth Erskine was sentenced to life in prison with no parole for forty years. After an appeal, Erksine's murder convictions were reduced to manslaughter in July 2009 due to diminished capacity.

Giudice, Giancarlo. Between 1984 and 1986, Giancarlo Giudice murdered seven prostitutes in Turin, Italy. Dubbed by the media as the "Devil of Turin," his victims had all been whipped and tortured before he killed them. On June 26, 1986, the thirty-two-year-old Giudice was arrested after a witness saw him toss a body over a bridge. Giancarlo Giudice confessed to seven murders and was sentenced to life in prison in June 1987.

Glover, John Wayne. Called the "Granny Killer," John Wayne Glover murdered elderly residents in Sydney, Australia, from 1989 to 1990. He would bludgeon them with a claw hammer and strangle them in their homes. After Glover had murdered his sixth victim on March 19, 1990, police discovered him lying unconscious in the bathtub of the victim's home with an empty bottle of pills and whiskey next to him on the floor. After the fifty-seven-year-old Glover recovered from the overdose, he was arrested and charged with murdering six elderly women, one count of attempted murder, and other charges. John Wayne Glover was found guilty of all charges in November 1991 and sentenced to six life sentences with no parole, plus nine years for robbery and assault charges. On September 9, 2005, Glover was found dead in his cell where he had hung himself.

Gonzales, Delfina, and **Maria de Jesus Gonzales**. From 1954 to 1964, Mexican sisters Delfina Gonzales and Maria Gonzales murdered as many as eighty young girls. Running a brothel in Rancho El Angel, Mexico, the sisters would abduct young teenagers, force them to take drugs, and perform sexual services for the clients. When the girls got sick, became unattractive, or caused trouble, they were killed. In 1964, police got a tip about the ranch run by the Gonzales sisters. When they got there, the sisters were gone but they discovered the bodies of more than eighty young women and numerous fetuses that had been forcibly aborted from the victims. Delfina Gonzales and Maria Gonzales were tried and each sentenced to forty years in prison. In

October 1968, Delfina died in prison. Maria was released from prison after she completed her sentence.

Grossmann, Georg Karl. Born in 1863 in Germany, Georg Grossmann was a sadist who preyed on children. Over the years, Grossmann murdered at least fifty women, mostly street girls. He would sexually assault and butcher them, selling their flesh on the black market and dumping their bones in the river. Known as the "Berlin Butcher," Grossmann had a hot dog stand near the rail station where he allegedly chose his next victim while selling his last victim in the form of a hot dog. He was captured in August 1921 when his neighbors reported screaming coming from Grossmann's apartment. When police arrived, they found a dead woman on his bed. He was tried, convicted, and sentenced to death. While awaiting execution, Georg Karl Grossmann went insane and hung himself in his cell.

Haarmann, Fritz. Known as the "Butcher of Hanover," Fritz Haarmann murdered at least twenty-seven young men and boys in Germany from 1919 to 1924. After the war ended, he viewed the many homeless, starving, refugees as a business opportunity. Haarmann would pose as a policeman and lure young male drifters to his home where he would sexually assault them and bite through their throats until they were dead. He sold their clothes and the meat from their bodies, throwing the skulls in the river. In 1919, Haarmann met Hans Grans. While living together, they began raping and butchering victims jointly, selling the meat to the black market. Haarmann was arrested in 1924 when he tried to molest a boy in the street. When they searched his apartment, they found piles of his victims' clothes waiting to be sold. Haarmann confessed and implicated Grans. Fritz Haarmann was charged with twenty-seven murders and, in December 1924, he was convicted and sentenced to death by decapitation. Hans Grans was sentenced to twelve years in prison for his part in the murders.

Haigh, John George. From 1944 to 1949 in England, John George Haigh murdered five victims for their money and valuables. Known as the "Acid Bath Murderer," he would kill his victims, rob them of their valuables, and dump them in a forty-gallon drum of sulfuric acid. The acid would reduce the bodies to a greasy sludge. After police questioned Haigh about a missing woman, they found enough evidence at his house to arrest him. He arrogantly told the police that he destroyed the victim with acid and murder couldn't be proven without a body. Haigh was eventually charged with her murder and four others when police were able to identify the dentures of his latest victim that hadn't yet been destroyed by the acid. John George Haigh was convicted and hanged on August 10, 1949.

Komaroff, Vasili. From 1921 to 1922, twenty-one bodies were found in empty lots in Moscow—all victims of serial killer Vasili Komaroff. The victims were all men who were either strangled or bludgeoned in the head. They had been tied up and doubled over so they would fit in a sack. Komaroff was suspected when the police linked the murders to a horse trader. He would pick up his victims at the horse trading market and take them home under the guise of selling them a horse. Police soon discovered a body in a sack in Komaroff's barn. After his arrest, he confessed to murdering thirty-three men and admitted that his wife, Sophia, was his accomplice. Vasili Komaroff and Sophia Komaroff were tried, convicted, and sentenced to death. They were executed by firing squad on June 18, 1923.

Kroll, Joachim. Born in West Germany in 1933, Joachim Kroll was a cannibal who sexually assaulted and murdered five young girls from 1959 to 1976. He was captured in 1976 when his toilet became clogged after trying to flush the remains of his four-year-old victim. When police arrived, they found bags of flesh in a freezer and a child's hand cooking in a pot on the stove with potatoes and carrots. Kroll confessed to five murders and admitted that he ate their flesh. He later confessed to murdering nine more victims, hoping he would get a brain operation and be set free. Instead, Joachim Kroll was convicted of murder in 1982 and received nine life sentences. In July 1991, Kroll died in prison.

Kurten, Peter. Born in Germany in 1883, Peter Kurten grew up in a violent household with an alcoholic, abusive father and twelve siblings. Dubbed the "Monster of Düsseldorf" by the press, Kurten's murderous ways began in 1929 when he stabbed to death a nine-year-old girl with scissors. He burned her body later and claimed to receive sexual gratification from it. Kurten stabbed his next victim and drank his blood while it spurted from his neck. He went on to murder at least seven more female victims. Kurten was captured in May 1930 when he suddenly stopped strangling a would-be victim and let her go. She was able to identify him and where he lived. After his arrest, Kurten confessed to the murders, rapes, and mutilations, claiming he would become sexually aroused while drinking his victims' blood. Charged with nine murders, his insanity plea was rejected when his trial began in 1931. Peter Kurten was found guilty of all nine murders and beheaded.

Landru, Henri Désiré. In France in the early 1900s, Henri Landru murdered at least eleven women and burned their bodies in the stove at his villa. Landru was a swindler who would advertise for a wife in the newspaper. He would swindle them out of their savings and possessions and then murder them. In 1919, Landru was captured when the sister of one of the missing victims reported she had gone off with Landru. Police investigated the villa and found 290 bone and teeth fragments in the stove, along with numerous clothes and possessions of his victims. Henri Désiré Landru was tried and convicted in 1921 and put to death by guillotine in February 1922.

Lopez, Pedro Armando. Called the "Monster of the Andes," Pedro Lopez admitted to strangling to death at least 300 girls in Ecuador, Columbia, and Peru. Born in Columbia to a prostitute, Lopez had a rough childhood and was obsessed with sex. In Peru, he kidnapped and strangled over 100 young girls, mostly from Indian tribes. Lopez was caught trying to kidnap a nine-year-old girl and sent back to Ecuador where he continued to kill. In April 1980, Lopez was captured when he was seen leaving a market with a twelve-year-old girl. In jail, he confessed and told police he liked to be the first to introduce sex to his victims. Pedro Lopez was convicted of murder in Ecuador and sentenced to life in prison.

Ludke, Bruno. Born in Germany in 1909, Bruno Ludke was involved in rape, murder, and necrophilia before he turned twenty. During the war, he was captured and sterilized because he was a suspected rapist and mentally defective. Ludke continued with his sex crimes when he relocated to a village near Berlin and was arrested in 1943 when a woman was found strangled near his house. He confessed and admitted to killing eighty-five other women between 1929 and 1943. Ludke claimed he had stabbed or strangled his victims and had sex with them after they died. Because he was deemed mentally incompetent, he was confined to a hospital in Vienna under Nazi law. There, he was used as a human guinea pig in their experiments. On April 8, 1944, Bruno Ludke died during an experiment when he was fatally injected.

Manuel, Peter. Born in Glasgow, Scotland, in 1927, Peter Manuel was a common criminal. From age twelve, he was charged with burglary, robbery, assault, and murder. In 1956, he shot to death three members of the Watt family during a bank robbery. In 1958, Manuel murdered the Smart family of three while robbing their house. He also sexually assaulted and murdered two seventeen-year-old girls. Manuel was arrested and confessed to the murders of the Smart family, along with five other incidents. He was tried and convicted in May 1958 and sentenced to death. While in prison, he confessed to three more murders. Peter Manuel was hanged in 1958.

McDonald, William. Born in 1924 in England, William McDonald eventually moved to Australia. From June 1961 to November 1962, four vagrants were found stabbed and sexually mutilated in Sydney—all victims of the "Sydney Mutilator." McDonald, diagnosed as a schizophrenic, sexually mutilated himself. Thought to be a surviving victim of the Sydney Mutilator, police talked to him and discovered that he had mutilated himself and had committed the four murders. McDonald was found sane and convicted of murder. While serving a life sentence in prison, he attacked and almost killed a fellow inmate. William McDonald was then labeled insane and confined to a mental hospital. He died of natural causes on May 12, 2015.

"Monster of Düsseldorf" *see* Kurten, Peter

"Monster of Florence". This unidentified serial killer murdered couples who were making love in their cars in Florence, Italy, between 1968 and 1985. All the murders occurred during a full moon. The couples were shot through the car window and their bodies mutilated with a scalpel. Sixteen couples were murdered before they inexplicably stopped in 1985. To date, the police have no suspects.

"Monster of Montmartre" *see* Paulin, Thierry

"Monster of the Andes" *see* Lopez, Pedro Armando

"Moors Murderers" *see* Brady, Ian, and Myra Hindley

Nesset, Arnfinn. From 1977 to 1980, twenty-five patients were murdered at the Orkdal Valley Nursing Home in Norway. Arnfinn Nesset was the manager of the home for elderly patients. The victims—age sixty-seven to ninety-four—all died from an overdose of a muscle relaxant. Nesset was arrested in 1981 after authorities became suspicious of the large amount of orders of the drug by the nursing home. He claimed he was only guilty of mercy killing, even though he had also embezzled money from some of his dead victims. Nesset was charged with twenty-two counts of murder and one count of attempted murder. On March 11, 1983, the forty-six-year-old Arnfinn Nesset was found guilty on all charges and received the maximum sentence of twenty-one years in prison. After completing his sentence, Nesset was released in 2004.

Nilsen, Dennis Andrew. Between late 1978 and early 1983, Scottish sexual serial killer Dennis Andrew Nilsen brutally murdered and dismembered as many as sixteen people in England. A civil servant, Nilsen's victims were all young men—many vagrants—whom he picked up at public houses or on the street. He would lure them to his flat where he would strangle and perform necrophilia acts on their corpses before dismembering the bodies. Some of the murdered men's remains were flushed down the toilet—causing a blockage in nearby flats in north London—which led to thirty-seven-year-old Nilsen's capture on February 3, 1983. He confessed his gruesome crimes to the authorities and went to trial in October 1983. A jury found Dennis Nilsen to be both insane and guilty on six counts of murder and two counts of attempted murder. On November 4, 1983, he was sentenced to life in prison with at least twenty-five years behind bars. His sentence was changed to a whole life tariff in 1994, which meant he would never be released. On May 12, 2018, Nilsen died in prison at the age of seventy-two.

Olson, Clifford. Forty-one-year-old Clifford Olson murdered at least eleven young boys and girls in Vancouver, Canada, from December 1980 to July 1981. An ex-con, he had a record of ninety-four convictions including fraud, armed robbery, and rape. Married with an infant son, Olson was arrested while attempting to pick up two girls. When the police searched his van, they found a notebook containing the address of one of the dead victims. In a strange turn of events, Olson offered to give police information on where the bodies were buried if they would pay him a set amount for each murder. They did agree to put some money in a trust for Olson's son if he would give them details of the murders. During his trial in 1982, Clifford Olson changed his plea to guilty of eleven counts of murder and was sentenced to eleven consecutive life sentences. He died of cancer on September 30, 2011.

Paulin, Thierry. Between 1984 and 1987, Thierry Paulin brutally murdered at least twenty-one elderly women in the Montmartre district of Paris, France. Dubbed the "Monster of Montmartre" by the press, Paulin would break into his victims' apartments, ransack them, and tie the women up before he suffocated, strangled, stabbed, or beat them to death. In December 1987, he left one of his victims barely alive. She was able to identify her assailant as Paulin and he was arrested. The twenty-five-year-old confessed to murdering twenty-one women. While awaiting his trial in prison, his health deteriorated rapidly. Authorities believed Paulin's gay lifestyle and drug abuse had made him a risk for AIDS. He went into a coma in March 1989 and was transferred to a prison hospital. On April 16, 1989, Thierry Paulin died of AIDS.

Petiot, Dr. Marcel. Born in France in 1897, Dr. Marcel Petiot murdered twenty-seven of his patients at his home in Paris by putting strychnine in their typhoid shots. A neighbor called the fire department in March 1944 when the furnace in Petiot's basement set his chimney on fire. When firemen went to the basement, they found a pile of dismembered bodies waiting to be burned in the furnace. Petiot was arrested in November 1944 and confessed to killing at least sixty-three people that he said were either German soldiers or collaborators. He was charged with twenty-seven murders and found guilty of twenty-four of them. Dr.

Marcel Petiot was executed by guillotine on May 25, 1946.

Popova, Madame. Born in the 1800s in Russia, Madame Popova killed over 300 men for profit. Between 1880 and 1909, she ran a serial killing business where she would murder unwanted husbands for a fee. Popova would poison the victim herself or use an accomplice. When one of her clients felt remorse over her husband's death, she told police. In 1909, Popova was arrested and confessed to killing more than 300 husbands over three decades. Madame Popova was executed by a firing squad in 1909.

"Red Spider" *see* Staniak, Lucian

Rendell, Martha. In 1907 and 1908 in Australia, Martha Rendell killed three of her boyfriend's children by swabbing their throats with hydrochloric acid. She moved in with her boyfriend, Thomas Morris, and his five children in 1906. Rendell was very strict and beat them with little provocation. She insisted they call her mother. In 1907, two of Morris's daughters became ill and were prescribed throat swabs by the doctor. Rendell happily complied and laced the drinks with acid, swabbing their throats with it. The two girls died months apart and the cause of death was diagnosed as diphtheria. A year later, the fourteen-year-old son also received swabbing treatments with hydrochloric acid. He died in October with the cause of death listed as diphtheria. Police finally grew suspicious and exhumed the bodies. It was revealed they had all died from hydrochloric acid poisoning. Martha Rendell was charged with three murders, found guilty, and hanged on October 6, 1909—the last woman executed in Western Australia.

"Rostov Ripper" *see* Chikatilo, Andrei

Sandwene, Ntimane. Between 1929 and 1936 in South Africa, Ntimane Sandwene murdered eight people. A Zulu servant, he would rob and murder his victims and then return to his master's home under the guise of a good and faithful servant. Sandwene planned to rob victims until he got enough money to buy his own farm. In 1936, he made the mistake of not killing one of his victims. The man was able to identify his attacker as Sandwene. After being arrested, Sandwene confessed and told authorities he was only trying to gain a more secure financial future. He asked them for another chance. The authorities were not impressed and found him guilty. Sentenced to death, Ntimane Sandwene was hanged at Pretoria Central Prison in May 1937.

Sodeman, Arnold Karl. Described as a loving father and husband and well-liked by neighbors and co-workers, Arnold Sodeman was a child sex murderer in Melbourne, Australia. He sexually assaulted and murdered his first victim—a twelve-year-old girl—in November 1930. He went on to sexually assault and murder three more young girls, luring them with sweets while riding his bicycle. Sodeman was arrested on suspicion and made a full confession to the four murders. He pleaded insanity, but was convicted of the charges and hanged on June 1, 1936. After an autopsy, it was discovered that Arnold Sodeman suffered from an inflammation of the brain caused by heavy alcohol consumption that may have contributed to his "Jekyll and Hyde" personality.

Staniak, Lucian. In Poland, Lucian Staniak brutally murdered at least twenty women from 1964 to 1967. His victims were all raped and sexually disemboweled, and most of the murders occurred on Poland's public holidays. Because he wrote letters to the police in red ink in a thin spidery way, the press called him the "Red Spider." The letters taunted police with the location of the most recent victim's body and dared them to catch him. Staniak, a twenty-six-year-old artist, was arrested on February 1, 1967, after police traced him to the ink. He bragged and confessed to authorities that he had murdered twenty people. He was tried and convicted of six murders and sentenced to death. Lucian Staniak was later found to be insane and committed to an asylum.

"Stockwell Strangler" *see* Erskine, Kenneth

Sutcliffe, Peter. Born in England in 1946, Peter Sutcliffe was known as the "Yorkshire Ripper." He murdered thirteen young women from October 1975 to November 1980. Sutcliffe's victims were bludgeoned to death with a hammer, stabbed, and slashed multiple times, with the genitalia mutilated. Eight of his victims were prostitutes. The murders resulted in one of the largest and most expensive manhunts ever by British police. Sutcliffe was finally caught in January 1981 when police found him in a car with a prostitute. While routinely questioning him, they discovered knives and a hammer. He readily confessed to thirteen murders. Peter Sutcliffe was convicted and sentenced to life in prison in May 1981.

"Sydney Mutilator" *see* McDonald, William

Szczepinski, Waldemar. From late 1983 to early 1984, Waldemar Szczepinski murdered six elderly women in West Berlin. Known as the "Doorbell Killer," he would ring the doorbell of an elderly woman and force his way inside. He would then strangle the victim and steal anything he could find. Szczepinski was arrested in 1984 when police were able to trace him to a store receipt found in his last victim's home. The twenty-two-year-old confessed to three murders, but denied three other murders. Waldemar Szczepinski was tried and convicted of three murders and sentenced to life in prison on June 7, 1985.

Torinus, Metod. Farmer Metod Torinus murdered five young women in Yugoslavia from 1977 to 1979. The women were disappearing from the village with no trace, panicking residents. Torinus was discovered when a man he had beaten and robbed identified him to police. They went to his farm and searched his house. When they looked inside the large baking oven, they discovered the charred bones and skulls of the missing women. Torinus confessed to raping, torturing, and strangling the five women and incinerating them in his oven. He was tried and found guilty of five counts of murder in December 1980. Metod Torinus was executed a few days later.

Wagner, Waltraud, Maria Gruber, Irene Leidolf, and **Stefanija Mayer**. In Vienna, Austria, nursing assistants Waltraud Wagner, Maria Gruber, Irene Leidolf, and Stefanija Mayer murdered at least forty-two patients at Lainz Hospital between 1988 and 1989. The women claimed they were merely ending the misery and suffering of their patients. It is estimated they may have murdered hundreds of patients over six years. The women would murder their patients by giving them overdoses of drugs or by literally drowning them (one person holds the patient's head back while the other pours water down their throat until they drown). Each of the four women confessed and went to trial in 1991. Waltraud Wagner, thirty-two, was found guilty of fifteen counts of murder, seventeen counts of attempted murder, and two counts of aggravated assault. She was sentenced to life in prison, which is usually fifteen years in Austria. Irene Leidolf, twenty-nine, was found guilty of murder and also sentenced to life. Stefanija Mayer, fifty-two, was found guilty and sentenced to twenty-two years. Maria Gruber, twenty-seven, was sentenced to fifteen years. In August 2008, Waltraud Wagner and Irene Leidolf were released from prison due to good behavior. Maria Gruber and Stefanija Mayer were released a few years prior to that.

Weber, Jeanne. Growing up in the slums of Paris, France, Jeanne Weber lost two of her three young children to death by natural causes. From March to April 1905, she had four children die under her care, including her only remaining child. Each death was ruled as either convulsions or diphtheria. However, the mother of one of the victims charged Weber with murder. She was acquitted in January 1906. Weber then moved in with a man who had three young children. When one of them died in her care, she was again charged with murder. Weber was again acquitted when the doctor felt the child had died of typhoid fever and had not been strangled. In 1908, Weber was again caring for a young child who was staying at an inn. The innkeeper heard screams and broke into her room, finding the seven-year-old child bloody and dead. Weber was standing there covered in blood. Labeled insane and committed to an asylum in 1908, Jeanne Weber died in 1910 after trying to strangle herself.

Weidmann, Eugen. Born in Germany in 1908, Eugen Weidmann was a swindler who moved to Paris in 1937 after serving five years in a German prison. From July to November 1937, he murdered six people while robbing them. He was arrested when he murdered a real estate agent who was showing him property. Weidmann confessed to the murders and implicated his companions—two Frenchmen, Roger Million and Jean Blanc, and his girlfriend, Colette Tricot. Charged with six murders and found guilty, Eugen Weidmann was executed by guillotine in May 1939—the last person publicly executed in France. Roger Million was charged with two murders and sentenced to death, though it was later changed to life. Jean Blanc was found guilty of harboring criminals and sentenced to twenty months in prison. Colette Tricot was acquitted of receiving stolen property.

West, Frederick, and **Rosemary Pauline West**. Between 1971 and 1987, British husband and wife sexual serial killers Fred and Rosemary West murdered at least ten females and as many as eighteen in England. The murderous pair—who had eight children—combined sexual assault, sadism, and torture in murdering their young victims, many of whom were runaways. They lured the victims to their home under false pretenses of lodging or work as a nanny. Rosemary West—still in her teens and sexually abused by her father when she met the twenty-seven-year-old Frederick West—joined her husband in sexually molesting and murdering girls and women. The victims' corpses were often mutilated and buried thereafter. Among the homicide victims were the Wests' eldest child, sixteen-year-old Heather, and Fred West's stepdaughter, Charmaine. The serial murderers were arrested at their home in Gloucester in 1994 and charged with multiple homicides. On January 1, 1995, Fred West killed himself in his prison cell while awaiting trial and facing additional murder charges, including killing his ex-wife. On November 22, 1995, Rosemary West, who was charged with ten counts of murder and proclaimed her innocence, was convicted on all counts and sentenced to life in prison. In 1997, a whole life order was imposed, ensuring that West would never be released from prison.

"Yorkshire Ripper" *see* Sutcliffe, Peter

Young, Graham. Growing up in England and always intrigued by explosives and chemistry, Graham Young soon became interested in poisons and how they worked on humans. In 1961, at age fourteen, he began poisoning his sister, stepmother, and father by putting arsenic in their food. In 1962, his stepmother died. His father and sister became seriously ill and were put in the hospital, diagnosed with arsenic poisoning. Young was arrested and confessed to poisoning his family. He was found insane and put in a mental institution. After spending nine years there, he was pronounced cured and released in 1971. Young got a job and began poisoning several of his co-workers, two of whom died. When medical staff came to investigate the poisonings at the plant, Young told them the symptoms were consistent with thallium poisoning. Authorities checked him out and discovered he had recently been released from a mental hospital. In custody, Young readily confessed. In July 1972, he went to trial for two counts of murder. He was found guilty and sent to prison. In August 1990, Graham Young was found dead in his cell from a heart attack at age forty-two.

TERRORIST ATTACKS

Bombing of U.S. Embassy in Beirut. On April 18, 1983, in a terrorist-suicide attack, a truck carrying a 2,000 pound bomb exploded at the U.S. Embassy in Beirut, Lebanon, killing sixty-three people inside, including seventeen Americans. Hezbollah—a terrorist group—was responsible for the attack with the approval and financial support of top Iranian officials.

Bombing of U.S. Marine Barracks in Beirut. On October 23, 1983, a truck bomb exploded outside the U.S. Marine headquarters building in Beirut, Lebanon, killing the driver of the truck and 241 American soldiers who were there as part of a peacekeeping force. In May 2003, it was ruled by a U.S. federal judge that Hezbollah perpetrated the deadly attack, which was orchestrated by the government in Iran.

Bombing of Pan Am Flight 103. On December 21, 1988, a bomb exploded on a Pan Am jetliner over Lockerbie, Scotland, killing all 259 passengers and eleven people on the ground in the town of Lockerbie.

The plane had been en route to the United States from Britain. After an exhaustive investigation, two Libyans—Abdel Basset al-Megrahi and Al-Amin Khalifa Fahima—were charged with carrying out the bombing. In May 2000, both men went on trial at a special Scottish court in The Netherlands. In 2001, Megrahi was convicted of 270 counts of murder. He was sentenced to life in prison, but eligible for parole after twenty-seven years. Fahima was acquitted. In 2009, amid much controversy, Megrahi was freed and returned to Libya on compassionate grounds because he had terminal cancer and was only expected to live for about three months. Instead, he died three years later in May 2012 still proclaiming his innocence.

Bombing of U.S. Military Complex in Saudi Arabia. On June 25, 1996, a fuel truck packed with 5,000 pounds of explosives was detonated outside a U.S. military complex in Dhahran, Saudi Arabia, killing nineteen U.S. service personnel and wounding more than 400 others. According to U.S. officials, the Iranian-backed Saudi Hezbollah terrorist group was responsible for the bombing of the Khobar Towers housing complex.

Bombing of U.S. Embassies in Africa. On August 7, 1998, two powerful car bombs exploded at U.S. embassies in Nairobi, Kenya, and Dar es Salaam, Tanzania, killing 224 people, including twelve Americans, and injuring more than 1,000 people. Believed to be responsible for the deadly attack was the terrorist group Al Qaeda under the leadership of Osama bin Laden. On November 4, 1998, a federal grand jury indicted the forty-one-year-old bin Laden on charges in connection with the bombing. Placed on the FBI's Ten Most Wanted Fugitives list, a five million dollar reward was offered for information leading to bin Laden's arrest or conviction. At least two other alleged terrorist men believed to be associates of bin Laden or members of Al Qaeda—Saddiq Odeh and Mohamed Rashed Daoud—were extradited to the United States to face charges for their involvement in the deadly East Africa bombings. They were both convicted in 2001 and sentenced to life in prison without parole. Osama bin Laden was killed on May 2, 2011, by U.S. Navy SEALs at his compound in Abbottabad, Pakistan.

GLOSSARY OF TERMS

Bandit - A robber, usually one who is armed.

Black Hand - A gang of extortionists, kidnappers, and killers who usually victimized Italian and Sicilian immigrants from 1890 to the early 1920s in large urban regions of the United States.

Black Widow - A cunning, calculating female serial killer who, like the female spider of the same name, systematically kills her mate—usually by poison and often for profit.

Celebrity Killer - One who kills a famous, infamous, or prominent person.

Child Killer - One who kills a child or children.

Digitalis - A drug obtained from the leaf of the foxglove plant that is used to stimulate the heart. In large doses, it will kill a person.

Familial Killer - One who kills within the family.

Familicide - The murder of a family member.

Filicide - The killing of one's children.

Gangster - An organized criminal mobster or racketeer or a member of a crime syndicate.

Hate Crime Killer - A person who is motivated to kill in whole or in part by the ethnicity, religion, sexual orientation, or other personal characteristic of the victim.

Homicide - The killing of a person by another.

Infanticide - The killing of an infant.

Intimate Killer - One who kills a spouse, lover, or previous romantic partner.

Juvenile - One who is under the age of eighteen.

Lady Bluebeard *see* Black Widow

Mass Murderer - A person who kills three or more people in the same place or setting in a short time span.

Munchausen syndrome by proxy - A rare disorder where one creates or imagines physical ailments in their children, usually bringing the children to doctor's offices or hospitals for treatment. It is a form of child abuse.

Murder - The intentional and unlawful killing of another person.

Murder, Inc. - A group of professional hired killers who worked for the national organized crime syndicates from the 1920s to 1940s.

Necrophilia - Sexual relations with a dead person.

Organized Crime - Crime that is systematic or institutionalized and structured, usually on a wide scale, involving racketeering, including extortion, prostitution, narcotics, loan sharking, and murder.

Outlaw - A fugitive from justice whose freedom depends on avoiding capture. Usually associated with robbers and killers from the Old West.

Pair and Group Killers - A person acting with one or more persons who systematically kill another or others as a team or group for shared purpose, motives, or results.

Parricide - The killing of one's father, mother, or both.

Politically Motivated Killer - One who kills for reasons of politics or government related reasons.

Serial Killer - A person who kills repeatedly and obsessively, typically with a sexual motivation.

Sexual Killer - One who is motivated by sex or sexually-related reasons to kill.

SIDS *see* Sudden Infant Death Syndrome

Spree Killer - A mass murderer whose killings occur over a matter of time, usually hours or days.

Sudden Infant Death Syndrome - The sudden, mysterious death of an infant that remains unsolved after a comprehensive investigation. SIDS is the primary cause of death in children age one month to one year.

Suicide - The taking of one's own life.

Terrorist Killer - One who kills using violence, kidnapping, and/or bombing to achieve a political purpose.

REFERENCES

Abadinsky, Howard. *The Criminal Elite: Professional and Organized Crime*. Westport, Conn.: Greenwood Press, 1983.

_____. *Organized Crime*. 4th ed. Chicago: Nelson-Hall, 1994.

Abernathy, Francis E., ed. *Legendary Ladies of Texas*. Dallas: E-Hearst Press, 1981.

Allen, William. *Starkweather*. Boston: Houghton Mifflin, 1976.

Anderson, Chris, and Sharon McGehee. *Bodies of Evidence*. New York: Lyle Stuart, 1991.

Anslinger, Harry J. *The Murderers*. New York: Farrar, Straus & Cuddhy, 1961.

Barnes, Bruce. *Machine Gun Kelly: To Right A Wrong*. Perris, Calif.: Tipper, 1991.

Begg, Paul. *Jack the Ripper*. London: Robson Books, 1988.

Blackburn, Daniel J. *Human Harvest*. New York: Knightsbridge, 1990.

Bloch, Herbert A., ed. *Crime in America*. New York: Philosophical Library, 1961.

Boar, Roger, and Nigel Blundell. *The World's Most Infamous Murders*. New York: Exeter Books, 1983.

Bolitho, William. *Murder For Profit*. London: Cape, 1934.

Brearley, H. C. *Homicide in the United States*. Chapel Hill, N.C.: University of North Carolina Press, 1932.

Brown, Wenzell. *Introduction to Murder*. London: Dakers, 1953.

Buck, Pearl. *The Honeymoon Killers*. London: Sphere Books, 1970.

Bugliosi, Vincent. *Helter Skelter: The True Story of the Manson Murders*. New York: Bantam, 1974.

Capote, Truman. *In Cold Blood*. New York: Random House, 1965.

Carpozi, George, Jr. *Gangland Killers*. New York: Manor Books, 1979.

Christie, Trevor. *Etched in Arsenic*. Philadelphia: J. B. Lippincott, 1968.

Claitor, Diana. *Outlaws, Mobsters and Murderers*. New York: M & M Books, 1991.

Clayton, Merle. *Union Station Massacre*. New York: Bobbs-Merrill, 1975.

Cohen, Daniel. *The Encyclopedia of Unsolved Crimes*. New York: Dorset Press, 1988.

Cox, Bill G. *Crimes of the 20th Century*. New York: Crescent Books, 1991.

Cox, Mike. *The Confessions of Henry Lee Lucas*. New York: Pocket Books, 1991.

Cray, Ed. *Burden of Proof*. New York: Macmillan, 1973.

Crockett, Art, ed. *Serial Murderers*. New York: Pinnacle, 1991.

Cromie, Robert, and Joseph Pinkston. *Dillinger: A Short and Violent Life*. New York: McGraw-Hill, 1962.

Daigon, Arthur. *Violence U.S.A.* New York: Bantam, 1975.

Daly, Martin, and Margo Wilson. *Homicide.* New York: Aldine Degruytler, 1988.

Davis, Don. *The Milwaukee Murders.* New York: St. Martin's Press, 1991.

De la Torre, Lillian. *The Truth About Belle Gunness.* New York: Gold Medal, 1955.

DeFord, Miriam A. *Murderers Sane and Mad.* New York: Abelard-Schuman, 1965.

Detlinger, Chet, and Jeff Prugh. *The List.* Atlanta: Philmoy, 1983.

Dickson, G. *Murder by Numbers.* London: Robert Hale, 1958.

Dietz, M. L. *Killing for Profit.* Chicago: Nelson-Hall, 1983.

Dietz, Park. "Mass, Serial and Sensational Homicides." *Bulletin of the New York Academy of Medicine* 62 (1986): 477-91.

Douthwaite, L. C. *Mass Murder.* London: John Long, 1928.

Duke, Thomas S. *Celebrated Criminal Cases of America.* San Francisco: James H. Barry, 1910.

Egger, Steven A., ed. *Serial Murder.* New York: Praeger, 1990.

Egginton, Joyce. *From Cradle to Grave.* London: W. H. Allen, 1989.

Ellroy, James. *The Black Dahlia.* New York: Mysterious Press, 1989.

Engstrom, Elizabeth. *Lizzie Borden.* New York: St. Martin's Press, 1997.

Everitt, David. *Human Monsters: An Illustrated Encyclopedia of the World's Most Vicious Murderers.* Lincolnwood, Ill.: Contemporary Books, 1993.

Ewing, Charles P. *Fatal Families: The Dynamics of Intrafamilial Homicide*. Thousand Oaks, Calif.: Sage, 1997.

_____. *Kids Who Kill*. New York: Avon, 1990.

Fido, Martin. *The Chronicle of Crime: The Infamous Felons of Modern History and Their Hideous Crimes*. New York: Carrol and Graf, 1993.

Flowers, R. Barri. *Jealous Rage: Stunning True Tales of Intimates, Passion, and Murder, Vol. 1*. Paradise House Press, 2018.

_____. *The Dynamics of Murder: Kill or Be Killed*. Boca Raton, Florida: CRC Press, 2013.

_____. *The Sex Slave Murders*. New York: St. Martin's Press, 1996.

Fortune, Jan. *The True Story of Bonnie and Clyde*. New York: Signet, 1968.

Fox, Stephen. *Blood and Power: Organized Crime in Twentieth Century America*. New York: William Morrow, 1989.

Frank, Gerold. *The Boston Strangler*. New York: New American Library, 1967.

Franke, David. *The Torture Doctor*. New York: Hawthorn Books, 1975.

Franklin, Charles. *The World's Worst Murderers*. New York: Taplinger, 1966.

Freeman, Lucy. *Catch Me Before I Kill More*. New York: Crown, 1955.

Gaute, J. H. H. *Murderers Who's Who*. New York: Methuen, 1979.

_____, and Robin Odell. *The New Murderers' Who's Who*. London: Harrap, 1989.

Gilmore, John. *Severed: The True Story of the Black Dahlia Murder*. Los Angeles: Amok Books, 1998.

Ginsburg, Philip. *Poisoned Blood.* New York: Warner, 1987.

Glaister, John. *The Power of Poison.* New York: William Morrow, 1954.

Godwin, J. *Murder USA.* New York: Random House, 1978.

Goodman, Jonathan, ed. *Masterpieces of Murder.* New York: Carrol and Graf, 1992.

Granlund, Nils T. *Blondes, Brunettes and Bullets.* New York: David McKay, 1957.

Green, Jonathan. *The Directory of Infamy.* London: Mills and Boon, 1980.

_____. *The Greatest Criminals of All Time.* New York: Stein and Day, 1982.

Gribble, Leonard. *The Deadly Professionals.* London: John Long, 1978.

Gross, Kenneth. *The Alice Crimmins Case.* New York: Alfred A. Knopf, 1975.

Gurwell, John K. *Mass Murder in Houston.* Houston: Cordovan Press, 1974.

Heide, Kathleen M. *Young Killers: The Challenge of Juvenile Homicide.* Thousand Oaks, Calif.: Sage, 1998.

Heimer, Mel. *The Cannibal.* New York: Lyle Stuart, 1971.

Helmer, William, and Rick Mattix. *Public Enemies: America's Criminal Past.* New York: Checkmark Books, 1998.

Hickey, Eric W. *Serial Murderers and Their Victims.* Pacific Grove, Calif.: Brooks/Cole, 1991.

Holmes, Ronald M., and James E. De Burger. *Serial Murder.* Beverly Hills, Calif.: Sage, 1988.

_____, and Stephen T. Holmes. *Murder in America.* Thousand Oaks, Calif.: Sage, 1994.

Jenkins, Philip. "Serial Murder in the United States, 1900-1940." *Journal of Criminal Justice* 17 (1989): 377-97.

Jennings, Dean. *We Only Kill Each Other: The Life and Bad Times of Bugsy Siegel.* Englewood Cliffs, N.J.: Prentice-Hall, 1967.

Joey. *Killer: Autobiography of a Hit Man for the Mafia.* Chicago: Playboy Press, 1973.

Jones, Ann. *Women Who Kill.* New York: Holt, Rinehart & Winston, 1980.

Jones, Richard G., ed. *Killer Couples.* Secaucus, N.J.: Lyle Stuart, 1987.

_____, ed. *The Mammoth Book of Murder.* New York: Carrol and Graf, 1989.

Jones, Valarie, and Peggy Collier. *True Crime: Serial Killers and Mass Murderers.* Upland, Penn.: DIANE Publishing Company, 1997.

Kahaner, Larry. *Cults That Kill.* New York: Warner, 1988.

Kelleher, Michael D., and C. L. Kelleher. *Murder Most Rare: The Female Serial Killer.* New York: Dell, 1997.

Keppel, Robert D., and William J. Birnes. *Signature Killers: Interpreting the Calling Cards of the Serial Murderer.* New York: Simon & Schuster, 1997.

King, Jeffrey S. *The Life and Death of Pretty Boy Floyd.* Kent, Ohio: Kent State University Press, 1998.

Klausner, Lawrence D. *Son of Sam.* New York: McGraw-Hill, 1981.

Kobler, John. Capone: *The Life and World of Al Capone.* New York: Putnam, 1971.

Kohn, George C. *Encyclopedia of American Scandal.* New York: Facts on File, 1989.

Krivitch, Mikhail, and Ol'gert Ol'gin. *Comrade Chikatilo: The Psychopathology of Russia's Notorious Serial Killer.* New York: Barricade Books, 1993.

Kuncl, Tom, and Paul Eisenstein. *Ladies Who Kill.* New York: Pinnacle, 1985.

Lane, Brian, and Wilfred Gregg. *The Encyclopedia of Serial Killers.* New York: Berkley, 1995.

Lane, Roger. *Murder in America.* Columbus, Ohio: Columbus University Press, 1997.

Langlois, Janet L. *Belle Gunness: The Lady Bluebeard.* Bloomington, Ind.: Indiana University Press, 1985.

Larson, Richard W. *Bundy: The Deliberate Stranger.* New York: Pocket Books, 1980.

Lasseter, Don. *Killer Kids.* New York: Pinnacle, 1998.

Lassieur, Allison. *Serial Killers.* San Diego, Calif.: Lucent Books, 2000.

Lavergne, Gary M. *A Sniper in the Tower: The Charles Whitman Murders.* Denton, Texas: University of North Texas Press, 1997.

Lester, David. *Serial Killers: The Insatiable Passion.* Philadelphia: Charles Press, 1995.

Levin, Jack, and James A. Fox. *Mass Murder.* New York: Plenum, 1985.

Leyton, Elliot. *Compulsive Killers: The Story of Modern Multiple Murder.* New York: Washington Mew Books, 1986.

_____. *Hunting Humans.* London: Penguin, 1989.

Linedecker, Clifford L. *Killer Kids: Shocking True Stories of Children Who Murdered Their Parents.* New York: St. Martin's Press, 1993.

_____. *Night Stalker.* New York: St. Martin's Press, 1991.

_____. *Serial Thrill Killers.* New York: Knightsbridge, 1990.

_____, and William A. Burt. *Nurses Who Kill*. New York: Pinnacle, 1990.

Livsey, Clara. *The Manson Women*. New York: Richard Marek, 1980.

Louderback, Lew. *The Bad Ones: Gangsters of the '30s and Their Molls*. Greenwich, Conn.: Fawcett, 1968.

Lucas, Norman. *The Child Killers*. London: Barker, 1970.

_____. *The Sex Killers*. London: W. H. Allen, 1974.

Lunder, Donald T. *Murder and Madness*. New York: Norton, 1979.

Mackenzie, Frederick. *Twentieth Century Crimes*. Boston: Little, Brown, 1927.

Maddox, Web. *The Black Sheep*. Quannah, Texas: Nortex, 1975.

Manners, Terry. *Deadlier than the Male: Stories of Female Serial Killers*. New York: Macmillan, 1997.

Markman, Ronald, and Dominic Bosco. *Alone With the Devil*. New York: Doubleday, 1989.

Masters, Robert E. L., and Eduard Lea. *Perverse Crimes in History*. New York: Julian Press, 1963.

McDonald, R. Robin. *Black Widow*. New York: St. Martin's Press, 1986.

McDougal, Dennis. *Angel of Darkness*. New York: Warner, 1991.

McGinniss, Joe. *Fatal Vision*. New York: Putnam, 1983.

Monaco, Richard, and Lionel Bascom. *Rubouts: Mob Murders in America*. New York: Avon, 1991.

Munn, Michael. *The Hollywood Murder Case Book*. New York: St. Martin's Press, 1987.

Nash, Jay R. *Almanac of World Crime*. New York: Doubleday, 1981.

_____. *Murder, America: Homicide in the United States From the Revolution to the Present*. New York: Simon & Schuster, 1980.

_____. *World Encyclopedia of 20th Century Murder.* New York: Paragon House, 1992.

Newton, Michael. *Bad Girls Do It!: An Encyclopedia of Female Murderers.* Port Townsend, Wash.: Loompanics Unlimited, 1993.

_____. *The Encyclopedia of Serial Killers: A Study of the Chilling Criminal Phenomenon, from the "Angels of Death" to the "Zodiac" Killer.* New York: Facts on File, 2000.

_____. *Hunting Humans: An Encyclopedia of Modern Serial Killers.* Port Townsend, Wash.: Loompanics Unlimited, 1990.

_____. *Mass Murder.* New York: Garland, 1988.

Nicholas, Margaret. *The World's Wickedest Women.* New York: Berkley, 1988.

Norris, Joel. *Arthur Shawcross: The Genesee River Killer.* New York: Windsor Publishing, 1992.

_____. *Serial Killers.* New York: Anchor, 1989.

O'Brien, Darcy. *Two of a Kind: The Hillside Stranglers.* New York: New American Library, 1985.

O'Donnell, Bernard. *The World's Worst Women.* London: W. H. Allen, 1953.

Odell, Robin. *Landmarks in 20th Century Murder.* London: Headline, 1995.

Patterson, Richard. *The Train Robbery Era: An Encyclopedic History.* Boulder, Colo.: Pruett, 1991.

Peterson, Virgil W. *The Mob: 200 Years of Organized Crime in New York.* Ottawa, Ill.: Green Hill, 1983.

Plaidy, Jean. *A Triptych of Poisoners.* London: Robert Hale, 1958.

Radin, Edward D. *Crimes of Passion.* New York: Digit Books, 1953.

Rappaport, R. G. "The Serial and Mass Murderer." *American Journal of Forensic Psychiatry* 9, 1 (1988): 39-48.

Ressler, Robert K., Ann W. Burgess, and John E. Douglas. *Sexual Homicide: Patterns and Motives*. New York: Lexington, 1988.

Rule, Ann. *The Stranger Beside Me*. New York: New American Library, 1980.

Rumbelow, Donald. *Jack the Ripper: The Complete Casebook*. Chicago: Contemporary Books, 1988.

Schechter, Harold. *Deviant*. New York: Pocket Books, 1989.

_____, and David Everitt. *A to Z Encyclopedia of Serial Killers*. New York: Pocket Books, 1997.

Scott, Gini Graham. *Homicide: 100 Years of Murder in America*. Lincolnwood, Ill.: Roxbury Park, 1998.

Segrave, Kerry. *Women Serial and Mass Murderers*. Jefferson, N.C.: McFarland, 1992.

Sifakis, Carl. *The Encyclopedia of American Crime*. New York: Facts on File: 1982.

_____. *The Mafia Encyclopedia*. New York: Facts on File, 1987.

Simpson, Philip L. *Psycho Paths: Tracking the Serial Killer through Contemporary American Film and Fiction*. Carbondale, Ill.: Southern Illinois University Press, 2000.

Smith, Carlton, and Thomas Guillen. *The Search for the Green River Killer*. New York: Penguin, 1991.

Sparrow, Gerald. *Women Who Murder*. New York: Abelard-Chuman, 1970.

Steele, Phillip W., and Marie Barrow Scoma. *The Family Story of Bonnie and Clyde*. Gretna, La.: Pelican Publishing, 2000.

Sullivan, Terry, and Peter T. Maiken. *Killer Clown*. New York: Dunlap, 1983.

Thompson, Charles J. S. *Poison Mysteries in History, Romance and Crime*. London: Scientific Publications, 1925.

Tithecott, Richard. *Of Men and Monsters: Jeffrey Dahmer and the Construction of the Serial Killer*. Madison, Wis.: University of Wisconsin Press, 1997.

Toland, John. *The Dillinger Days*. New York: Random House, 1963.

Treherne, John. *The Strange History of Bonnie and Clyde*. New York: Stein and Day, 1984.

Tulley, Andrew. *The FBI's Most Famous Cases*. New York: William Morrow, 1965.

Turkus, Burton B., and Sid Feder. *Murder, Inc.: The Story of the Syndicate*. New York: Farrar, Straus and Young, 1951.

Watkins, J. G. "The Bianchi (L.A. Hillside Strangler) Case." *International Journal of Clinical and Experimental Hypnosis* 32 (1984): 67-101.

William, Patrick. *Murderess*. London: Michael Joseph, 1971.

Williamson, W. H. *Annals of Crime: Some Extraordinary Women*. New York: M. Evans, 1981.

Wilson, Colin. *The Mammoth Book of True Crime*. New York: Carrol and Graf, 1998.

_____, and Damon Wilson. *The Killers Among Us: Sex, Madness, and Mass Murder*. New York: Warner, 1995.

_____, and Donald Seaman, eds. *The Encyclopedia of Modern Murder, 1962-1982*. New York: Putnam, 1985.

_____, and Patricia Pitman. *Encyclopedia of Murder*. New York: G. P. Putnam's Sons, 1961.

Wilson, Patrick. *Murderess*. London: Joseph, 1971.

Winn, Steven, and David Merrill. *Ted Bundy*. New York: Bantam, 1980.

Wolf, Leonard. *Bluebeard*. New York: C. N. Potter, 1980.

INTERNET REFERENCES

20th Century America.
   http://members.aol.com/TeacherNet/20Cen.html
APB Serial Killer Bureau: Tracking America's Serial
   Killers.
   http://www.apbonline.com/serialkiller/index.html
APBNews.com. http://www.apbnews.com
Assassinations.
   http://dir.yahoo.com/Arts/Humanities/History/By
   _Subject/Assassinations/
Britannica.com. http://www.britannica.com/
CharlesManson.com. http://www.charliemanson.com/
Chicago Tribune. http://www.chicagotribune.com/
CNN.com. http://www.cnn.com/
Court TV Online. http://www.courttv.com/
Crime Library.
   http://www.crimelibrary.com/index.html
Crime Magazine: An Encyclopedia of Crime.
   http://www.crimemagazine.com/
Crime Spider: Murder and Other Crimes.
   http://www.crimespider.com/
Criminology and Criminal Justice.
   http://www.geocities.com/~sociorealm/criminolog
   y.htm
Famous Trials - UMKC School of Law.
   http://www.law.umkc.edu/faculty/projects/ftrials/f
   trials.htm
Federal Bureau of Investigation. http://www.fbi.gov/
Internet Crime Archives.
   http://www.mayhem.net/Crime/

Jack the Ripper.
http://dir.yahoo.com/Regional/Countries/United_Kingdom/Society_and_Culture/Crime/Types_of_Crime/Homicide/Serial_Killers/Jack_the_Ripper/

Juvenile Violence Time Line.
http://www.washingtonpost.com/wp-srv/national/longterm/juvmurders/timeline.htm

Leopold and Loeb Trial Home Page.
http://www.law.umkc.edu/faculty/projects/FTrials/LEOPLOEB/LEOPOLD.HTM

Mass and Serial Murderers.
http://www.crimelibrary.com/serialkillers.htm

Mass Murder WebSite.
http://srd.yahoo.com/srst/24277243/mass+murderers/1/6/

Mass Murderers and Serial Killers.
http://crime.about.com/cs/massmurderers/

Mcall.com. http://www.mcall.com/library/search.htm

Millennium Time Traveler 1900-2000.
http://www.calgaryherald.com/millennium/index.html

Modus Operandi - Serial Killers. http://www.mo-serialkillers.com/

Murder in the UK. http://www.terryhayden.free-online.co.uk/murder/

MurderInc.com. http://www.murderinc.com/

Real-Life Monsters.
http://members.tripod.com/~VanessaWest/

San Diego Union-Tribune.
http://www.signonsandiego.com/

Scratchin' Post Serial Killers Archives.
http://www.tdl.com/~kitty/crimes.html

Serial Killer Hit List.
http://www.mayhem.net/Crime/serial1.html

Serial Killer Info Site. http://www.serialkillers.net

Serial Killer Page.
http://www.geocities.com/serialkillers101/

Serial Killer Webring.
http://nav.webring.yahoo.com/hub?ring=serialkiller
s&list

Serial Killers and Murderers.
http://www.geocities.com/SunsetStrip/Mezzanine/
2991/murder/killers.htm

World Wide Serial Killer Home Page.
http://hosted.ray.easynet.co.uk/serial_killers/

Violent Kids. http://violentkids.com

Washingtonpost.com.
http://www.washingtonpost.com/

# # #

ABOUT THE AUTHOR

R. Barri Flowers is a well-respected criminologist and bestselling author of more than one hundred books, including enthralling true crime and criminology books, as well as gripping mystery, suspense, and thriller fiction, and young adult mysteries.

True crime titles include The Sex Slave Murders; Masters of True Crime (editor); Murder and Menace: Riveting True Crime Tales (volumes 1-3); Murder Chronicles: A Collection of Chilling True Crime Tales; Murders in the United States; Serial Killer Couples: Bonded by Sexual Depravity, Abduction and Murder; and The Dreadful Acts of Jack the Ripper and Other True Tales of Serial Murder and Prostitutes.

Mystery and thriller fiction titles include Before He Kills Again, Dark Streets of Whitechapel, Dead in Pukalani, Dead in Wailuku, Killer in The Woods, Murder in Maui, Murder in Honolulu, Murdered in the Man Cave, Murdered in the Gourmet Kitchen, Murder of the Hula Dancers, Murder on Kaanapali Beach, Persuasive Evidence, Seduced to Kill in Kauai, State's Evidence, and Justice Served.

As an expert on violent criminality, R. Barri Flowers has appeared on the Biography Channel, Investigation Discovery, and Oxygen television documentary crime series.

Follow R. Barri Flowers on Twitter, Facebook, LinkedIn, Pinterest, YouTube, Flickr, Goodreads, and LibraryThing. Learn more about the author in Wikipedia and www.rbarriflowers.com.

# # #

Made in United States
North Haven, CT
17 May 2023

36680955R00222